IPP Studies in the Frontiers of China's Public Policy

IPP Studies in the Frontiers of China's Public Policy combines original research and theoretical innovation to provide fresh insights into the fast-changing landscape of China's public policy. Books in the series, written by scholars based inside China or commissioned by the IPP, draw on local Chinese experiences to generate empirical findings and theoretical insights. The field of China's public policy is broadly defined to include all aspects of the country's social, economic, technological and foreign policies. The series encourage interdisciplinary approaches to public policy, with a special but not exclusive focus on the study of south China, especially the Guangdong, Hong Kong, Macau Greater Bay Area, one of the most vibrant regions of growth and innovation in China.

Wei Zhao

Remade in South China

Bottom Up Innovation in Guangdong

palgrave
macmillan

Wei Zhao
South China University of Technology
Guangzhou, China

IPP Studies in the Frontiers of China's Public Policy
ISBN 978-981-95-7276-2 ISBN 978-981-95-7277-9 (eBook)
https://doi.org/10.1007/978-981-95-7277-9

Cover Credit: Xiaodong Qiu

This Palgrave Macmillan imprint is published by the registered company Springer Nature Singapore Pte Ltd.
The registered company address is: 152 Beach Road, #21-01/04 Gateway East, Singapore 189721, Singapore

Foreword

Readers of this volume hold in their hands a rare work. It deals with industrial development not on the basis of statistics and economic simulations, but rather on the basis of impressive research informed by field surveys and in-depth reflections on China's industrial development. I met Zhao Wei, the author of these pages, when he was starting this work in Guangzhou at Sun Yat-Sen University. We joined forces in 1999, and that allowed me to appreciate Zhao Wei's qualities as a socio-economist whose work is strongly based on fieldwork. During my stay in Guangzhou between 2000 and 2004, we conducted together numerous case studies and surveys among industrial companies in the Pearl River Delta, a region emblematic of the explosive growth that would take place in the years to come. This fieldwork enabled us to challenge the so-called "Chinese miracle" by using concrete examples explaining how companies obtained what they needed in order to produce, grow, acquire technology, and access markets. In this way, we were describing the material basis for the country's prosperity, as well as its weaknesses, often linked to fierce competition between companies, a lack of policy coordination, and disagreements between national and local levels. This was not theory-laden research, but empirically informed fieldwork on specific case studies. We showed, contrary to popular belief at that time, how, under certain conditions, technology would not be the main bottleneck to growth. We believed difficulties always arise when companies can't find a profitable position in international trade, or didn't have access to foreign companies, since the latter provided basic models and technologies, when, attracted by low labor costs, were becoming the clients of the Chinese companies.

Since then, China has created what Zhao Wei calls an ecosystem, a complex and genuine indigenous industrial multi-level system. The challenges and trends of industrial development have profoundly changed in these last 25 years. I am pleased to detect in these pages the author's same desire to understand the strengths and weaknesses of industrialization in China. After obtaining a doctorate on industrialization in the electronics and automotive industries, Zhao Wei continued his research efforts by working closely with economic actors. He thus offers us an analysis that is deeply rooted in reality, while allowing us to benefit from his keen intuition and knowledge, which enable him to connect the dots that others cannot see.

He is able to link the detailed micro-level observations of companies and actors in the field involved in the implementation of public policies to promote industry with grand theory. He shows the correspondence between the learning process of firms, which enables them to develop an absorptive capacity, and the same learning process of policy people who are gradually learning to manage local industrial policies. The 2008 financial crisis had an adverse effect by concentrating economic decisions within central government, and that has tended to hamper China's growth engine, namely the close ties that companies forge not only with their clients but also with all local players (providers, R&D centres, innovation centres, including local and regional authorities,) thereby developing what Zhao Wei calls an « innovation ecosystem ». It remains to be seen whether and how the return to the local level will be completed as the author of this book predicts and recommends. But crises always occur, and no man is a prophet in his country!

It is no coincidence that I mention engines here: we are talking about firms producing automobiles, machines, computers, electronic products, and many other common consumer products, and these are the main part of basis of Guangdong's industrial production, as well as part of our everyday lives. We are not talking of heavy industrial sectors that are mainly located in the central and north-eastern parts of China. The great value of this book lies precisely in its focus on Guangdong and Southern China, its unique characteristics, and its industrial landscape, which is mainly not one of high technology. Of course, companies such as Huawei and ZTE, and many more large providers to the world corporations, appear as counter-examples. But in fact, Zhao Wei's analysis applies to these larger firms as well as to the SMEs in the Pearl River Delta. All of them developed technological capabilities in the same way, by adapting products to the local markets and thus surviving fierce competition, through aggressive commercial strategies geared towards the needs of customers—most of whom are consumers like you and me, but also foreign client companies that somehow represent foreign markets. Moreover, by demonstrating the local innovation capabilities—in the sense of novelty for local companies and markets—Zhao Wei shows how both large and small companies emerge in a relatively low-tech environment. As he so aptly puts it: "The capability of learning how to economically use technologies to meet customer needs was the foundation of Guangdong firms' competitiveness." This is also why I believe this work compares to Alice Amsden's famous analysis of South Korea's learning economy.

Zhao Wei does not attempt to draw comparisons with Japan or South Korea, or any other Asian economy. He focuses on the unique characteristics of the Pearl River Delta, which is the birthplace of this great "workshop of the world" where a new economy emerged at the end of the 20th century that astonished the entire world. This is where Zhao Wei began his career, but I believe it is also here that China's industrial power takes its roots. Of course, some unique geographical features in this region of the world played an important role: the proximity of Hong Kong and the flow of foreign investment in the early 2000s mainly from overseas Chinese certainly facilitated the initial steps of Chinese local firms. The companies mushrooming in the Southern frontier had easier access to what were the new management practices and to knowledge on how a market economy works. This was decisively important at the beginning of the new economy rather than in later stages, particularly after 2010, when more strategic skills based on one's own experience need to be developed, and when R&D and innovation need to be introduced. Similarly, Hong Kong was a gateway to the world that was much easier to open than anywhere else in China. In the same vein, the policy of welcoming overseas Chinese (huaqiao) certainly played an important role, and the local authorities in Guangdong did everything they could to facilitate their arrival. But these factors cannot explain the success of this industrial ecosystem over such a long 40 years period.

Zhao Wei suggests the formation of an industrial universe with increasing endogenous factors, and the capability to build upon the external technical and economic linkages with foreign and domestic clients. Ultimately, this is what has stabilized a rather crude but fast-paced production model, enabling it to take better advantage of the production cost differential with Western, Korean, and Japanese markets. Zhao Wei gives us numerous examples of companies that have learned from their foreign customers in the US, Europe, Japan, and Korea, since these are the "professors (laoshi) of the company," as a successful small business owner in the Shuikou industrial cluster once told us. Blueprints (product models to be manufactured), quality control, and variety design all became a reality that companies learned to understand and integrate. They also benefited from the expansion of this growing industrial universe, which allows any new SME to find everything it needs within a 30-km radius. Location plays an important role, as Paul Krugman teaches us, and here, the industrial economic system has abundant and increasingly complex resources for industry. Zhao Wei builds upon this specificity, and draws upon evolutionary economics. As these pages illustrate, innovation policies in Guangdong tried also, in many ways, to take advantage of this particular feature. Something similar happened later, when significant research activities, and R&D appeared as a necessary ingredient of Chinese successful companies.

But enough of my writing, since it will spoil Zhao Wei's fascinating account of this exceptionally interesting economic adventure. However, I must end by emphasising not only the originality of the author's method, as well as the richness of his analyses, but also the pedagogical qualities of this volume.

Paris, 1st March, 2026 Rigas Arvanitis

Contents

List of Figures

List of Tables

CHAPTER 1

Introduction: How to Make a "World Factory" Innovative?

Setting the Stages of Development

During the 1990s in China, the period when economy and business were the central focus of the whole country, many Chinese government officials were keen to get a business diploma such as MBA (master of business administration) or EMBA (executive master of business administration) than in public administration or political science. One of their books the most favorably read was *"The Competitive Advantage of Nations"* by Michael Porter (1990), a Harvard strategic management scholar. Within the book, a nation's economic development is described as a sequence of stages, each with a different set of competitiveness characteristics and challenges:

1. The first stage is the Factor-Driven Stage, in which national competitive advantage is based exclusively on endowments of labor and natural resources, supporting only relatively low wages.
2. In the second stage, the Investment-Driven Stage, efficiency in producing standard products and services becomes the dominant source of national competitive advantage. Economies at this stage concentrate on manufacturing and on outsourced service exports. They achieve higher wages, but are susceptible to financial crises and external, sector-specific demand shocks.

W. Zhao, *Remade in South China*, IPP Studies in the Frontiers of China's Public Policy,
https://doi.org/10.1007/978-981-95-7277-9_1

3. In the third stage, the Innovation-Driven Stage, the ability to produce innovative products and services at the global technology frontier using the most advanced methods becomes the dominant source of national competitive advantage. At this stage, industrial clusters become critical motors, not only in generating productivity, but also encouraging innovation at the world frontier. Institutions and incentives supporting innovation are also well developed, increasing the efficiency of cluster interaction. Companies compete with unique strategies that are often global in scope, and invest strongly in advanced skills, the latest technology, and innovative capacity.
4. There is the fourth and last stage of development: the Wealth-Driven Stage, represented by some developed economies with high social welfare and high revenues.

According to Porter, successful economic development is a process of successive upgrading and a developing country's business environment has to evolve accordingly to support and encourage increasingly sophisticated and productive ways of competing by firms. In China, Professor Porter's positive assertion became a normative guideline of Chinese officials in their policy practice. Now, 35 years after the publication of this national competitiveness theory, China found that its growth trajectory just conformed to the development stages described in the book: the country did experience the Factor-Driven Stage (from 1980s to 2006) and the Investment-Driven Stage (mainly from 2007 to 2017, but also even up to present), and is heading hard for the Innovation-Driven Stage (from 2014 till now), while there has been much social phenomena signaling that China's development is in fact entering into a Wealth-Driven Stage.

The ascendance of China to become the World Factory was initially due to successful mobilization of a particular set of inputs, or production factors: the unlimited availability of supply of surplus labor from rural areas from 1980s to 2006; the low and rapidly failing costs of land and raw materials due to scale economy; the massive expansion of domestic market for consumer durables; the wide use or incorporation of standardized technologies in products and processes in manufacturing firms; the building up of many infrastructure facilities, etc. One of the most important elements was that China caught the opportunity of economic globalization in the end of the twentieth century and integrated its production capacity with the world's most advanced markets, which was symbolized by its accession to WTO in 2001. China emerged as the most attractive geographic locus for export processing—basic assembly of products destined for abroad from components sourced from abroad—of global consumer products: electronics, office equipment, toys, furniture, footwear, apparel, and many others. The share of foreign trade in China's GDP rose from 10% in 1978 to 33% in 1990, 49% in 2002, and 67% in 2006. In 2016, China's foreign trade reached 4.3 trillion Yuan and represented 13% of world share. 30–40% of China's foreign trade was for process-exporting. Although currency undervaluation played a role in keeping the products "made in China" generally competitive in price in the factor-driven stage, it was the fast labor productivity as well as total factor productivity (TFP) growth that was a more important factor driving China's export success. For example, the average annual labor productivity growth was 20.4% between 1995 and 2003, and 8.7% for the period 2000–2005.

During the investment-driven stage, the year 2012 was especially important both politically and economically. That year witnessed the ascendance of the Chinese new top leaders. And China became, in the end of the same year, the second largest economy in the world by GDP size (nominal and PPP terms) just after the United States. However, it also recorded a GDP growth rate of 7.75%, apparently below its own average growth rate of 10% maintained over 30 years until 2011. Eventually, the year 2012 drew a splitting line in the recent Chinese growth history: before it, the country's high-speed growth era was over; after it, "the end of the China's economic miracle" just began (Pei, 2012).

By the year of 2014, the Chinese government confidently believed that its economy soon should and would enter into the new stage of "innovation-driven development." Since many years, the Chinese officials had aspired and desired entering into the innovation-driven stage. They elaborated a series of policy frameworks to push innovation to become the main driving force, such as National Mid- and Long-term Science and Technology Development Plan, Made in China 2025, National Innovation-driven Development Strategy, and the supply-side reform in broad sense.

Indeed, though the Chinese macro economy has suffered from consecutive growth-rate slowing down since 2020, the goal of innovation has been somehow achieved with 10-year efforts. In 2024, China filed 70,160 patent applications under the Patent Cooperation Treaty, surpassing the United States (ranked second) and Japan (ranked third) by 30% and 45%, respectively. The Innovation Composite Index released by the European Commission in July 2025 showed that China's score increased by 31.6 percentage points compared to 2020, a significantly higher rise than the

United States (15.8 percentage points) and the EU (10.8 percentage points). By 2025, China's ranking in the Global Innovation Index had risen from 34th in 2012 to 10th, making it one of the fastest-growing economies in terms of innovation over the past decade.

Two Policy Approaches

Currently, there is a widespread recognition that China's economic development from factor-driven and investment-driven to the current innovation-driven stages has largely been propelled by government policies. The policy-driven development does not add a new stage to Professor Porter's theory, but rather highlights that government policy (commonly referred to as industrial policy in standard economic theory) has always been a crucial factor in China's economic growth. A deeper observation and more nuanced analysis can reveal that the implementation of government policies in China actually follows two distinct pathways, which we may tentatively term as "top-down" and "bottom-up" approaches. The juxtaposing two policy approaches are identified in cluster policy researchers (Boekholt & Thuriaux, 1999; Fromhold-Eisebith & Eisebith, 2005). Top-down cluster policies are explicitly implemented by regional authorities and implicit initiatives are organized and financed bottom-up by groups of firms (Fromhold-Eisebith & Eisebith, 2005):

1. In the top-down approach of development, government (in consultation with industry and research agencies) sets national priorities, formulates a challenging vision for the future. Once national priorities have been set and the stakeholder groups implemented, the clustering process becomes a market-led process, with little government intervention (Boekholt & Thuriaux, 1999).
2. The bottom-up approach of development depends very much on market-induced initiatives, with the government acting as a facilitator and moderator but not setting national priorities (Boekholt & Thuriaux, 1999).

Regarding China's policy practice, the top-down approach has received widespread attention and discussion. Most observers, especially those outside of China, see the Chinese development policy in a top-down manner. But the biggest difference of China from the planned economy system of the former Soviet Union is the substantial role played by local governments in China's economic transformation, reform, and opening up, or a de facto federalist system (Zheng, 2007). China's reform trajectories have been shaped by regional decentralization. The central government has control over personnel, whereas subnational governments run the bulk of the economy; and they initiate, negotiate, implement, divert, and resist reforms, policies, rules, and laws (Xu, 2011). In fact, what happened in China, especially in the era of high growth, was the de facto domination of bottom-up policy practice. Although top-down policies were always important as base line, their actual implementation, supplementation, and even the generation of new policies were often carried out and completed through the bottom-up approach of local governments. The stage of innovation-driven development has very strong temporal and space characteristics. Chinese local government effectively drove up innovation of firms, by translating the national innovation strategy into local implementation. No other region than the Guangdong province in the southern China can better highlight the width and depth of the bottom-up approach in developing a local economy from factor-driven, to investment-driven, and to innovation-driven stages.

Putting Guangdong Under Spotlight

Geographically located in the very southern part of China, Guangdong is the province having the population of 108.49 million residents, the largest in the country. Within the Province, most of this dynamism occurred in the Pearl River Delta (PRD), a cluster of 9 cities (the yellow area in Fig. 1.1), which concentrates half of the total population of the province (59.27 million) and 85.4% of the provincial GDP. The Pearl River Delta gained the recognition of "the World's Factory," since it had the world's largest concentration of low- and medium-value-added manufacturing (OECD, 2010). Guangdong was therefore also famous for being one of the main receivers for China's incoming FDI (25% of China's total FDI from 1978–2008, in cumulative terms), and later for Chinese outbound investment. After 2019, the Pearl River Delta region, along with Hong Kong and Macau, was collectively referred to as the Guangdong-Hong Kong-Macao Greater Bay Area in official policy.

However, it should be noted that there is also a significant imbalance in innovation-driven development between the Pearl River Delta (PRD) and other regions in Guangdong. In terms of R&D investment, Shenzhen accounts for almost 40% of the province's total R&D expenditure.

Fig. 1.1 Guangdong province and the Pearl River Delta Region. (Source: Adapted from internet)

Excluding Shenzhen, Zhuhai, and Foshan, the remaining six cities in the PRD all have R&D expenditure as a percentage of GDP lower than the provincial average. The eastern, western, and northern regions of Guangdong exhibit even lower R&D investment, with only 0.7% of GDP allocated to R&D expenditure.

Today, almost 40 years after Guangdong took on its pioneering role in the country's transformation, it may no longer stand out from the rest of China quite as distinctly as it once did. Nevertheless, equivalent to a small-scaled prototype of industrializing country, Guangdong's three-stage development—world factory building, industrial upgrading, and innovation-oriented development—corresponds exactly to Professor Porter's three stages of factor-driven, investment-driven, and innovation-driven development, and represents typically the overall development phases and trajectory of contemporary China (Table 1.1).

Table 1.1 The development trajectory of Guangdong

Development Stage	*Policy Strategy*	*Industrial Dynamics*	*Technological Dynamics*
"World Factory" (1990s–2007)	• develop" world-class manufacturing base" and" world-class city cluster" • enlarge manufacturing base and increase foreign trade scale • develop heavy industries, high and new technology sectors, and service sector related to manufacturing • develop local clusters and specialized industrial towns	• engaged in assembly, processing, manufacturing sections in the global value chain • international market and export-oriented • organizational form of industrial cluster • complete and efficient supplier network and industry supporting system	• technology importation and foreign technology transfer • learning and imitating technology from foreign clients under the arrangement of OEM (Original Equipment Manufacturing)
Industrial Upgrading (2008–2014)	• relocating traditional manufacturing sectors elsewhere, while introducing more advanced industries • "double relocation strategy": relocating labor-intensive industries in Pearl River Delta to northern, eastern, and western Guangdong, while labors from these areas shall be relocated to the Pearl River Delta	• change from international market to domestic-market development. • upgrade from manufacturing process to more R&D and marketing activities (climbing up along the "Smile Curve") • industrial expansion in terms of geography and scale • give priority to develop modern service sectors and advanced manufacturing sector	• internal source: production and operation activities such as production scale expansion, plant relocation, and equipment upgrading, such as process • external source: domestic universities and research institutes, industry-academia alliance, key science and technology projects • forms: Re-innovation on the basis of technology importation, system integration, and patent development

(*continued*)

Table 1.1 (continued)

Development Stage	*Policy Strategy*	*Industrial Dynamics*	*Technological Dynamics*
Innovation-driven Development (2015–now)	• innovation-driven development strategy as general guideline • plan of the Pearl River Delta as National Demonstration Zone for Indigenous Innovation • emphasis on science and technology development • develop innovation service sector related to manufacturing • integrate innovation promotion and urbanization • implement Made in China 2025 Master-plan and Internet+ industrial plan	• the "whole industry chain" pattern of manufacturing is gradually formed, and the industrial and trade structures are steadily upgraded • massive emergence of new types of platforms and carriers with scientific and technological innovation to promote industrial development • rapid growth of manufacturing services, high-end services and activities related to internet technologies • future: advanced industrial clusters and local multinational companies capturing high added value in global competition	• diversified actors of innovation: large enterprises, small and medium enterprises, entrepreneurs and teams, universities, research institutions • various sources of knowledge: domestic, foreign, Hong Kong, and Macao networks • types of innovation: technological innovation, business model innovation, market innovation, management innovation, etc. • geographic concentration: the Pearl River Delta as a super-urban innovation ecosystem with Shenzhen and Guangzhou as growth poles.

Source: Author

"World Factory" Development (1990s–2007)

Since 1981 till the early 2010s, the Guangdong Province had registered an annual average around 12%, one of the highest output growth rates in China. The foundation of Guangdong's international competitiveness had been laid far before 2008. Its industry was basically oriented to the international market, firstly through the formation of the "Store-in front and Factory-behind" model with Hong Kong, and then through investment, subcontracting, foundry, and other international production arrangements with Taiwanese firms and large multinational companies in Europe and the United States. By integrated in global value chain with assembly production and processing manufacturing, Guangdong became one of the most important manufacturing bases for world industries in late 1990s. China's accession to the WTO in 2001 also brought Guangdong the label "World Factory" since. In terms of economic performance, from 2000 to 2007, on average, its annual social R&D expenditure accounted for 1.15% of GDP, the contribution rate of scientific and technological progress to GDP growth was 47.5%, the proportions of primary, secondary, and tertiary sectors were respectively 6.9:48.3:44.8, and the value-added by high-tech manufacturing industries accounted for 23.8% of the total industrial value-added (2004–2007).

During the period, the development goal of regional Government was to create a "world-class manufacturing base" and a "world-class city cluster." Its industrial strategy was to enlarge manufacturing basis and increase international trade scale, while vigorously developing heavy chemical industry and high-tech industries, and emphasizing industrial upgrading to high-end activities along the global value chain (research and development technology and brand sales), to cope with rising costs, land shortages, environmental quality decline, labor shortages, and other development bottlenecks. Decentralized power to local governments in Guangdong had turned them into development-oriented entrepreneurial actors. Main policy instruments included investment in infrastructure and investment attraction measures in various development zones operated by provincial, municipal, or township governments that could offer different kinds of incentives and benefits for foreign investors, including fiscal deductions, low-cost land, better physical infrastructure, relatively flexible administrative procedures, etc. Local governments' control over the right to approve land use allowed them to lease land to foreign investors to build factories. Local revenues from land lease were used to finance large-scale infrastructure provision, which in turn improved the transportation and logistics of manufactured goods.

After the initial industrial take-off, the governments in Guangdong began to promote highly geographical concentration of industrial activities, especially in the Pearl River Delta. With the strong government intervention in technology upgrading, industrial park construction, and collective brand building, the Pearl River Delta had gradually formed a local industrial ecosystem with complete upstream and downstream supply chain activities and supporting industries. For example, within a two-hour drive around Shenzhen, there distributed more than 2000 electronics manufacturers, more than 1000 manufacturers of electrical accessories and equipment, more than 300 apparel manufacturers, 1300 material producers, and a workforce up to 9 million with an average age of 33.

The technological progress of industrial clusters was driven by the local entrepreneurial spirit and rapid technological learning in workshops in local firms, who were privately owned and participated in global value chain. Through different forms such as subcontracting or foundry manufacturing, these firms interacted frequently with their foreign clients, and carried out technical imitation, product reverse engineering, and other learning activities. They learnt also how to establish commercial relations and how to take advantage of flexible production and low-cost condition to catch market opportunities. In technology development, they imitated or even copied clients but also competitors, while always positioning themselves behind the first-mover.

Industrial Upgrading (2008–2014)

Before the financial crisis of 2008 hit Guangdong by slump of market demand, local manufacturing firms had already suffered from rising wages, expensive lands, and difficulty of hiring and keeping high skilled workers since several years. But 2008 crisis formally pushed Guangdong to enter the so-called "transformation and upgrading" period.[1] In terms of statistics, from 2008 to 2014, on average, its annual social R&D expenditure accounted for 1.95% of GDP, the contribution rate of scientific and

[1] This vision has been reiterated in the "The Outline of the Plan for the Reform and Development of the Pearl River Delta region 2008–2020", the first central government sub-provincial regional development strategy produced in China's history.

technological progress to GDP growth was 50.4%. The proportions of primary, secondary, and tertiary sectors were respectively 5.0:48.3:46.7. The added value of modern services accounted 57.83% of the whole added value of the service sector. The added value of high-tech manufacturing industry was 22.7% of total industrial added value. The added value of advanced manufacturing was 47.8% of total industrial added value (2011–2014). During this period, the provincial strategy of "industrial transformation and upgrading" was based on two main pillars:

1. Upgrade the industrial base through "establishing modern industrial system programme," targeting the development of modern service sectors, high-tech industries, advanced manufacturing, and high-value-added manufacturing, meanwhile forcing firms to exit low-value-added export processing industry;
2. Develop lagging regions in Guangdong through the "double relocation policy," aiming at moving low value-added factories in the Pearl River Delta to lagging peripheral regions, while the labor force in the lagging regions of Guangdong would be transferred to the new industries in the Pearl River Delta, in the hope of benefiting from lower labor costs, raw material prices, and greater land availability while releasing land.

Government policy aimed on some key issues of industrial upgrading—scaling up; technological progress; and sales and distribution system building—, while the approach was very sectoral in using traditional policy instruments like picking pillar industries, investment in hard infrastructure, and investment attraction policies (different kinds of incentives, subsides to firms, etc.). During 2008 and 2014, Guangdong's "Industrial Transformation and Upgrading" strategy changed somehow the dynamics of its industrial development:

1. First of all, firms formerly only focusing on international market turned to explore the domestic market. Many of them established manufacturing bases in other provinces in China and increased production scale.
2. Secondly, firms formerly focusing on manufacturing activity turned to undertake higher value-added functions, such as technology development and branding. Although their geographical distribution was more dispersed than before, they began to have more

research capabilities, more domestic distribution network, and more brand awareness.

3. Thirdly, the modern service industry in Guangdong was also developed rapidly, especially the technical services and financial service related to advanced manufacturing and high-tech industries.

During this period, local firms had more internal sources for technological change, due to massive activities of production scale expansion, production plant relocation, and production equipment renewal and transformation, whose main content was using machine to substitute manpower. External sources of technological change formerly relied on foreign and international technology transfer, and then gradually local firms established more cooperation with domestic universities and research institutes, as well as formed a variety of technical alliances and platforms to search and transform new technologies. At the same time, the national innovation policy encouraged firms to develop indigenous innovation, based on technology import, through system integration, or even using proprietary intellectual property rights to have original innovation.

Industrial upgrading brought Guangdong significant achievement. In 2015, Guangdong had an import/export volume of 1241.9 billion US$, which was 29% of China's total foreign trade and contributed to 70% of China's trade surplus. Guangdong's goods exports were larger than that of the Russian Federation. Its total retail sales of consumer goods of 3151.8 billion Yuan made it also the biggest provincial domestic market in China.

Innovation-Driven Era (2015–Present)

In 2014, the government of Guangdong Province took the lead in China in issuing the decision on deepening the reform of scientific and technological system to drive Guangdong into innovation-driven development stage. In early 2015, the government clarified its innovation-driven development strategy as core strategy for Guangdong's economic restructuring and industrial transformation. In February, a number of policy measures on accelerating scientific and technological innovation were introduced, as well as key programs of accelerating innovation and development for 2015–2017. In September 2015, the State Council approved Guangdong's ambitious plan of the Pearl River Delta as National Demonstration Zone for Indigenous Innovation, aiming to create more advanced industrial clusters, promote the competitiveness of "Made in Guangdong" in the global value chain, increase Guangdong's international market share, extend vertical integration of industry to a global scope, and also drive related local service industry toward internationalization.

In 2015 and 2016, Guangdong's annual social R&D expenditure accounted for 2.5% of GDP, the contribution rate of scientific and technological progress was 56.8, and the proportions of primary, secondary, and tertiary sector were respectively 4.7:43.2:52.1. With their respective sectors, the proportion of value-added of modern service industry accounted for 61%, the added value of high-tech manufacturing accounted for 27.3%, the added value of advanced manufacturing accounted for 48.9%, and added value of strategic emerging industries accounted for 16.8%. Guangdong had seven billion-Yuan-worth sectors (new display, software, biomedical, new materials, new generation of communications, LED and energy-saving and environmental protection), nine World Top 500 companies, twenty-nine companies with sales exceeding 100 billion Yuan, and 19,857 national high-tech companies.

As Guangdong became number one in China in terms of authorized patents, its sources of technological innovation also turned to be further diversified. In addition to formal research and development institutions in large firms, small and medium in Guangdong set up own R&D facilities and research centers. Local entrepreneurial teams and individual entrepreneurs brought a large number of innovative projects, and cooperated with universities and research institutes to create innovative start-ups and joint ventures. Many local governments in Guangdong established offices in high-tech regions in Europe and the United States through cooperation with professional institutions, and used overseas teams to obtain cutting-edge information on technical knowledge. Thus, many companies, such as DJI which was world leader in drones, could take advantage of the trans-frontier knowledge network across Mainland, Hong Kong, and Macao in higher education and entrepreneurship.

Moreover, with super-urban agglomeration and megalopolis infrastructure development, the Pearl River Delta constructed a multi-level and diversified ecosystem of industrial innovation in China. Amazingly, the ecosystem was built up without first-class universities, national laboratories, and defense research institutions, just relying on its sections in global value chains and former manufacturing clusters. This urbanized local ecosystem was characterized by a variety of new forms of platform for promoting innovation:

1. industrial parks, science parks, smart cities, stylized towns, which integrated urbanization and innovation;
2. joint projects, new-type research and development institutions, talent teams, and other R&D institutes, which worked in the fields of big data, cloud computing, the internet of things, artificial intelligence, robotics, etc.;
3. incubators, makers spaces, industrial property developers, which provided services to entrepreneurial start-ups and idea creation; and
4. the traditional organizations which carried out innovation projects, such as research-university-industry alliances, research associations, university institutes, science and technology service agencies, emerging internationalized companies, etc.

The dynamics of such a rich innovation ecosystem in Guangdong embodied not only original innovation of new products and processes, but also innovations of flexible and diversified business models, novel marketing modes, and particular methods of organizational management, adapting to market demand and rapid environment change. Till the end of 2019, just before the outbreak of Covid-19, if Guangdong had yet generated a large number of world-class innovative companies, the Pearl River Delta would have been transformed to a world-class ecosystem of innovation.

The "Secret Formula" of a Successful Guangdong

Already in 2016, Guangdong generated the biggest part of China's GDP at provincial level—79.512 Billion Yuan—making its economic size equivalent to that of Australia and Turkey (GDP, PPP). Guangdong's economy, to a large degree, has successfully transformed from the factor-driven stage, through the investment-driven stage, and to the current innovation-driven stage. Over the last half-century, the province has also made an outsized contribution to the wider economic success of China. However, the mechanism or "secret formula" of Guangdong's late but catching-up industrialization is not well explained. The general impression about Guangdong's almost miraculous emergence always sticks to the vague concepts of private entrepreneurs, overseas Chinese investment, special economic zones and policies, its geographical proximity to Hong Kong, etc. The role of Guangdong local government and its interactive linkages to business firms in fostering development receives a fraction of the attention than the Chinese central government policies and strategy do. Yet this is the key to understand why and how Guangdong did not only emerge as the "world factory" of China after 1978, but also transformed smoothly into an innovation powerhouse after the global financial crisis of 2008 till the end of 2010s.

The purpose of this book is to give a detailed account and some theoretical explanation of Guangdong's innovative transformation. When both the company strategies and the government policy tools are put together in summative comparison all along the three major development stages of Guangdong (Table 1.2), it becomes super clear that a development model appears to the surface. In the book, this model is called "bottom-up innovation." The essence of the model is that contrary to what is often assumed to be the case, the continued success of Guangdong was due not solely to central government top-down policies, but mainly to "bottom-up innovation" in which companies and local governments have worked together closely over time to develop their appropriate strategies and policies. Understanding such an approach is vital if the whole of China or any other emerging economy is to head successfully toward their next stage of development.

From an innovation policy perspective, the model conforms of course to what is previously defined as a "bottom-up approach." That is to say, under the general background of reform and opening policy from the central government, the local governments in Guangdong made a series of policy adaptations and initiatives in favor of local firms and innovation activities from grassroots level. The local policy and implementation practice were so much richer than the written guidelines of central government that, during some time, the central government even tended to learn directly from the very local governments.[2]

But the whole model of bottom-up innovation contains not only government policies, but also business companies and their strategies. For example, the investment in R&D, learning technologies from foreign clients, and procurement of equipment and key components are all decisions from the very grassroots level of local business companies and supplier,

[2] For example, an anecdote is that in the summer of 2015, the book author helped a research team sent by the Ministry of Science and Technology of China from Beijing to carry out field visit in a district of Shenzhen in Guangdong. The objective of the field research was to discover find what "innovation ecosystem" meant in the implementation of innovation policy, a concept that the researchers heard of repeatedly from local government officials at that moment.

Table 1.2 Company strategy and policy tools in Guangdong

Development Stage	*Strategy of Small- and Medium-Sized Companies*	*Policy Tools of Regional or Local Governments*	*Relationship between local government policy and business strategy*
"World Factory" Development (1990s–2007)	**Technological learning (Chap. 4):** –shop-floor learning of production skills and know-how; –technology transfer, interacting with clients and finding markets; –learning from insertion in global value chain and interaction with equipment suppliers	**Industrial cluster (Chap. 5):** –promoting and facilitating business firms in marketing, technology development, and organizational change; –development local industrial districts as clusters; –pro-business local environment building	Policy imitating and learning business strategy
Industrial Upgrading (2008–2014)	**Dynamic capabilities building (Chap. 6):** –in-house R&D, product and process upgrading strategy; –strategy of integrating technical, market and organizational change within organization; –upgrading strategic management capabilities; –reconfiguring global value chain, supply chain upgrading, inter-sectoral upgrading, and new industry creation	**Industrial transformation and upgrading (Chap. 7):** –key projects investment –industrial targeting of more technology-intensive and emerging sectors, such as new electronics and robot industries –prioritizing service sector for manufacturing –industrial relocation ('freeing the cage for changing birds') –automation and advanced manufacturing system –public investment in R&D	Policy framing and guiding business strategy

(*continued*)

Table 1.2 (continued)

Development Stage	*Strategy of Small- and Medium-Sized Companies*	*Policy Tools of Regional or Local Governments*	*Relationship between local government policy and business strategy*
Innovation-driven Era (2015–now)	**Innovation platform and ecosystem building (Chaps. 9 and 10):** –heavily investing in formal R&D, and engineering –government-business-academia joint projects of innovation platforms; –creating new R&D institutes; –nnovation alliances and networks; –innovation chain and business ecosystem development	**Focusing on "ecosystems," constructinginnovation platforms, and resulting inregional innovation system (Chaps. 8 and 10)**: –establishing and financing jointly the new R&D institutes and platform projects. –incubation and entrepreneurship policies –fusion of innovation and industrial chains and activities –channeling and agglomerating innovation resources (talents and capital) in urbanized metropolitan areas and districts –multi-level governance structure of innovation policy –ntegrating previous innovation policy tools into a regional system of innovation as a development result	Policy and business strategy converging and jointly made

Source: Author

often small and mid-sized, even with sometimes policy interventions of local government.

And the most interesting part of the bottom-up innovation model of Guangdong is the continuous dynamic integration or interaction linkages of business firm strategies and local government policies over the three stages of development:

1. At the stage of "world factory" development, local companies mostly adopted the strategy of technological learning. They learnt how to produce from their foreign clients, who had direct access to the final markets. Their choice was to be technology followers and focus on being efficient production bases before going into the production and marketing of branded products. In viewing the companies' intents, local governments adopted policy of building local industrial clusters and district. They followed closely the footsteps of the local firms in promoting business and serving "customers," even imitated the business strategy by organizing exhibition markets, developing relevant technologies (testing and process improvement), and training local workers. There was a policy learning and mimicking of business strategy at this stage.
2. Then, at the stage of industrial upgrading, facing the severe decline of orders from international markets, local governments (firstly the provincial government, then the municipal and district/township governments) took initiatives to push the relocation of industrial firms and help them upgrade technologically but also commercially. Local governments made clear the prioritized sectors of investment and R&D areas, giving incentives and subsidies to local firms. Progressively, local firms reoriented their investment in those industries and projects targeted by governments. Many of them also joined the alliances or associations with other firms and research institutes set up by governments. The policy linkage to company strategies at this stage can be described as "framing and guiding."
3. When Guangdong's development entered into the innovation-driven stage, both business companies and local governments began to discover the usefulness of "innovation platforms" and the importance of "innovation ecosystem." Many companies were keen to create new ventures, R&D units, or research-intensive organizations under the label of "platforms." On the side local governments, following the national guideline of "massive entrepreneurship and innovation," they preferred to throw their own money as well as the venture capital from outside the region to construct new organizations of platforms and ecosystems, such as incubators, high-tech parks, innovation centers, and trendy start-ups. Local governments

were also interested in attracting large universities and research institutes to create local branches to commercialize their research outcomes and patents. In such a way, the local innovation policy and business strategies of companies were converging and mixed up. Local governments and companies often jointly created new ventures and platforms. Local governments became definitely a stakeholder of the whole local innovation "ecosystem."

In sum, there was a mutual co-evolution of local business strategies and government policies over time in Guangdong. Instead of simply making industrial policy decisions and then wait for the reaction from local industry, local governments in Guangdong pro-actively interwove their interventions into companies' action. They first learnt and imitated the business strategy, then framed and tried to guide business investment, and finally got deeper involvement in creating new organizations with companies. Together, the policy-strategy interplay reinforced each other, formed a closed-loop cycle of interactive learning, inducing, and converging between companies and governments, and jointly fostered innovation and change in the region. This is maybe the core ingredient of the "secret formula" of Guangdong.

How to Read This Book

The subsequent content of this book is divided into two parts.

Part I gives a general background of China and its development toward innovation economy in a top-down perspective, including Chaps. 2 and 3.

Chapter 2 analyzes the formal research and development activities of Chinese companies when China R&D investment began to soar in mid-2010s. But behind the splendid statistical numbers, Chinese companies were facing big hurdles of lacking external connections and absorption capacity, which used to lead to low quality and efficiency of research and development. How did the Chinese companies eventually overcome this institutional and organizational obstacle to develop from imitation to innovation? Chapter 2 only raises the question, but the answers could only be found in Part II of the book.

Chapter 3 reviews the issues with China's growth model and illustrates how the change of macroeconomic situation after 2010s forced the Central Government to adopt innovation-centered policy strategy, which required fundamentally to be localized and decentralized for designing and implementation, i.e., a bottom-up process in nature. This strategic dependency on innovation-centered policy has been kept even till today when China is struggling to go through the slow-down period. This time, China is trying to solve the Keynesian problem with a Schumpeterian solution, contrary to the era before 2015 when the country worked out a Keynesian solution to the Schumpeterian problem (Zhao & La Pira, 2013).

Part II, containing the seven chapters from 4 to 10, details the bottom-up innovation model of Guangdong and the chapters are arranged in time sequence.

Chapters 4 and 5 respectively describe the learning strategies of local companies and the cluster policies of local governments during the factor-driven stage.

Chapters 6 and 7 respectively analyze the management strategy toward dynamic capabilities for mastering technological change and local government industrial upgrading policies for promoting innovation in the investment-driven stage.

Entering into the innovation-driven stage, Chap. 8 identifies how local governments achieved to construct local innovation ecosystems with all kinds of policy tools.

Chapter 9 focuses on how companies, research organizations, and local governments made joint efforts in creating and operating various innovation platforms and projects.

Based on the experience of bottom-up model of Guangdong, Chap. 10 opens up a future road for a new generation of innovation policy, suitable for further innovation-driven development.

Policy makers are encouraged to read Chaps. 3, 5, 7, 8, 9, and 10. These chapters constitute in fact a policy handbook of bottom-up innovation, a unique policy strategy based on the practice of Chinese local governments.

Business executives may be more interested in Chaps. 2, 4, 6, and 9. These chapters contain some practical strategies of technological learning, innovation management, and project organization for running business, all based on empirical cases of ordinary Chinese local companies.

For my academic colleagues, peers, and the students, any chapter can be read directly and independently, because each is based on published papers with some thorough theoretical reflexion.

However, the essence of this book is the empirical facts. So, I hope that readers can digest it in a "bottom-up" way. As George Soros says,

"Thinking can never quite catch up with reality; reality is always richer than our comprehension."

References

Boekholt, P., & Thuriaux, B. (1999). Public policies to facilitate clusters: Background, rationale and policy practices in international perspective. In OECD (Ed.), *Boosting innovation: The cluster approach* (pp. 381–412). OECD.

Fromhold-Eisebith, M., & Eisebith, G. (2005). How to institutionalize innovative clusters? Comparing explicit top-down and implicit bottom-up approaches. *Research Policy, 34*(8), 1250–1268. https://doi.org/10.1016/j.respol.2005.02.008

Pei, M. (2012, July 9). The End Of China's Economic Miracle. *Newsweek.* https://ww.newsweek.com/end-chinas-economic-miracle-65591

Porter, M. E. (1990). *The competitive advantage of nations.* Free Press.

OECD. (2010). *OECD Territorial Reviews: Guangdong, China 2010*, OECD *Territorial Reviews.* OECD Publishing. https://doi.org/10.1787/9789264090088-en.

Xu, C. (2011). The fundamental institutions of China's reforms and development. *Journal of Economic Literature, 49*(4), 1076–1151.

Zhao, W., & La Pira, F. (2013). Chinese entrepreneurship: Institutions, ecosystems and growth limits. *Advances in Economics and Business, 1*, 72–88. https://doi.org/10.13189/aeb.2013.010204

Zheng, Y. (2007). *De facto federalism in China: Reforms and dynamics of central-local relations* (460 p.). World Scientific Publishing

PART I

The Top-Down Perspective of China's Innovation

CHAPTER 2

Behind the National Innovation System: R&D and Absorptive Capacity of Firms

Introduction: Explaining China's Jump from Imitation to Innovation

Macro statistic data shows that China's technology capabilities have improved dramatically in recent decades. China now sits first among 36 upper-middle-income economies and 3rd in the Asia-Pacific, trailing only Singapore and South Korea. From 2010 to 2025, China's rank in the Global Innovation Index, the gold standard for tech development, rose from 43rd to 10th. Its number of patents, number of publications, and ratio of R&D expense over GDP are all impressive. The number of high-level international journal articles and invention patents ranks first in the world, the integration of technological innovation and industrial innovation is accelerating, and the advantages of enriching application scenarios are constantly emerging. Its patent conversion rate is steadily increasing, and cutting-edge technological achievements are constantly being transformed into production.

The original version of this chapter "Is R&D Upgrading China from Imitation to Innovation? An Institutional Analysis of Absorptive Capacity" was published in *Journal Transition Studies Review*, Vol.22, No. 2 (2015), pp. 81–110. DOI: https://doi.org/10.14665/1614-4007-22-2-006

W. Zhao, *Remade in South China*, IPP Studies in the Frontiers of China's Public Policy,
https://doi.org/10.1007/978-981-95-7277-9_2

Now, the number of high-level scientific and technological talents in China ranks among the top in the world, with over 5 million graduates trained annually in science, technology, engineering, and mathematics (STEM) majors. In 2017, China's scientists for the first time published more papers than their US counterparts. By 2022, their papers also were being cited more often by other scholars. China has long led the world in the number of filed patents but since 2019 has led with the most filings of globally recognized "PCT" (Patent Cooperation Treatment) patents, an objective sign of quality. China's spending on research and development (R&D) jumped 475 percent between 2007 and 2023, placing it just behind the United States. In 2024, China's R&D investment has exceeded 3.6 trillion yuan, with investment intensity close to the average level of OECD countries.

In one word, it can be said that after 2010s, the Chinese economy has largely evolved from imitation to innovation in terms of technological capabilities. How was this leap achieved? A common view is attributed to China's top-down establishment of a strong national innovation system (NIS) and the relevant policy of high-intensity R&D investments. At macro level, the perspective of national innovation system focuses on interactive institutional arrangement upon which firms develop their innovation capabilities. The institutional aspect of NIS occupies most of the OECD reports. Indeed, within this enumerative vision of institutional system, the micro-dynamics underlying technological development and interaction between economic and technical actors disappear. Technological capability is translated into national plan set out by official innovation policy. A country is supposed to gain innovation capability through completing a national institutional structure composed by various functions, such as provision of R&D results, formation of new product markets, articulation of new product quality requirements, creating and changing organizations, networking through markets and other mechanisms, creating and changing institutions, incubating entrepreneurial activities, financing of innovation processes, and provision of consultancy services (C. Edquist, 1997). If innovation capacity emerges through only the building of such a system, China should have already reached the level since the country had finished the whole picture of NIS with these pieces of institutions many years ago.

Related to NIS argument, R&D investment is another explanation of China's leap from imitation to innovation. After all, the success experience from East Asian economies, such as Japan, South Korea, and Singapore seems to prove the idea that heavy R&D will naturally lead to more innovation. Innovation depends on the translating and commercializing of inventions (patents and publications are most obvious forms) into new products by firms. The firms in all these economies have made intensive investment in in-house R&D or other R&D equivalent activities for creating new products and services in market, then rapidly moved their whole economies up to innovation ladder. South Korea is even ranked as the most innovative country in the world in 2013.

There is no doubt that from the end of the twentieth century China became a world giant in R&D. Its gross domestic expenditure on R&D jumped from 1% of GDP in 2000 to 1.75% of GDP in 2010. Amount invested in R&D was multiplied by 6.6 between 2000 and 2010 (reaching 700 billion Yuan). There were 3.1 million people working in R&D in 2010. Already in 2012, China ranked number 1 in terms of patents registrations: 526,412 applications were filed with an increase of 41.3% from 2010s.

On the other hand, firms from Taiwan and Hong Kong developed active and closed interactions among their networks of firms, instead of increasing dramatically their formal R&D investment. Yet these "dragon" economies have been also approaching the innovation-driven stage. R&D for their innovation capabilities seems not to be a necessity. This paradoxical view of R&D is due to the fact that usually people substitute "innovation" simply and directly by "R&D" in assuming a country's scientific and technological capabilities become sufficient conditions of its innovation capacity. More detailed analysis shows that R&D is just one of many inputs in the complicated process of innovation; and scientific and technological capabilities need to be integrated into a country's production system to make firms innovative, especially for those in a more or less globalized competitive market. From a national economic development perspective, R&D itself is hardly to be said as a purpose, but rather a means which can lead the country to a new growth model. What finally counts for a country is the economic growth driven by its competitive firms as a result. If it is important to know the state of art of China's R&D activities as an "input" and its patents and publications as "potential sources," it should be even more important to detect the dynamic and innovation capacities of Chinese firms as an "output" of these efforts.

This brings us to the third way to explain China's innovation leap: the technological capabilities of firms. As Kline and Rosenberg (1986) rightly pointed out, innovation is a complicated linked-chain process of activities from research to market need detection, invention & design, development, engineering, production, distribution, market commercialization, etc. The successful process is determined by many critical linkages across these activities in the economy, such as linkages among the internal activities of firms at different stages of innovation development, among scientific activities and industrial invention & design, among firms' market detection activities and society's research activities, among a society's research activities and internal development activities of firms, and finally among distributing and consuming activities and firms' market searching activities, etc. Therefore, a country's innovation capacity shall not be evaluated at simply aggregate level with statistical indicators or official policy announcement, but at a more down-to-earth firm level which reflects often the unofficial but realistic behavior and quality of linkage building by innovation actors within the country.

Upon closer examination of China's R&D investments, it will be found that the performance of R&D requires some "absorptive capacity" at the firm level. In fact, the huge R&D investment brought about by China's strong national innovation system was able to play a role precisely because some companies had adopted R&D strategies based on absorptive capacity. These companies were initially some leading large ones, but this R&D strategy would eventually be adopted by a large number of local small- and medium-sized enterprises in China, as described in detail in Part II.

We will come back to discuss the firm capability explanation in the later part of this chapter. Before that let us first check the NIS explanation and the critical R&D history in China.

Constructing China's National Innovation System

Macro statistics illustrates the extremely important role of Chinese government in leading and organizing R&D activities. Since the reform of 1979, China has its S&T policy focusing on science and technology as premier force of production, and enacting the nation through science and education. Science and technology has been the cornerstone of China's development strategy since the 1980s, with a heavy initial emphasis on public funding of projects and investment in infrastructure. The structure of China's national R&D system has evolved from a central-planning model in which industrial R&D centers are located in ministries and organized by product. This structure separated and prevented interactions among scientific research and industrial application of R&D results.

Since the mid-1980s government has encouraged closer integration among R&D institutes and science parks through investment in R&D clusters, and mergers of R&D institutes into enterprise groups (some such as Huawei, Datang, and Lenovo subsequently evolved into major IT enterprises). As a result of such policies and China's openness to foreign direct investment, technology market transactions increased, as did in-house R&D. Outsourcing of science and technology from universities and research institutes to various types of domestic enterprises and to international enterprises expanded. Even in 1985 China has begun to reorganize its research and development (R&D) structure through reducing the numbers, downsizing the scales, and directing to lucrative purpose of its R&D institutions.

During all the 1990s, the government encouraged the creation of all sorts of technological poles and industrial parks in the coastal provinces, then the scientific incubators and economic and technological development zones in major urban areas. The State financed and established national and local-level laboratories in all disciplines across the whole country. It controlled often directly the most important research laboratories, universities, and technical centers, as well as maintained in its arms the strategic and military sectors. Combined with national industrial policy, the Chinese government searched to build up "national champions" in terms of technology and research capability, often State-owned enterprises, but also some selected non-State enterprises, such as the Chinese giant companies in telecommunication industry, in petrochemical industry, in transportation industry, etc.

From late 1990s, the Chinese government implemented a series of policies to build an "innovative nation." According to the Chinese official definition, the innovative nation concept included original innovation, integrated innovation, and innovation based on introduction, assimilation, and absorption of foreign technology.

National Innovation Policies

Since 1999, in adopting the concepts and frameworks of "national innovation system", China's national science and technology was transformed into innovation policy and the investment in R&D activities was greatly accelerated. This "big push" of China's R&D expenditure since 2006 was in fact the result of the continuing investment efforts and R&D system reform of Chinese government. The same year, Chinese government announced a national "Mid to Long Term Science and Technology Development Plan, 2006–2020" with the following goals by 2020:

1. R&D input should achieve 900 billion Yuan
2. R&D/GDP ratio should achieve 2.5%
3. To build an "Innovative Nation"
4. High R&D input (annual increase rate of 10%)
5. High contribution of S&T to economy (more than 70%)
6. Indigenous innovation capability (reduce the reliance on foreign technologies from 60% to 30% in terms of licenses fees)
7. High S&T output like patents

Shortly after the announcement of the Plan, 99 supporting policies were presented which define concrete action plans to implement the strategy. Each supporting policy was under the responsibility of one lead government institution. Main priority was given to the development of technologies on energy conservation, water resources, environment protection, biotechnology, space, and aviation, on the mastering of core technologies, on the comprehension of intellectual property in the manufacturing sector, and on the strengthening of basic and strategic research. Alongside the identification of priority fields for future research activities in detail, the plan also defined 16 key projects (mega-projects), for example sending a Chinese astronaut to the moon or developing the next generation of large planes. In 2010, the Chinese government specified seven sectors as strategic emerging industries and reemphasized R&D investment in these sectors:

1. energy efficiency and environmental protection,
2. next generation IT,
3. biotechnology,
4. high-end equipment manufacturing,
5. new energy,
6. new materials, and
7. new energy automotive.

Since 2006 China's innovation policy was labeled as "indigenous innovation." The Plan stated that it could be achieved through various approaches (including innovation through originally creating newness, innovation through creatively integrating technologies, and innovation through renewing imported and assimilated technologies), but the chosen term "indigenous" implied also some intentions of the Chinese government underlying its innovation strategy. First, "indigenous" implied "independent" and "self-determined" development of certain sectors identified as strategic through organizational coordination and heavy State investment in science and research activities of universities, institutes, and State-owned enterprises. The implementation of such kind of science policy essentially divided technological R&D from industry production, with universities and research institutes actively engaged in downstream industrial projects and enterprises focusing on fulfilling assigned producing quota. Compared to developed countries where firms are a major source of innovation, the extensive involvement of public research in industry R&D in China constituted an important character of its national innovation projects. As a result, the process of research–invention interactions in China was often unidirectional, with the knowledge flowing from university to industry.

But "indigenous" had another implication. It means also that the innovation should be original, not copied, and constitute intellectual property rights owned by Chinese organizations, especially Chinese enterprises. This concern reflected the facts that till then most of the so-called innovations in China were imitated from foreign technologies. In fact, during the 1990s till 2005, the Chinese technology strategy in practice could be summarized as "market in exchange of technology."

Automobile industry was a typical case of this State strategy. In 1984, when China granted foreign auto manufacturers market access, it imposed foreign companies to form joint ventures with Chinese local partners, often State-owned enterprises designated by the authorities or to obtain their consent. China knew its car makers were behind the curve on precision manufacturing, so it hoped that the State-owned car producers could learn through contact with foreign partners to bolster domestic technology expertise, and gradually take ownership of the learnt technologies. Similar obligations of technology transfer were also imposed to heavy equipment vendors. As the country invested in acquiring aerial fleets, thermal and nuclear power stations, and modern rail network, the State always required forming joint ventures in order to have access to the most advanced technologies. Yet the Chinese car companies still found it tough to improve their quality, in part because they lagged on in-house research and development spending. Most Chinese companies just thought several years out with their R&D spending and try to compete with international companies that were already doing R&D 20 to 25 years out. Chinese JV partners spent less on nurturing innovative engineering and design. Instead of creating a car from scratch, which would allow them to claim half the patent rights, Chinese JV partners would take existing foreign vehicle blueprints, make a few changes, and call it a new JV auto: GM and SAIC's first JV car, Baojun 630, was built on the old Buick Excelle, while Dongfeng and Nissan's first Venucia vehicle was fashioned after Tiida. Chinese JV car companies wanted to gain quickly consumers' confidence through their reliance on foreign tech for quality. The government wanted to see the domestic capabilities in car industry, but many of the Chinese companies were just happy on successful foreign joint ventures to contribute to their profitability.

National Mega-Projects of R&D

To change this situation, the Chinese government translated the implementation of this "indigenous" innovation strategy into a series of mega-industrial projects with ambitious "techno-nationalist" goals and public funding: high-speed railway, big commercial aircraft C919, new generation of nuclear enter, wind power energy, etc., were all examples. In history, Chinese government had habit and experience in organizing and implementing national mega-projects. During the period of 1978 to 1985, it organized and implemented 108 sectional science and technology projects. Since 1986, it launched 3 basic national R&D projects and 2 supplementary projects. The 3 basic projects were: 863 Programme, Tackling Programme, and 973 Programme; and the 2 supplementary projects are: Torch Programme and Spark Programme.

Since 2000, Chinese government realized that its R&D projects aiming at scientific "big bangs" or leaps needed to be connected to the country's production system and extended to downstream activities of industrial chain. Therefore, 12 National Specific Programmes of Significant Technologies were established. Comparing with former S&T projects emphasizing research and science activities, these projects of national significant technologies directly contained industrialization and commercialization of R&D results. They emphasized the participation of enterprises in order to implement the activities of design, development, production, and commercialization. Enterprises should not only participate, but also behave as project leaders. Covering very different technological fields, the 12 national projects gave priority to the market formation of national

R&D outcomes. The Chinese high-speed train was in fact one of the fruits of these national projects of significant technologies. Encouraged by the success of these projects, the Chinese government decided in 2006 to establish another 16 national projects of significant technologies to be implemented till 2020. The new projects correspond in fact to the 16 strategic industrial sectors with technological importance, in which 3 are in military fields, identified by the 2006 national innovation strategic plan.

Over time, China's new generation of techno-nationalist mega-projects achieved to mobilize the country's resources at a very exceptional speed and scale to integrate science and technology in industrial production. Nevertheless, beyond the apparent effectiveness, they encountered some hidden problems and limits. The implementation and organization of such projects depended almost completely on the technocratic administration structures of Chinese government and State-owned enterprises. National innovation policy was then elaborated through 3 central ministries: National Commission of Reform & Development, Ministry of Science & Technology, and Ministry of Finance. The formation and execution of projects needed coordination among more ministries and involvement of local governments. Powerful ministries such as Commission of Reform & Development, Ministry of Industry and Information, and departments of Ministry of Science & Technology were all chasing big projects with allocation of big budget.

The continuous R&D investment promoted the emergence of a stabilized class of technocrats with their interests related to China's R&D system. Traditionally, Ministry of Science & Technology had more influence on the direction of national R&D projects. It had tendency to emphasize the scientific and technological aspects of projects and public institutes and universities became naturally main undertakers of the projects. Thus national innovation objective was easily translated into academic research activities. Within the closed circle, the technocrats established their own criteria of project. The S&T technocrats transplanted directly the government's performance evaluation system to R&D system, using quantitative methodology, setting up complicated indicators, and executing strict paper-work auditing over researchers in laboratories. Time and energy of researchers were used to deal with administration. Besides, the class of technocrats itself was a big spender of R&D budget.

For example, in 2009, 83.91% of total R&D expenditure was for ordinary administrative expense such as traveling, meeting, buying stationary, etc. (486.88 billion Yuan), which was five times more than expense on assets. It was only in the end of 2000s, after some policy reports done by international organizations (IDRC, World Bank, OECD, etc.) and the diffusion of national innovation system approach in Chinese academia, that some top leaders recognized that the majority of inventions recorded as patents were never introduced on a commercial basis and most of successful innovations were initiated as the result of perceived market needs. So the former projects driven by scientific or technical breakthroughs were redirected to have linkages with industrial production and market commercialization, but mainly in State-owned enterprises.

In terms of organization, China's national mega R&D projects inherited the legacy of its centrally planned economic system. Plan failed to recognize the importance of non-high-technology, incremental innovation, driven by market competitive forces that was widespread among non-State-owned enterprises. Through tailored government policies and assured funding, national R&D projects became always vertically integrated enterprises by linking public institutes' research and State-owned enterprises' production. The industrialization of R&D outcomes was normally found in a domestic monopolistic market or with government as final purchaser, such as transportation, telecommunication infrastructure, aircraft, energy, petroleum, etc., so that risks and costs of projects can be internalized by government itself. But wider linkages with other domestic non-State enterprises and international markets were not established.

However, because science, research, and technological activities were vertically linked to industrial development, production, and distribution within the government projects, China was able to quickly catch up the targeted technological fields once the industrial-technical system was well identified. Thus, this kind of project was especially suitable to the development of technical complex product systems, which required much interactions between central activities along the innovation linked chain and a society's research activities and knowledge base. However, the Chinese technological catch-up through these projects happened only in the existing techno-economic paradigm such as high-speed train and nuclear power station. Even with an initial preference to high-tech content, China's mega-projects have not created any new-to-the-world techno-economic paradigm, but replicated the existing ones through developing its own technological capabilities. It should be mentioned that much of these technological capabilities were also originally obtained by learning from foreign partners, of which the establishment of numerous Sino-foreign joint ventures within the framework of China's grand airplane projects is a proof. In fact, China's national R&D projects represented a transition from a "process driven by scientific and technical breakthroughs" to a state of combing the "process of essential development activities" with the "process of research and knowledge exploitation."

According to the conceptual framework of Kline and Rosenberg (1986), China's national R&D projects would help effectively develop science and technology capabilities in the upstream of the innovation chain. This was proved to be true by the famous "Made in China 2025" plan to accelerate its indigenous capabilities and market share in a wide range of high-tech sectors, launched in 2015. The Chinese State thus had a full intervention at national and local levels in the domain of science and technology development to a variety of enterprises (developing endogenous projects, assimilating foreign tech transfer, as well as inserting in global value chain, etc.), especially through its State-owned enterprises (SOE). Analyses by Bloomberg, the Information Technology & Innovation Foundation, the U.S. Chamber of Commerce and Rhodium Group, the Wire China, and others showed that the risky initiative largely paid off, with substantial advances in domestic technical capabilities, value-added, and market share in most of the targeted industries by 2025, 10 years after.

China's Investment in R&D

The History of R&D Surge During 2005 and 2015

Related to the establishment of China's national innovation system is the sudden increase of R&D investment. The experience of East Asian newly industrialized economies, especially that of Japan and South Korea, has suggested that the key of enterprise' jumping from the stage of imitation to stage of innovation is intensified in-house research and development (R&D) activities, even though R&D activities can be very costly and their results are uncertain. Taking the Japanese companies as examples, in fact, their continuous investment in reverse engineering is a special form of R&D efforts. Reverse engineering involves taking apart something (a mechanical device, electronic component, computer program, or biological, chemical, or organic matter) and analyzing its workings in detail to make a new device or program that does the same thing without using or simply duplicating the original. Through reverse engineering, Japanese enterprises often added new functions or features to imported products and tailored them to fit local demand. This process needs deep understanding of the technological and scientific logic of the product and system, and often leads to formal R&D. From the 1950s to the 1970s, China also used reverse engineering to try to acquire technology. However, because of the State-owned companies, there was less incentive to invest in R&D. The government did say that there was a need for reverse engineering, but reverse engineering failed to become the popular or dominant way to develop indigenous technologies. Since then, the potential bridge between in-house R&D and foreign technology transfer and importation has been broken within the Chinese enterprises. The lack of attention to R&D efforts led Chinese enterprises to import new technology or products from advanced economies or rely on joint-venture partners to provide new technologies. As a result, technology imports still play an important role in China and the share of expenditure on technology importation is still high. Compared to Japanese and South Korean enterprises, during long time Chinese enterprises spent little money on assimilating the imported technology. The allocation of resources for assimilation was then increased over years.

Compared to Japan or South Korea, the Chinese government was capable of mobilizing massively all kinds of resources to invest in R&D activities. Even China had no official statistics of industrial R&D before the year of 2000, the country's national R&D policy could always be described as a "Big Push" approach.

Since late 1990s, Chinese central government began to make tremendous efforts in R&D investment. Then by 2010, China had the world's biggest number of professional R&D staff (3.2 million people) and its annual R&D budget had already been number 3 in the world since 2010. Potentially, the country had a stock of 51 million scientific and technical persons as human resources to get involved in R&D and the aggregate R&D expenditure was even accelerated after 2005 with an average growth rate over 20%. During 2000 and 2012, China's R&D intensity (ratio of R&D expense over GDP) jumped from 1% of 2000 to 1.97% of 2012 (see Table 2.1). In 2012, the country's R&D budget reached 1024 billion RMB Yuan, of which 74% was expended by enterprises. Its output value of high-tech industrial production had exceeded 1 trillion Yuan and counted more than 30% of its total export. The overall average annual growth rate for R&D expenditure of large and medium-sized enterprises had been more than 25% since 2006.

Policy measures were implemented concretely over the country, often with fixed quantitative goals to achieve. For example, between 1997 and

Table 2.1 China's Surge in National R&D Expenditure (2006–2012)

	2006	*2007*	*2008*	*2009*	*2010*	*2011*	*2012*
R&D Expenditure (Billion RMB Yuan)	300.31	371.02	461.6	580.21	706.26	868.7	1024
Ratio to GDP (%)	1.42	1.49	1.54	1.7	1.76	1.84	1.97

Source: National Bureau of Statistics and Ministry of Science and Technology (ed.), China Statistical Yearbook of Science and Technology (Beijing: China Statistics Press, various years)

2007 patent subsidies were introduced in 27 provinces to stimulate the usage of intellectual property rights and boost provincial and national patent statistics. The result was tremendous growth of patent applications. In 2010, China recorded 363,329 patent applications and 1,423,545 scientific publications with an average citation count of 6.21 times for the Chinese international publications (about 14.84 million papers), lower than the world average count of 10.71 times for international publications. Chinese industrial enterprises applied 266,000 patents, 10.2 times more of the patent application in 2000. The applications included 92,000 invention patents, 11.6 times more of invention patent applications in 2000. In 2012, patent applications reached 526,412, an annual increase of 41.3%, and made China number one in terms of patent volumes, although patenting in China has only a small impact on productivity growth and the problem of quality of research and its commercial relevance still exists.

However, with the expansion of R&D activities, China's R&D quality became problematic. For example, in most of the high-tech sectors, China's R&D intensity was lagging behind the major players in the world. In the aircraft and spacecraft industry, the R&D intensity just reached half of those in Germany, France, and the United Kingdom. China's focus in R&D activities mainly concentrated on applied research and especially experimental development. Experimental development expenditure over total R&D spending increased from 68% in 1995 to 87% in 2008. In 2009, this ratio decreased to 82.75% and remained at 83.5% in 2011. The fact that most R&D expense was used in the experimental development showed that R&D activities in China mainly concentrated in the latter-end of R&D.

Meanwhile, the expense of fundamental research in total R&D expense stayed at the level of 4.7% after 2009, even its absolute amount increased steadily after that year. Basic research might not have immediate commercial success, but is often essential for progress and constitutes the foundation for innovative products. China's spending on basic research as a percentage of the GDP was ten times lower than basic research expenditures in the United States. The weak fundamental research capability in China was reflected by the fact that China's patents and scientific papers per population are maintained on a low level compared to developed countries and also quality issues remain, though the quantity of scientific articles and patent applications were increasing rapidly. Regarding the famous growth of Chinese patents in those years, the share of "invention" patents over total registered domestic patents fluctuated. It climbed up at 25.9% in 2004 and fell to 22.7% in 2008, then jumped up to 34.8% in 2010. Besides, the Chinese patent explosion was driven by a small group of companies in the information and communication technology equipment industry.

Another characteristic of China's R&D was the nature of activity. In 2009, 50.7% of national R&D budget was spent for developing brand new product, 30.3% for increasing product functionalities and improving quality, 6% for energy using reduction, 3.3% for improving labor productivity, 2.7% for pollution reduction, 2% for technical theorem research, and 1.7% for raw material using reduction. Roughly speaking, 80% of Chinese R&D budget was allocated for product innovation and 15% for process innovation, and 5% for long-term non-commercial development. Chinese R&D projects preferred much the short-term economic returns.

The major financial source of China's R&D activities was government's fiscal budget. In 2010 and 2011, the government fiscal source of R&D was 411.4 billion Yuan and 490.2 billion Yuan, representing respectively 58% and 48% of the national R&D expenditure. The shares of R&D expenditure by enterprises, government-owned institutes, and public universities in national expenditure remained around 75%, 15%, and 8% respectively, which indicated the then institutional structure of R&D activities. Chinese academic circle was made up of its 3900 research institutes, university laboratories, and national key laboratories (there were 220 in total, mostly from universities). They were related, even intermingled with firms and worked for corporate R&D in the form of research contracts. In 2012, this type of contract carried a total amount of over 600 billion Yuan in China.

The Institutional Constraints of R&D

Regarding enterprises, in 2009, there were 36,387 industrial enterprises which carried out 194,000 R&D projects. This number of enterprises having R&D function was only 8.5% of total number of enterprises in China. Within these firms having R&D activities, 12,434 were middle and large sized enterprises, representing 30.5% of total middle and large sized enterprises. All these R&D projects by enterprises spent 377.6 billion Yuan of which 85% were spent by middle and large sized enterprises. Averagely, enterprises in China spent 0.7% of their sales on R&D if they do, while middle and large sized enterprises spent 0.96% of their sales on R&D if they do. Among the enterprises having R&D activities, 4.8% were State-owned enterprises (1737) while they had 17.1% of industrial R&D budget (64.46 billion Yuan); 72.6% were non-State-owned enterprises (26,418) while they had 56.5% of industrial R&D budget (213.44 billion Yuan); 22.6% were foreign-invested enterprises, including investment from Hong Kong, Macau, and Taiwan (8232), while they had 26.2% of industrial R&D budget (99.68 billion Yuan).

As early as in 1997, the Chinese government was already well aware that the key of making China an indigenous innovation machine was to upgrade the capacities of its enterprise sectors. But it was until 2010 that it recognized that it was especially the non-State and private sectors that remained a weakest part in the national innovation system. A quick look on the list of most R&D intensive enterprises in China will demonstrate that most of them are State-owned enterprises in the non-competitive market. Since then, policies of favorable tax policies and various other fiscal incentives are elaborated to increase investment in in-house R&D and enhance the innovation capabilities in the enterprise sector. Since 2010, the government encouraged all kinds of enterprises to participate in the development of the "strategic emerging industries" identified since 2010, including energy saving and environmental protection, new generation of information technology, biology, high-end equipment manufacturing, new energy, and new energy vehicles. These sectors traditionally reserved only to State R&D investment now solicit more private participation. In the beginning of 2013, the central government called on companies to make greater efforts to upgrade and innovate. By 2015, the government helped enterprises establish their "technological innovation system" which combined the functions of research, development and production. To do this, the government directly set up R&D utilities for industrial sectors, supported small and medium enterprises, trained more qualified talents, and improved the financial policies. The government also required other public institutions, such as universities and technical centers, to cooperate with enterprise sectors, which were not only State-owned sectors, but also included the non-State and private sectors.

A glance at the top Chinese companies in terms of R&D investment in 2012 would show that most of them were State-owned enterprises who often got involved in national mega R&D projects, and the very few private companies were those whose names had begun to be known in international market, such as Huawei, ZTE, Lenovo, and BYD. These namely superstar private enterprises also participated in national R&D projects and undertook projects of new product development and technological studies (see Table 2.2).

Table 2.2 Top 20 Chinese Companies in R&D Investment (The 2012 EU Industrial R&D Investment Scoreboard)

	Company	*World Rank*	*R&D Expenditure (Million Euros)*	*R&D Intensity (%)*
1	Huawei	41	2906.5	18.6
2	PetroChina	68	1622.0	0.7
3	ZTE	99	1129.8	10.7
4	China Railway Construction	106	1039.2	1.9
5	SAIC Motor	151	702.3	1.4
6	China Railway	157	655.6	1.2
7	China Petroleum & Chemicals	169	596.4	0.2
8	Dongfeng Motor	223	424.3	2.6
9	CSR China	251	363.2	3.7
10	Lenovo	259	347.7	1.5
11	BYD	277	326.3	5.7
12	HBIS	299	298.5	1.9
13	China Communications Construction	310	283.8	0.8
14	Metallurgical of China	316	275.1	1.0
15	China CNR	323	267.7	2.5
16	Chongqing Changan Motor	392	197.6	6.4
17	Shanghai Electric	435	173.0	2.1
18	Dongfang Electric	494	147.3	2.8
19	Huyau Automotive	560	129.3	2.0
20	Great Wall Technology	643	107.7	0.9

Source: European Commission (2012)

The disproportionally high percentage of R&D budget for State-owned enterprises in China raised the question about the role of privately owned Chinese domestic enterprises in technology development. Although China's privately owned enterprises were expanding rapidly and in terms of absolute amount of R&D expenditure they were bigger than the State-owned enterprises, they were still lagging behind their State-owned counterparts in terms of R&D investment intensity. This was due to institutional constraints in China such as limited access to finance for non-State-owned enterprises and government preference of grants to State-owned enterprises.

The Firm-Level Efficiency of R&D

During the period 2000 and 2012, the Chinese government strengthened the patent law and legal protection of technologies to give bigger incentive to enterprises to innovate. One the other side, Chinese enterprises responded to government policies by increasing dramatically R&D investment and application of all forms of patents, as demonstrated by macro statistics.

For most of Chinese non-State-owned manufacturers, they had traditionally had a manufacturing-led focus on reapplying existing business models to deliver products for fast-growing markets. Furthermore, their success depended on local resources—for example, lower cost labor, inexpensive land, and access to capital or intellectual property—that were difficult to replicate elsewhere. The main sources of technologies were from technology importation. If there was R&D in these enterprises, its main content was in fact absorption and assimilation of imported technologies. And even the investment on technology absorption through internal R&D was very low. For instance, for a long period of time the expenditure for assimilation and absorption in Chinese textile industry was below 1.5% of the machine and equipment importation expenditure.

The innovation process in these enterprises, if there were one, was based on the linear chain activities from design to development to industrialization, without much investment in formal R&D, without much links to the country's research activities, and without multiple feedbacks from distribution and market detection. For example, in consumer electronics sector, China purchased 33% of the world's chips ($100 billion worth), using them both in products sold domestically and in exports. But most of the Chinese industry competed in commoditized areas such as chip assembly and testing, and Chinese semiconductor companies held 4% or less of the most prized segments of the global value chain in chip design and manufacturing. Chinese enterprises exerted little influence on semiconductor design, technology standards, or chip selection for major product categories such as mobile phones, laptop computers, and LCD televisions. Most decisions about design and functionality came from global champions and reflect the preferences of consumers in Europe, Japan, and the United States.

Local enterprises' R&D projects tended to be derivative—refining products developed in Japan and South Korea instead of developing fundamentally new products (Shanzhai products). Innovation based on careful study of consumer preferences was rare, especially when the consumers were outside of China. Chinese companies placed much focus on expanding market share with just-good-enough products instead of creating markets with totally new products. In most cases, the skills and capabilities of these companies were oriented toward the domestic market which was so large, that even if they want to expand globally, they would face high hurdles. Most of Chinese private entrepreneurs were uncomfortable doing business outside their own geography and language.

After 2000, the investment of R&D by Chinese enterprises exceeded 60% of the country's total R&D spending and increased rapidly. Some sectors experienced intensive development of R&D. For example, the top 100 domestic electronics and information enterprises spent on average about 3% of annual sales revenue on R&D, with telecom equipment manufacturers such as Huawei Technologies, Datang Telecommunications, and Zhongxing Telecommunications (ZTE) leading the way, each devoting above 10% of the sales revenue to R&D. Nationwide, of the more than 10 million medium- and small-sized firms in electronics and information sector, 150,000 allocated more than 5% of sales to technological development. Although R&D expenditures, patent applications, and high-tech exports had markedly risen, the overall technological capabilities of Chinese enterprises remained poor. Impressive absolute R&D expenditure growth failed to reveal the quality and efficiency of R&D investment of Chinese enterprises. In 2011, only 11.5% of all industrial enterprises carried out R&D activities, in which only 30.5% of large and medium-sized enterprises were active in R&D. The R&D intensity (R&D expenditure over sales revenue) was 0.71% for all industrial enterprises, and averagely 0.96% for large and medium-sized enterprises, much lower than the average 3–5% in developed countries, even though it had been increasing steadily since 2000 (see Table 2.3). It should be mentioned that R&D activities were very rampant in the State-owned sector. Although they had 14.6% of enterprise R&D budget, the State-owned enterprises counted 81% of total number of enterprises having R&D and 66% of national R&D personnel.

The limit of R&D deepening of Chinese enterprises was also reflected by the investment structure and outcome efficiency of R&D. The share of basic and applied research expenditure over total R&D spending was always small. It declined from 32% in 1995 to 17% in 2008, to 17.3% in 2009 and 2010, to 16.5% in 2011. The shares of fundamental research, applied research, experiment, and development were respectively 0.1%, 2%, and 97.9% for the industrial enterprise sector. During 2000 and 2009, the R&D intensity of Chinese enterprises increased from 0.71% to 0.96%, while its ratio of new product over sales revenue increased from 11.1% to 12.1%, with less amplification effect. The share of "invention" patents over total domestic patents registered was 30.4% in 2000, dropped to 25.9% in 2004 and 22.7% in 2008. Encouraged by the government policy, the share of "invention" patents dramatically jumped up to 34.8% in 2009, but fell back to 27.3% in 2011. It is estimated that enterprises had then a

Table 2.3 Technology-Related Expenditure of Chinese Large and Medium—Sized Enterprises (RMB 100 million, 2004–2011)

	2004	*2005*	*2006*	*2007*	*2008*	*2009*	*2010*	*2011*
R&D Expenditure	954.4	1250.3	1630.2	2112.5	2681.3	3210.2	4015.4	5031
Technology Renovation	2590	2792.9	3019.6	3650.9	4167.7	3671.4	4293.7	4292.1
Technology Importation	367.9	296.8	320.4	452.5	440.4	394.6	449.0	449.4
Adaptation and Assimilation of Imported Technology	54.0	69.4	81.9	106.6	106.5	163.8	202.2	201.4
Purchase of Domestic Technology	69.9	83.4	87.4	129.6	166.2	174.7	220.5	222.1
R&D Expenditure / Sales Revenue (%)	0.71	0.76	0.77	0.81	0.84	0.96	0.93	0.96

Source: National Bureau of Statistics and Ministry of Science and Technology (ed.), China Statistical Yearbook of Science and Technology (Beijing: China Statistics Press, various years)

share of 25% of patent applications in China. Even the most patented enterprises preferred to produce patents of utility new models and external design rather than “invention” patents. A check on the top 20 enterprises which registered biggest number of patents in 2011 showed that only 5 of them had more “invention” patents than other forms of patents (On the list they were: ZTE as number 1; Huawei as number 2; Hongfujin as number 5; China Chip International as number 17; and Hangzhou Huasan as number 18). Chinese R&D stagnated in bringing more auxiliary improvements based on design instead of coming out with product innovation based on core technology development. Except that several enterprises progress with strong integration capability from R&D to marketing, most of Chinese enterprises began to invest in R&D but quickly found it difficult to deepen their R&D fields, to increase the efficiency of projects, and to upgrade the quality of outcomes. They were stuck in the halfway of imitation to innovation. A survey in 2012 in the Pearl River Delta region (Guangdong Province) of 1201 industrial enterprises showed that 44% of these enterprises set up new R&D utilities after 2008 as a response to crisis, but still 55% of enterprises reported that their R&D activities contained imitation of foreign technologies.

The Absorptive Capacity of Catch-up Firms

The Meaning of "Absorptive Capacity"

Academically, evidence from empirical studies supports the argument that explicit investment in endogenous and formal R&D activities of latecomer firms always matters, particularly when local firms intend to jump to upper level in the value chain. Li (2011) shows that investment by Chinese firms in foreign technology alone does not enhance innovation in domestic firms, unless it is coupled with own in-house R&D. Through the case of a Mexican company Vitro, the largest glass company in the world after Owen-Illinois, Gabriela Dutrénit (2000, 2004) argues that there is no simple linear progression from the early stage of accumulation of the minimum levels of innovative capability to the management of knowledge as a strategic asset and the deployment of core capabilities. On the contrary, the transition process is complex and while latecomer firms make that transition, they have to build deeper and broader specialized knowledge and develop new ways of strategic integration. The innovation capability can be reached only through a specific kind of “spontaneous” actions rather than a succession of different stages of formation of technological capabilities. In using South Korea's transition from imitation to innovation, Linsu Kim (1997, 1998) argues that cumulative learning of firms takes place through learning by doing, but discontinuous learning takes place in crisis. Effective learning firms (such as Hyundai) construct a crisis (by setting ambitious targets) intentionally to develop organizational systems and manage their processes to make the crises truly creative. Although creative imitation (producing knockoffs and clones) through reverse engineering is still important, it is the continuous increase in in-house R&D investment that plays the key role in leap from coping imitation to indigenous innovation. He suggests that latecomer firms shall intensify dramatically their formal R&D activities to engage in independent product innovation and participate actively in global alliances.

In fact, R&D not only generates new knowledge but contributes to the firm's absorptive capacity. According to Cohen and Levinthal (1989, 1990), absorptive capacity is the ability of a firm to recognize the value of new, external information, assimilate it, and apply it to commercial ends is critical to its innovative capabilities. Absorptive capacity may be a byproduct of R&D investment or manufacturing or through training. Generally, it depends on the firm's own R&D. In big firms, specific R&D projects will often be triggered by practice (problems with a product, new user needs, problems with producing) but almost immediately attempts will be made going through its earlier work as well as looking for insights that can be drawn from outside sources. Therefore, absorptive capacity will in return condition the success and sustainability of its innovative activity, or R&D in the narrow sense. Because a firm's absorptive capacity influences the effects of appropriability and technological opportunity conditions on its R&D spending, it becomes the essential condition of R&D deepening.

The continuous reinforcement and development of absorptive capacity itself also need appropriate conditions external to the firm. These external conditions are mainly the nature of linkages and interactions that the firm establishes with potential knowledge sources. Vertical linkages are interactions in terms of new product development with suppliers, buyers, end-users, channel members, and downstream manufacturing customers, while horizontal links are collaborations with other companies, industrial research laboratories, public research institutes, universities, technical consulting firms, and even competitors, among others. Together, the vertical and horizontal linkages are often termed as ecosystem of innovation of "world" of innovation. Though vertical linkages can be vital for elementary technological learning, horizontal linkages offer more opportunities for firms to gain access to complementary knowledge that tends to lead to more innovations.

Vertical and horizontal linkages together can be termed as ecosystem or "world" of innovation (Arvanitis et al., 2014). Shu (2003) uses examples of Taiwanese IT firms to show that these OEM/ODM manufacturers receive product specifications from their customers such as IBM, Dell, and HP in terms of design, manufacturing, and delivery of finished products, but their intensive horizontal linkages and interactions with other Taiwanese firms and public research institutions within the network were so important that it substituted partially the formal internal R&D activities. In fact, the horizontal linkage with other Taiwanese firms was found to be the most significant contributor to both the technical and marketing knowledge for commercial ends.

More precisely, the development of such absorptive capacity depends on the easiness and quality of linkage building. For firms, external linkages should be neither too difficult, nor too easy to establish. A survey about the South Korean automobile industry (Kim, 1997) found that compared with wholly owned firms, joint-venture firms were lagging behind in terms of developing absorptive capacity, due to their easier access to technical knowledge from foreign partners. On the contrary, having no quick access to foreign technology, Hyundai Motor Company had to accumulate more prior knowledge, invest more resources in R&D resources, and adopt a more aggressive attitude toward knowledge learning and acquisition. As a result, Hyundai developed a stronger capacity of technology absorption and R&D than joint ventures.

For upgrading to innovation, of particular importance is the quality, i.e., form and nature of these external linkages (Furman et al., 2001). Absorptive capacity building needs sustained interactions that go beyond arm's length market transactions and that involve more than the information about prices and volumes. These include what Lundvall (1988, 1992) called as user-producer interactions, i.e., direct cooperation and exchange of qualitative information based on mutual trust and codes of communication in relationship. Storper (1997) called these different types of linkages and interactions "conventions" and identified five forms:

(a) inter-firm "hard" transactions, as in buyer-seller relations that involve market imperfections;

(b) inter-firm "soft" transactions, as in the sharing or diffusion of non-traded information about the environment or about learning;
(c) hard and soft intra-firm relations, as the bases for the functioning of large firms which are "internally externalized";
(d) interactions in factor markets, especially labor markets, which involve skills that are not entirely substitutable on an inter-industry or inter-regional basis, i.e. where there are industry- or region-specific dimensions to workers skills; and
(e) economy-formal institution relationships, where universities, governments, industry associations, and firms are only able to communicate and coordinate their interactions by using channels with a strong relational-conventional content.

Callon et al. (1995) put them together under the concept of "socio-technical network," which contains two elements:

(a) Form of coordination: acquisitions, purchasing, through licensing and contractual agreements, and interorganizational relationships, including R&D consortia, alliances, and joint ventures.
(b) Content of interaction: it may be written documents (scientific articles, reports, patents ...), embedded skills (researchers, engineers from one firm to another ...), more or less developed technical objects (prototypes, machines, products for final consumption ...), money (cooperation agreements between a research center and company, financial loans, paying customer of a good or service ...), and informal orders or exchanges (hierarchy and trust).

More broadly, laws, regulations, social rules and norms, technical standards, and cultural habits constitute the institutional context within which firms and organizations interact. Such institutions may foster or hinder the interactive learning and linkage essential for absorptive capacity, R&D, and upgrading to innovation. Here institutions include not only the more formal laws and regulations, judicial decisions, and enforcement of contracts, but also the less formal norms, commercial conventions, and preconscious cognitive and ideational elements that are embedded in culture and widely accepted in a society (North, 1990). In fact, commonly held commercial norms and cultural conventions as informal institutions themselves often are the linkages and used to replace formal contracts, and a variety of legitimizing activities to secure the firm's position in the market. As all these institutions, interactive linkages, firms' absorptive capacity, R&D investment, and national innovation capacity co-evolve over time, they constitute the fundamental dynamic nature of the whole economy at a macro level (Nelson, 2008).

The Problem of Absorptive Capacity of the Chinese Firms

When approaching 2010s, the Chinese government policy pushed a big surge of R&D investment. However, the splendid statistics was not translated into high-quality and efficient innovation activities at firm level. The Chinese enterprises had tendency to continue their trajectory of imitation instead of indigenous innovation. Why? The answer may lie in the fact that enterprises in China in general only had low levels of "absorptive capacity" for R&D. The absorptive capacity is, as defined above, a specific way that enterprise carries out its R&D activities. When an enterprise begins its in-house R&D projects and at the same time makes continuous effort to identify, assimilate, and exploit knowledge from outside knowledge such as basic research findings, instead of keeping every effort inward without external interaction, the enterprise is said to have "absorptive capacity." This open-door strategy of doing R&D will in return induce more R&D spending on future options, thus condition the success of ongoing R&D projects. Otherwise, despite the domestic knowledge production at universities and research institutes, enterprises will fall short in absorbing this knowledge and its own in-house R&D will be lack of dynamic inputs. If innovation is an aircraft, indigenous R&D capability and absorptive capacities are like two wings. Missing either of them will make the aircraft unworkable.

During the years of early 2010s, although Chinese enterprises had begun to invest more in R&D, they tended to do it by closing the door, i.e., to cooperate less with other organizations. A survey research of 42 enterprises in the region of Central China in 2010 showed that the new ideas of R&D projects were mainly from three sources: first the end-users, then the enterprise itself, then the competitors (see Table 2.4). Suppliers, universities, and research institutions were all of low importance as technology sources searched by enterprises (Ren et al., 2010). The 2012 survey of 1201 enterprises in the Pearl River Delta region of Guangdong Province in the South China also demonstrated that compared with efforts of upgrading the in-house independent R&D capabilities (effort value of

Table 2.4 Technology sources of R&D projects of enterprises in the Pearl River Delta (Guangdong)

Technological sources of R&D projects	*Frequencies*		*Percentage (%)*		*Total number of enterprises giving responses*
	No	*Yes*	*No*	*Yes*	
Independent R&D	368	808	31.29	68.71	1176
Cooperation with colleges and universities	987	148	86.96	13.04	1135
Cooperation with professional research institutes	985	149	86.86	13.14	1134
Cooperation with customers	428	735	36.80	63.20	1163
Cooperation with other enterprises	806	340	70.33	29.67	1146
Participation of multi-party R&D cooperation with other enterprises, colleges and universities, and research institutes	1032	102	91.01	8.99	1134
Purchase of technology patents and equipment	892	243	78.59	21.41	1135
Imitation of others' technology (without possessing private patent or purchasing others' patent)	970	164	85.54	14.46	1134

Source: Qiu et al. (2012)

6.17 of 10), enterprises made much less efforts to cooperate with universities, research institutes and other companies in R&D (effort value of 3.26 of 10). This survey also revealed that for the enterprises in the Pearl River Delta region, independent R&D and cooperation with customers who were generally foreign companies as clients constituted major sources of R&D projects. Only less than 14% of enterprises searched R&D sources through cooperation with universities and research institutes. Less than 10% of enterprises participated in joint R&D projects with other enterprises, universities, and research institutes. In terms of searching and absorbing external knowledge for the R&D projects, Chinese enterprises were like isolated islands standing alone in the ocean of science and technology. Without nurture from this ocean, its R&D propensity would eventually fade away.

Literally, the development of absorptive capacity in enterprises depends on two things: enterprises' own efforts and orientations of R&D projects and external conditions which permit enterprises to establish various linkages with other organizations. A Chinese national survey of R&D resources in 2009 reported that in terms of R&D project expenditure, 69.4% of enterprise projects were accomplished by enterprises themselves independently, 10.3% of enterprise projects were accomplished by enterprises in cooperation with domestic universities, 5.6% of enterprise projects were accomplished by enterprises in cooperation with domestic research institutes, 4.5% of enterprise projects were accomplished by enterprises in cooperation with other domestic enterprises, 3.8% of enterprise projects were accomplished by enterprises in cooperation with foreign organizations, and 6.4% of enterprise projects were accomplished in cooperation with other organizations. From the perspective of industrial enterprises, since 2009, both private and State-owned enterprises decreased their expenditure part of external R&D projects in cooperation with universities, public institutes, and other enterprises. In private sector, the external R&D expense share decreased from 5.5% in 2009 to 4.7% in 2010; in State-owned sector, the share of external R&D decreased from 8.6% in 2009 to 7.3% in 2010. Chinese enterprises were not good in developing external cooperation in R&D, which was a sign of their weak absorptive capacity, but is also the cause of the low-quality output of R&D projects with a "closed" management style.

In 2011, in whole China, there were 81,615 projects of cooperation among enterprises, universities, and research institutes. Though 30% of the project budgets were spent on external R&D cooperation, the Chinese enterprises didn't appreciate very much the role of these domestic R&D partners in developing innovation, especially domestic universities and research institutes. The 2012 Pearl River Delta survey (see Table 2.5) showed that the 1201 enterprises gave a lower evaluation of the service provided by universities and research institutes in their innovation (average value of 4.77 of 9) than the evaluation of the service provided by public technology platforms of local government (average value of 4.87 of 9) and cooperation provided by other local enterprises (average value of

Table 2.5 Assessment of external linkages by enterprises in the Pearl River Delta (Guangdong)

Type of organizations	*Average contact frequency (evaluation scores between 1–9)*	*Average level of trust (evaluation scores between 1–9)*
Competitors in the same industry	4.80	4.82
Local suppliers, supporting vendors, and subcontractors	6.89	6.43
Local distributors, domestic traders, and retailers	5.50	5.54
Overseas customers	5.81	5.93
Local governmental departments	6.07	6.71
Industry associations and chambers of commerce	5.55	6.18
Local centers of technological innovation	4.17	5.07
Domestic universities and research institutes	3.62	4.87
Local education, training and recruitment services organizations	5.12	5.52
Local financial services organizations	6.04	6.39
Local management consulting and information services organizations	5.01	5.53
Related local organizations to solve labor dispute	5.12	6.16
Mass media	3.22	4.66
Local exhibition and marketing organizations	4.62	5.39

Source: Qiu et al. (2012)

5.2 of 9). Regarding the frequency of contacts and level of trust with a series of other organizations in local environment, enterprises showed the second lowest level of trust to domestic universities and research institutes, and had fewer contacts with them than with other organizations.

In fact, Chinese enterprises lacked interest in engaging domestic universities and research institutes with respect to R&D efforts. There was almost 16% of enterprise R&D budget spent on joint projects with universities and institutes in 2009 because either the projects were organized by government, if the enterprises were State-owned or the participant enterprises would get money from the State, if they were non-State enterprises. But the aversion of enterprises to universities and research institutes was also due to the situation of these science and technology organizations themselves. For the big R&D projects financed and coordinated by the government, State-owned enterprises and universities and research institutes which were also State-owned are under the same roof and obliged to cooperate for innovation. Besides this kind of imposed linkage, local Chinese universities and research institutes, except as suppliers of engineers, had contributed very little to R&D activities of enterprises, especially the non-State and private enterprises. The reforms in the science and technology system since the mid-1980s had to some extent activated the enthusiasm of researchers in these institutions, but enterprises found soon that the coordination with universities and research institutes was even more difficult than negotiation with other enterprises. The academic mode of production was undermined and replaced by a profit-oriented mode of behavior, where pecuniary incentives became more important. These science and technology organizations aggressively searched for profits and tried to maximize every single piece of their knowledge when they saw enterprises having potential to acquire technology from them.

The deeply rooted problems of separation between R&D and the economy, and of organizational rigidity between enterprises and S&T institutions, had thus been overlapped by the new problem of marketization of research and industry cooperation. Such a problem may be due to the very unique Chinese model of capitalism in which the State itself behaved like a special interest group with lucrative objective in a market place, competing with other non-State groups for resources by elaborating all kinds of rules in favor of itself. If within the State sector enterprises had to cultivate vertical relationships with bureaucrats and politicians for subsidies and other favors, outside the State sector the Chinese society was like a pure laissez-faire market where non-State enterprises have to rely on traditionally inherited personalized trust and networks (the famous Guanxi) to establish links with research institutions, financiers, partners, suppliers and customers in transforming knowledge, capital, products, and talent for innovation (Gilboy, 2004). The "selfish" State left beyond its own controlled system a free market absent of reliable legal framework that could be used to enforce contracts. If the Chinese State top-down intervention had greatly promoted the country's catch-up through coordinating the interactions between its production system with the national research and knowledge system, the remaining part of relationship in China found it difficult for innovation to weave efficient linkages among organizations based on institutionalized trust.

New R&D Strategy: Domestic Firms

Till 2015, to the Chinese government, how to mobilize the non-State sectors to develop more dynamic linkages with the State-owned sector of science, technology, and knowledge seemed still to be a big challenge. If the government was capable of making efficient and rapid technological catch-up in the domestic, monopolistic, and infrastructure sectors (artificial satellite, high-speed railway, grand airplane, nuclear station, etc.) through its research-based mega-projects in mobilizing maximum financial, knowledge, and organizational resources, it seemed not so skillful in promoting further R&D investment and activity of non-State-owned enterprises in competitive markets (consumer electronics, automobiles, machine tools, food processing, textiles, fast moving consumer products, etc.). Whereas in these sectors, Chinese enterprises had accumulated enormous technological capabilities of manufacturing and distribution and the general technological level seemed to be approaching the world frontier. But it was this distance of "the last 100 yards" that constituted the most difficult part of catching-up. The challenge in this sector was uniquely difficult because of the complexity of science-based design and engineering-based manufacturing.

To create innovative outcomes, Chinese enterprises needed to combine their operational excellence with high-level research of science and technology, often under the form of formal and well-planned R&D projects. Thus, contrary to the common feeling, Chinese enterprises in the mature, traditional, and labor-intensive sectors still had a long way ahead of them to catch up the world's technology and innovation frontier at that time; even they were taking most of the market share in these fields. As a matter of fact, some Chinese domestic firms had been good in establishing strong linkages with customers, including both domestic consumers and foreign companies as clients. Chinese government then tried to support these indigenous firms in establishing more linkages other than those with customers, especially with domestic and foreign research institutions.

For example, to adequately match customer needs from different regions, urban and rural users, and income levels, household appliance producer Haier offered over 400 refrigerator models in China. Haier developed a dual-use washing machine that can be used to wash vegetables in addition to clothes. This was driven by "listening" to the "abnormal" users of their products. Thus, Haier's innovation capacity is creating more product models to match different market needs rather than being technology-intensive.

Lenovo, the Chinese company which bought the PC business of IBM in 2004, started by selling foreign computers such as AST, HP, and IBM in Chinese market, while losing money in their own PC business till 1993. The boss Liu Chuanzhi then made Yang Yuanqing as the GM of its own PC production. Yang, as a top salesman in Lenovo Company, learnt from selling foreign brands such as HP that the key in Chinese market was to create a nationwide network of sales agents. He fired all but 18 of the one hundred sales people in Lenovo. Then he reformed Lenovo's operation and asked the engineers to cut product costs in half. He purchased components in bulk from Samsung, used Intel and AMD CPU to cut price. He substituted heavy but cheap steel sheets for plastic computer cases. He even imitated the local small PC boutiques in assembling components to customerize PC products. By this strategy of imitation based on lowest price and customerization, Lenovo rose as number 1 in the Chinese PC market in 1997 and has kept this position till today.

Huawei, the leading telecommunication company established in 1987, first started as a distributor of the HAX switch produced by a Hong Kong company. Huawei's first product of its own was the C&C08 switcher with 2000 lines, and the customer was a small city in Zhejiang, a market neglected by the multinationals. In 1993, Huawei launched their C&C08 switchers with 10,000 lines, which were sold very well in rural areas. Ren Zhengfei, the boss of Huawei, always said that the user and customer are the source of innovation for Huawei. Later, Huawei set up a lot of joint laboratories with Texas Instruments (TI), Motorola, etc., and a joint venture with 3COM, thereby outsourcing more its technology from foreign companies buying than buying technology from university and research institutes.

As Huawei, some other leading Chinese firms also began to expand in global market and search for developing indigenous innovative products abroad. By acquisition of foreign firms and R&D facilities and the establishment of R&D and design labs in technologically advanced countries, these enterprises hope to benefit from spillovers abroad. Through M&A or joint R&D, they expect to monitor new development trends and transfer new technology to China, and thus speed up inverse technology transfer and promote domestic upgrading. In 2010, 188 Chinese outbound M&A transactions worth 38 billion USD took place which is a 30% increase compared to 2009. Chinese M&A targets are widespread globally with one focus on the United States, but also on the European Union, Asia, Africa, and developing countries with strong R&D infrastructure such as India.

For example, Haier's global network consists of R&D, manufacturing, supply chain, marketing, and service. It had 15 industry zones, 30 oversea plants and manufacturing sites, 8 oversea R&D centers, and 58,800 sales offices. But the international R&D outsourcing of Chinese enterprises had its own constraints. The first was the investment destination of other developing countries, especially South Asian economies (Vietnam, Cambodia, and Laos), Middle, Russia, and Africa. These markets could not provide powerful information and technology inputs to high-level R&D projects. Chinese enterprises had little habit of making dynamic linkages with a variety of institutions in the environment and found it even harder in a foreign context. For the acquired R&D laboratories and competences, Chinese enterprises also had difficulty in finding pertinent organization to carry out inverse technology transfer. Thus, in most cases, the overseas R&D activities of internationalized Chinese enterprises were mainly concerned of local product adaptation to consumer preference, collecting foreign technology and standard information for the home base, and assisting commodity manufacturing and marketing in the host country.

New R&D Strategy: Foreign-Invested Firms

Other potential linkages of innovation were found in exogenous firms in China. Chinese government had always policies to attract significant R&D activities of foreign companies. While previously most FDI was used for green-field investments or acquisitions in production and distribution facilities, in early 2010s an increasing portion of foreign investments flowed into the development of R&D facilities. China's universities graduated more than 10,000 science PhDs each year, and increasing numbers of Chinese scientists working overseas were returning home. Multinational firms were then to take advantage of these abundant supplies of low-cost skilled researchers in Beijing and Shanghai. The percentage of R&D expenditure of foreign-funded projects stayed constant at around 27%. A large portion of foreign spending on R&D was concentrated in a few regional clusters in China namely Shanghai and Beijing. However increasing R&D investments in other provinces (Guangdong, Jiangsu, and Tianjin City) created a close link to the concentration of MNC investments in production capacities. The number of foreign R&D centers in China increased drastically from around 50 in 2000 to approximately 1100 at the end of 2007, 1200 at the end of 2009, and 3300 at the end of 2012. 346 of the Fortune 500 companies established R&D facilities in China. Many multinationals established in China one of their main centers of global R&D, which was the case of Microsoft and SAP (IT), Alcatel Lucent (telecommunications), BASF (chemicals), Novartis (pharmaceuticals), Matsushita, Sanyo (electrical equipment), PSA (automobile), etc.

The strategic focus of these foreign R&D activities had evolved during the years of rapid investment growth in China. The initial motivations of establishing R&D centers in China were to innovate by commercialization, as opposed to constant research, perfecting development, and critical designs which were controlled by multinational R&D headquarters. Multinational companies were to put a new product or service into the Chinese market quickly and improve its performance through subsequent generations. It was common for products to launch in a fraction of the time that it would take in more developed markets. While the quality of these early versions may be variable, subsequent ones improved rapidly.

This approach of R&D was to focus on local product development in partnership with downstream players such as domestic manufacturing suppliers. This strategy helped multinationals meet local technology requirements, but above all do research and applied development close to the biggest market in the world. This kind of R&D projects in fact reinforced the multiple feedback process with the innovation chain. It helped multinationals have capabilities of domestic-market knowledge or relationships needed to apply R&D results effectively to adapt to Chinese domestic needs. The general idea was to be closer to Chinese customers and the network of institutions and universities from which multinationals source talent.

The Buick GL8 minivan introduced in Chinese market was a good example. General Motor quickly developed the model through capability built in China, in using a combination of on-the-job mentoring, coaching, and expert assistance from overseas, as well as a very structured development process from their global team. The GL8 was an old GM architecture that no one else wanted, but it had turned into an unbelievably good-looking and highly desirable car in China.

Normally foreign R&D centers had the functions of technology monitoring and corporate R&D representation. But with the strong competition for talent, resources, and markets between foreign and domestic enterprises, foreign companies began to launch indigenous R&D centers with Chinese universities and institutes and to focus these facilities on developing technologies for unproven but promising next-generation domestic markets. There were even a few examples that some multinational companies developed through local R&D new models and incorporated some of the features they could transfer to other markets.

Multinationals that participated in such ventures aligned themselves with China's goals while they have concerns about protecting intellectual property rights (IPR). Most of the foreign R&D labs in China were then independent wholly foreign owned for better protection of intellectual property rights. These labs did not apply for patents to avoid disclosure of the technology know-how. Foreign R&D centers were reported to have limited interest in sharing knowledge with domestic firms and R&D labs.

On the other side, since 2006 China issued a variety of policies which allowed Chinese companies to apply non-inventive patents (utility model patents, design patents) and impeded foreign products from the Chinese market by compulsory testing, certification, and standard requirements. The Chinese government even created a bigger web of interrelated policies by issuing requirements for the disclosure of foreign proprietary technologies.

For example, China enacted an "Anti-Monopoly Law" in 2008 which exempted monopolies in sectors which were dominated by State-owned enterprises and in sectors where monopolies were deliberate by the State as they were critical to the Chinese economy. As shown earlier, the Chinese government also supported the "indigenous" innovation projects. To be eligible for the indigenous innovation catalogue (including computers and application equipment, telecom products, modern office equipment, software, new energy equipment, and high-efficiency energy-saving products) to participate in public procurement, the product must, among other criteria, have full ownership of IP in China and have a trademark that was owned by a Chinese company registered in China. Chinese government sought to use transferred IP and manufacturing methods to create its own champions that could compete with global countries around the world, not just in the local market.

All these measures raised the concerns about the intellectual property rights of foreign R&D in China and impeded the more aggressive investment decisions. The purpose of the Chinese government was to push the foreign R&D activities upgrading from the focus on market feedback process to adding new process of more research and knowledge mobilization. However, the majority of foreign R&D centers were not conducting indigenous technology R&D yet and the innovation capacity was rather in the downstream along the linked-chain process.

Conclusion: From the Top to the Bottom

Some scholars such as William Baumol (2002) asserted that innovation as the capitalist growth engine was possible thanks to the free market mechanism, the laissez-faire competition, and the body of rules guaranteeing private properties; while others saw the State capitalism as compatible with creativity and innovation. China complied with neither. In the end of 2000s, with the industrial upgrading strategy based on more R&D, China was positioning itself as a follower and adopted a pragmatic strategy in terms of increasing investment quantity of R&D to serve the restructuring of its industries. Contrary to the classic Schumpeterian entrepreneurial capitalism characterized by "creative destruction," its so-called State capitalism impeded the country's development of innovation capacity, though it accelerated enormously the technological catch-up process and industrial structural upgrading. With huge R&D investment, Chinese innovation dynamics was still characterized by "imitative construction." Its rapid R&D quantitative expansion overwhelmed the quality improvement of R&D.

In this chapter, we reviewed the practical challenges faced by enterprises during China's rapid increase in R&D investment during its catching-up process. At the micro level, there is an institutional inertia of linking research activities by S&T organizations with industrial activities by firms. Chinese firms are generally lack of the so-called "absorptive capacity" for carrying out high-quality R&D projects. Relying solely on macro-level national innovation systems and R&D investment policies is insufficient to address the challenge of transforming R&D into innovation capabilities for enterprises. More precisely, the lack of or weak external linkages impeded the development of a strong absorptive capacity of firms, which is in fact the key to R&D quality and effectiveness.

In the business world, when market mechanism on an arm's length basis is no longer reliable, enterprises and organizations prefer to internalize their transactions instead of linking outside. Until 2010s, most of Chinese enterprises relied on their linkages with customers or clients in the market as the main source of innovation, in the absence of dynamic linkages with research and knowledge institutions. The feedback loops from distribution activities and market demands became the most important inputs of the innovation process from market detection, to product design, and to development. Large quantity of small- and medium-sized enterprises counted on American, Korean, European, and Japanese enterprises as foreign clients to teach them how to employ technologies. The leading big companies adopted the strategy based on market-oriented product diversification and technology outsourcing (buying innovations of others) as their primary approach of innovation. The technology may come from anywhere, although most of the core, proprietary technology came from the United States, Japan, Europe, and Korea. The most famous Chinese multinationals such as Huawei, Lenovo, and Haier grew up not because of their strong capabilities in in-house technology development, but thanks to their ability to survive market competition by understanding and responding to specific market needs. Put in another way, their success was not based on the technological capability of innovation promoted by the State, but on the emerging Chinese and global market opportunities. As these big three, many other big Chinese enterprises entered into the market first as distributors and sellers, not inventors or innovators in technology. This spirit of commercial trader was kept even in the following stages of enterprise development. During the 10 years between 2005 and 2015, numerous emerging Chinese enterprises such as Chery Automobile and Bird Mobile-phone announced that they made radical innovations but simply by buying various foreign developed technologies and putting them in a product shell designed for the Chinese or other under developed markets.

Then, most of Chinese enterprises got so used to the competitive and transaction-nature relations in market that they did not know what other kinds of linkage that they could have had with other organizations in the economy. For example, the very popular form of organizing R&D activities through strategic alliance found very few cases in the Chinese industry. When there was something like innovation network in China, it was always the relationship of competition which prevailed over cooperation and communication among network participants.

On the other side, with the establishment of a top-down national system of innovation, Chinese economy became rich of organizations of different natures, different levels, and different locations. It had well-established universities and institutes, a variety of intermediate organizations, newly created science and technology parks and incubators, well financed State-owned enterprises with their R&D centers, accumulated FDI with their R&D facilities, emerging Chinese big companies with their overseas R&D hubs, and a large number of private enterprises with regional public technology centers set up by local authorities. However, the Chinese top-down NIS was characterized by the conjunction of an opportunist State and a networked society which together excluded institutionalized trust among firms and organizations. To make China a Schumpeterian innovation machine, the big challenge to the Chinese government was whether it could overcome its long traditional "paternalism over the State sector" in innovation policy and find an institutional substitute to correct the market failure effect in innovation capacity building of all Chinese enterprises. With almost everything being done to promote innovation in China, it might still leave the dynamic linkages outside enterprises for R&D cooperation to be built.

References

Arvanitis, R., Villavicencio, D., & Zhao, W. (2014/3). L'apprentissage technologique dans les pays émergents, Au-delà de l'atelier et de l'entreprise, *Revue d'Anthropologie des Connaissances, 8*(3), 495–521.

Baumol, W. (2002). *The free-market innovation machine* (p. 336). Princeton University Press.

Callon, M., Larédo, P., & Mustar, P. (1995). Réseau technico-économiques et analyse des effets structuraux, dans. In *La gestion stratégique de la recherche et de la technologie*. Economica.

Cohen, W., & Levinthal, D. A. (1990). Absorptive capacity: A new perspective on learning and innovation. *Administrative Science Quarterly, 35*(1), 128–152.

Cohen, W. M., & Levinthal, D. A. (1989). Innovation and learning: The two faces of R&D. *The Economic Journal, 99*(397), 569–596.

Dutrénit, G. (2000). Learning and knowledge management in the firm. In *From knowledge accumulation to strategic capabilities* (p. 330). Edward Elgar.

Dutrénit, G. (2004). Building technological capabilities in latecomer firms: A review essay. *Science, Technology & Society, 9*(2), 209–241.

Edquist, C. (1997). *Systems of innovation: technologies, institutions and organizations.* Pinter Publishers / Cassell Academic.

European Commission. (2012). *The 2012 EU industrial R&D investment SCOREBOARD* (p. 126). Technical report by the Joint Research Centre of the European Commission.

Furman, J. L., Porter, M. E., & Stern, S. (2001, September 26). *The determinants of national innovative capacity.* Working paper of Northwestern University & NBER.

Gilboy, G. F. (2004). The myth behind China's miracle. *Foreign Affairs, 83*(4), 33–48.

Kim, L. (1997). *Imitation to innovation. Cambridge* (p. 303). Harvard Business School Press.

Kim, L. (1998). Crisis construction and organizational learning: Capability building in carching-up at Hyundai motor. *Organization Science, 9*(4), 506–521.

Kline, S. J., & Rosenberg, N. (1986). An overview of innovation. In R. Landau & N. Rosenberg (Eds.), *The positive sum strategy: Harnessing Technology for Economic Growth* (pp. 275–305). National Academy Press.

Li, X. (2011). Sources of external technology, absorptive capacity, and innovation capability in Chinese state-owned high-tech enterprises. *World Development, 39*(7), 1240–1248.

Lundvall, B. A. (1988). Innovation as an interactive process: From user-supplier interaction to the national system of innovation. In e. a. Dosi (Ed.), *Technical change and economic theory* (pp. 349–369). Francis Pinter.

Lundvall, B. A. (1992). *National Innovation System: Toward a theory of innovation and interactive learning.* Pinter Publishers.

Nelson, R. R. (2008). What enables rapid economic progress: What are the needed institutions? *Research Policy, 37*(2008), 1–11.

North, D. C. (1990). *Institutions, Institutional Change and Economic Performance.* Cambridge University Press.

Qiu, H., Zhao, W., et al. (2012). *Guangdong industrial development report (2011–2012): Industrial upgrading and transformation* (p. 380). Guangdong Provincial Government.

Ren, L., Zeng, D., & Krabbendam, K. (2010). Technological innovation Progress in Central China: A survey to 42 firms. *Journal of Knowledge-Based Innovation in China, 2*(2), 152.

Shu, S.-T. (2003). *Examining relationships between external linkages, absorptive capacity and gains in new product knowledge and impacts on new product innovativeness* (p. 355). Doctoral Thesis, Business School of Loughborough University.

Storper, M. (1997). Industrial policy for latecomers: Products, conventions, and learning. In L. Tsipouri, S. Thomadakis, & M. Storper (Eds.), *Industrial policy for latecomers*. Routledge.

CHAPTER 3

"Back to Local": Growth Model Crisis and Innovation Policy

Introduction: The Stock Market Crash in 2015

In 2015, when the Shanghai Stock Exchange Composite Index jumped from less than 3000 points in March to more than 5000 points in June (Fig. 3.1), Chinese official press argued that the soaring bull market was supported by the so-called "reform bonus," "policy bonus," and the benefits released from accumulated institutional changes, new leadership, and emergence of new industries based on technological revolution in China. However, the sudden crash of Shanghai Composite back to less than 3000 points in August proved that it was not a "normal" burst of bubbles of emerging technologies and industries, but simply and purely a financial manipulation taking use of investors' wishful thinking. Then, after accusing foreign banks' hostile speculations in market, the Chinese government finally admitted that within its own system, there existed some insider "evils" and financial giant "crocodiles" who speculated over the whole stock market. In 2016, some millionaires, the Chairman of China Assurance Supervision Committee, and the Assistant to Chairman of

This chapter is rewritten of the paper "Managing the Chinese Economy in 'Post-Miracle' Era: Crisis of Growth Model and Policy Responses", co-authored with Joel Ruet and published in *Post-Communist Economies,* 33:7, 820–841. DOI: 10.1080/14631377.2020.1867427.

W. Zhao, *Remade in South China*, IPP Studies in the Frontiers of China's Public Policy,
https://doi.org/10.1007/978-981-95-7277-9_3

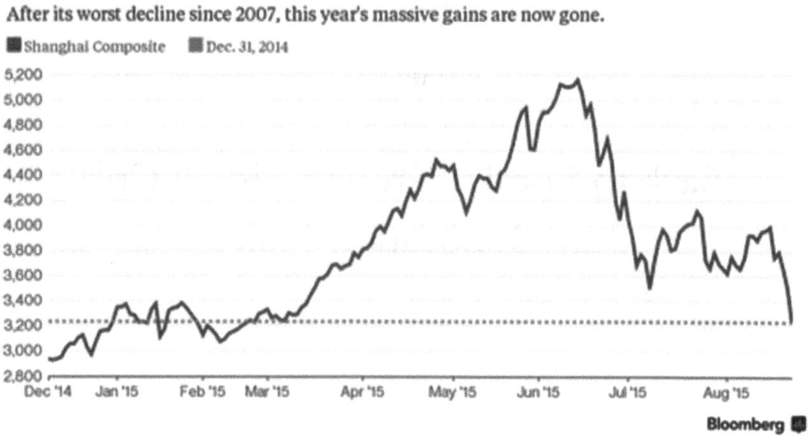

Fig. 3.1 The Shanghai Composite Meltdown

China Banking Supervision Committee were arrested. The Chairman of China Securities Supervision Committee stepped down as well.

Would this market crash in 2015 have become the Chinese version of 2008 financial crisis, if there had been no immediate and strong government intervention by force? The answer seemed to be yes. So what on hell happened to the Chinese economy? Anyhow, financial crisis was avoided, or was forbidden by the Chinese government, but did the 2015 summer financial disturbance represent the beginning of a more profound crisis in the Chinese economy, which would endure for a long term? And the answer seemed also to be yes. Literally, by crisis economists distinguish between two types: cyclical and structural. Which type did the crisis in China belong to?

Technology-Based Cyclical Crisis

The cyclical or technology-based crises can be very perturbing, and are often due to an external event or shift of techno-economic paradigm. Techno-economic paradigm, according to the Neo-Schumpeterian macroeconomics, is a combination of interrelated product and process, technical, organizational, and managerial innovations, capable of embodying a quantum jump in potential productivity for all or most of the economy and opening up an unusually wide range of investment and profit opportunities. Such a paradigm implies a unique combination of decisive technical and economic advantages. In history, the five techno-economic paradigms resulted from the diffusion of five waves of technological revolution that multiplied their impact across the economy and eventually modified the socio-institutional structures. The formation of a techno--economic paradigm system requires mutual adaptation and matching of the following three interrelated components (C.f., Perez, 2002; Freeman & Perez, 1988; Perez & Soete, 1988):

1. an industrial system or real economy, which contains an economy's science and technology capabilities, industrial structure, fixed assets, equipment, labor, labor costs, productivity, profitability, export trade, domestic market, the relative prices of the required inputs, the relative wage rates and the size and characteristics of the domestic market, etc.;
2. a financial system, which contains capital market, real estate market, foreign reserves, exchange rate and interest rate, etc.; and
3. a social system or a system of social institutions, which contains legal, social, and institutional framework, such as government regulations, standards, taxes, subsidies, tariffs, and other relevant policies or laws; trade-union organization and practices; the values of the local population in terms of willingness to accept or reject the innovation or its consequences; etc.

Cyclical crisis have their origin in the role of technological life cycles in providing changing amounts and qualities of investment and profit opportunities. All along the different phases of the big-bang, frenzy-bust and renewal of a techno-economic paradigm, the relationship between financial and production capital changes with a similar pattern of financial crisis as follows (Perez, 2002):

1. At the end phase of each techno-economic paradigm, production capital, including the revolutionary industries, often becomes one object of manipulation and speculation; the decoupling between financial and production capital is almost complete.
2. Nevertheless, a new paradigm emerges and opens vast opportunities for new products, processes, and services. It is also the time of fast development of infrastructure of the new paradigm, which facilitates a host of other related innovations.

3. Accordingly, during this period of irruption, financial capital generates a powerful magnet to attract investment into the new areas, hence accelerating the hold of the paradigm on what becomes the "new economy." In the world of capital gains, real estate bubbles and foreign adventures with money, all notion of the real value of anything is lost, when the decoupling between financial and production capital is extreme. Uncontrollable asset inflation sets in while debt mounts at a reckless rhythm; much of it to enter the casino. Thus grows the vast disproportion between paper wealth and real wealth, between real profits or dividends and capital gains.
4. But the illusion cannot last forever and these tensions are bound to end in collapse. This can happen in a series of partial crises in one market after another, in one huge crash or a combination of both; however it happens, the bubble needs to burst. Normally, the truly major collapses located about two or three decades after the big-bang of each technological revolution. This type of collapse is directly connected with the shift of techno-economic paradigm.
5. The painful process of implosion that marks the end of the frenzy phase brings paper values in line with real values and brings reluctant financial capital back to reality. What follows can be a time of reckoning and acceptance, when regulation of various sorts is put in place or generalized, in particular that which puts order in the behavior of financial capital and tends to re-establish the proper connections with production capital.

According to the above theory, the 2000 dot-com fever-and-bust is regarded as such a crisis due to the emerging revolution of internet, while the 2008 crisis is rather the result of decoupling between financial and production capital in the end period of the current techno-economic paradigm.

Structural or Regime Crisis

Different from cyclical crisis, structural crisis is due to the problems of mode of regulation and even of the fundamental accumulation regime in an economy. According to the French Regulation Theory (Boyer & Saillard, 2001; Boyer, 2011), "accumulation regime" is the way how production, circulation, consumption, and distribution organize and expand capital in a way that stabilizes the economy over time. For example, the accumulation regime of the Fordist mode of production was composed of mass-producing, a proportionate share-out of value-added, and a consequent stability in firm's profitability, with the plant used at full capacity and full employment. An accumulation regime is often supported by its corresponding "mode of regulation," which is a set of institutional laws, norms, forms of State, policy paradigms, and other practices that provide context for operating the accumulation regime. Typically, it is said that a mode of regulation comprises institutional forms related to money, market competition, wage-labor combination, State-society interaction, and relation to international economy.

Structural crisis happens when the mode of regulation doesn't match well the accumulation regime anymore, or when the accumulation regime is no longer effective, facing long-term diminishing return of capital due to the maturity of current techno-economic paradigm. The best example is the crisis of 1929, where the free play of market forces and competition did not lead to a renewed phase of expansion. The interwar period marked the passage from an accumulation regime characterized by mass production without mass consumption to a new regime incorporating both mass production and mass consumption. Another example is the crisis in 1971, which represented the end of Fordist accumulation regime, relying simultaneously on mass production and mass consumption. The crisis in 2008 was regarded as the result of an over-developed finance-dominated accumulation regime in Western economies. Thus, to overcome the structural crisis, institutional forms and the ways the State intervenes in the economy must be modified. It is impossible to continue long-term growth without major upheaval of accumulation regime.

Then, how about China? Did the 2015 stock market crash signal a cyclical financial crisis due to the techno-economic paradigm shift, or an enduring structural crisis due to the misalignment of accumulation regime? The following analysis reveals that it contained both, and unfortunately, more structural than cyclical. In 2015, some financial capital was speculated in the name of innovation. China was in fact suffering from the severe decoupling between financial capital and production capital in the end period of its already mature paradigm. It began to be trapped in a financial-dominant accumulation regime, which became eventually the kind of "middle-income trap" in China.

How Did China Fall into the Middle-Income Trap?

The "middle-income trap" refers to the fact that after enjoying a period of strong growth, many low-income countries have developed rapidly into middle-income status, but far fewer have gone on to high-income status. For example, growth of emerging countries slows by 2 points a year when their per capita income reaches about $17,000. Most economies in Latin America and the Middle East reached middle-income status as early as the 1960s and 1970s, but have remained there ever since. The factors and advantages that propelled high growth in these countries during their rapid development phases—low-cost labor, sectoral reallocation, and easy technology adoption—eventually exhausted and disappeared when they reached middle- and upper-middle-income levels. If countries cannot increase productivity through innovation (rather than continuing to rely on foreign technology) as new sources of growth, they find themselves trapped.

Factor-Driven Stage (Before 2008)

As for Chinese industrial productivity growth, it had been achieved by a large variety of firms: by 2008, roughly 30% of output was produced by foreign-invested firms, 45% by domestically held private firms, and 25% by State-owned firms. Their typical plant-level organization was the continuous-flow assembly line turning out massive quantities of identical products, with a separate and hierarchical managerial and administrative structure which required large numbers of low and middle skills in both the blue- and white-collar areas. The rate of return on capital was high throughout two decades and expected profitability was high enough to induce high physical investment.

Entrepreneurial expectations of rapid economic growth were crucial for investing in real economy during 1980s to 2008 (Zhao & La Pira, 2013). At origin, this remarkable development of industrial firms and entrepreneurial activities was initiated or conditioned by Chinese local governments, rather than the Central Government's strategy or policy. During 1978–2006, the main characteristics of the Chinese policy reform was decentralization. The cluster-based local innovation policies emerged during this period. In fact, China's factor-driven development stage was largely formulated by the so-called local State corporatism (Oi, 1992): the Central government gave freedom to key local governments to explore industrial development paths and let the successful experiments diffuse; the decentralization of decisions and making of industrial policies at the provincial level; a quasi-federal-type fiscal system which minimized central spending and induced local governments to maximize their revenues.

In such a circumstance, Chinese local governments limited their excessive taxation and competed to attract firms by offering them to get around all regulatory hurdles, and by granting them local market power. Contrary to other developing countries, Chinese local governments were competent, hard-working, and powerful, in the sense that they were "general managers" of local economic development. In the second half of the factor-driven development stage, to many local governments, foreign economic relations were more for the purpose of appropriation of frontier technologies than simple mercantilist objectives.

With a decentralized economic regulation system and industry focused policies in place, over the period of the 1980s–2006, a specific "accumulation regime" was progressively deployed in China, while its micro-institutional foundation was already laid down by the local governments, and its basic mode of production adopted by different types of firms. The formation of such an accumulation regime can be summarized as follows:

1. Reform on former planned economic system, opening to outside world, and especially active local government policies led to continuous creation of new firms;
2. These firms took use of China's surplus labor from rural areas and built up low-cost advantage for export manufacturing;
3. The export to international markets and foreign direct investment in China brought in large amount of foreign exchange;
4. The Chinese foreign exchange regime increased both Central government's foreign reserves and domestic money supply;
5. Fiscal decentralization, land revenues, and increased domestic credit encouraged local governments to invest in infrastructure development, which in turn attracted more private and foreign direct investment for export manufacturing.

It should be noted that at that moment, the Chinese techno-economic paradigm was very much based on the strengths of its industrial system—its real economy, when firms learnt and used globally diffused and standardized manufacturing technologies. The industrialization was due to the fact that the necessary technical knowledge for mass production of most of the products had been simplified and has become common knowledge. In 2001, China joined the WTO and business confidence was pushed high. Returns on capital improved and a lot of "hot money" flooded in the country. An industrial system based on export-oriented manufacturing had been built up, characterized by numerous incremental innovations and upgraded progressively toward higher level until the breakout of 2008 crisis. Through this capital accumulation circle, a kind of development dynamics of relationship between markets, firms, and State was established, with the local governments residing at its core. The Chinese industrialization process reached its climax in 2008, the year when Olympics Games was held in Beijing.[1]

Intrinsically, this Chinese industrial system had the tendency to evolve further to capture higher added-value activities. From 2000 to 2007, hundreds of local industrial clusters emerged in China's most developed regions of export-focused manufacturing. The clusters were boosted by pro-active local government policies, mainly in areas of technological progress and, to a less extent, in relevant institutional changes such as labor, education, medical care, social securities, etc.

The local government of Guangdong Province, for example, started some industrial programs even in 2005 to transform its labor-intensive firms to capital- and technological-intensive firms. This industrial upgrading required continuous (re)investment in fixed assets, in closing the knowledge gap in science and technology, in closing the experience and skills gap, and in physical infrastructure.

However, after 2006, China's industrial system development was disrupted by two historical events. First, low-cost surplus labor supply from rural areas had been exhausted. More than 10% of population was above the age of 65 and the labor population decreased by 2 to 3 million annually. Moreover, China stipulated a new Labor Contract Law at national level in 2007, which greatly reduced the employment flexibility in labor market and increased the minimum salaries of labor. The new Labor Contract Law dramatically raised the costs of manufacturing activities in China, which were even lower than in India before 2006.

[1] It is interesting to mention that the Olympics Games held in Asia seem to be related with the successful export-oriented development. In 1964, Tokyo hosted the Olympics that, typically, indicated that the host country is on the threshold of developed status. In 1972, Japan became the second largest economy in the world. In 1988, Seoul hosted Olympics when South Korea was about to become Asia's industrial giant.

Investment-Driven Stage (2008–2015)

But it was the other event that had more direct and consequent impact on Chinese manufacturing industries: the financial crisis in 2008, which suddenly reduced the developed economies' market demand of Chinese export. Facing the challenge of GDP growth rate slowing down, the Chinese central government turned to more pro-active fiscal and monetary policies: its anti-crisis package included a government budget expenditure of 4 trillion Yuan backed up by bank credit support of 10 trillion Yuan. With such an unprecedented liquidity injection, the central government took over the managing power of Chinese economic development from the hands of local governments. A change of mode of regulation began.

Even far before 2007, both central and local governments in China had become more and more GDP-ist. From 1978 to 2007, except during the period of 1997 Asian crisis, China's fiscal and monetary policies were contractionary by nature: their main objective was to cool down the fever of investment pulse and prevent the economy from hyperinflation. Fiscal policy was to control fiscal deficit and reduce fiscal expenditure; monetary policy was to reduce money supply. In the 1990s, compared with local governments, the central government was not so aggressive in terms of promoting GDP growth through massive industrialization. However, with the reform of taxation system after the mid-1990s, the central government's fiscal situation became stronger and stronger. By the end of 2000, the central government's total fiscal assets reached 23 billion Yuan, including 12 billion Yuan financial assets, 6 billion Yuan land revenues, and 5 billion Yuan assets of State-owned firms. Progressively, the central government had more incentive and resources to assert macroeconomic control through expansionary policies, termed as "active fiscal policy and stable monetary policy." Since the financial system had always been the central government's management mechanism to restrain lending and reduce inflation in the past, it certainly became the core part of macroeconomic policies to achieve the goal.

Thus, the Chinese central government began to manage the so-called aggregate demand, by playing on a few monetary keys—government spending, the interest rate, the required reserves ratio, the exchange rate, and the volume of credit or the quantity of money in circulation—in order to maintain the GDP growth rate. At operational level, the aggregate demand was decomposed into export, investment, and consumption, the three classic contributors to GDP growth. Export was primarily targeted as major driver of growth, which made China often criticized for manipulating its exchange rate for export promotion. Investment was another driver: both central and local governments invested vastly in infrastructural network of motorways, service stations, airports, and oil distribution systems, creating enormous demand for automobiles, consumer durables, synthetic materials, and petroleum products. After 2003, Chinese economic growth counted more heavily on investment, which has increased from around 35% to around 40% of GDP, higher than comparable countries, such as Japan and South Korea, at the equivalent stage of development.

The 2008 external crisis stimulated the Chinese central government to reinforce its controlling power over macroeconomic management and exploit fully its previous Keynesian fiscal and monetary policies to maintain the growth rate above 8% (Zhao & La Pira, 2013). China's investment hit a peak level of 48% of GDP in 2011, two years after the re-launching package in 2009. In terms of fixed assets investment, from 2013 to 2016, China recorded 44.6 trillion Yuan, 51.2 trillion Yuan, 56.2 trillion Yuan, and 59.7 trillion Yuan, representing 75%, 79.5%, 81.6%, and 80.2% of GDP respectively. 40% of this fixed assets investment was undertaken by governments and State-owned enterprises, and investment in infrastructure remained a growth rate of 17% to 20% since 2013. In fact, China's annual infrastructure investment was far greater than the United States, Europe, and other emerging markets. It was two times bigger than in India, four times bigger than in Latin America.

After 2007, as the Chinese growth was driven by investment, its investment was mainly financed by credit expansion. From 2008 to 2011, China released 28 trillion Yuan bank credits, more than half of the total credit amount during 1949 to 2011. Since then, money supply as measured by M2 had increased with an average rate of 16%, from 85.16 trillion Yuan in 2011, to 122.84 trillion Yuan in 2014, to 155 trillion Yuan in 2015 and exceeding 200 trillion Yuan in 2019. The increased M2 supply equaled the double value of China's GDP.

The huge supply of money in domestic market was structurally due to the Chinese foreign exchange regime. In 2014 Chinese national foreign reserve reached 3.84 trillion US Dollars. The central bank had to issue new money to commercial banks in exchange for the foreign exchange deposited by exporters. Large amounts of bank credits were channeled to State-owned firms and big infrastructure projects, such as roads, railways, airports, power generation, and buildings, which all involved land allocation and intermediate inputs. In 2015, for example, the Central Bank lowered interest rate and required reserve ratio for five times, and the National Commission of Development and Reform approved additional infrastructure projects of more than 2 trillion Yuan.

Local officials also seized on the stimulus package and the huge expansion of bank lending to initiate their local projects as rapidly as possible. Many local firms were created only for acting as financing platforms in order to enjoy greater access to bank loans and channel the financial resources to local property and infrastructure projects.

Thus, the excess money supply flooded into Chinese property market and capital market, creating asset bubbles. In 2009, around half of the investment is in property. In 2015, 98.7% of the 11.72 trillion Yuan new credit flowed in property-related markets: mortgage loans, infrastructure projects, real estate development, etc., making property-related credits have a share of 28% of the 100 trillion Yuan total credit. In 2016, the value of Chinese properties was 250% of its GDP. China's capital market value also reached 70 trillion Yuan in the same year. In 2015, Chinese Academy of Social Sciences reported that the total debts of China were 150.03 trillion Yuan, including 20 trillion debts of local governments. China's ratio of total debts over GDP had risen from 170% in 2008 to 235.7% in 2014.[2] Some international companies such as McKinsey and Moody's estimated that China's debt/GDP ratio was already over 250% in 2016.

Financializing the Chinese Economy (After 2015)

From 2008 to 2015, the injection of huge liquidity quickly financialized the whole Chinese economy: rapid growing dominance of financial institutions and markets over industrial firms and employees. Monetary factors—deficits, capital, credit, taxes—rather than goods and services, had become the determinants of allocation of resources. Huge financial capital was speculated in the name of innovation. The Chinese economy was suffering from severe decoupling between financial capital and production capital, trapped into a financial-dominant accumulation regime at home while being price taker on international markets—with a less marked

[2] Li, Y. (2015) National Balance Sheet of China 2015: Leverage Adjustment and Risk Management (《中国国家资产负债表2015:杠杆调整与风险管理》), Chinese Academy of Social Sciences Report: Beijing

burden though on the latter element. This risk then materialized into debt crisis of Evergrande, the biggest real estate company in China (Fig. 3.2).

The short-term counter-crisis macroeconomic measure and the consequent series of policies of Chinese central government crafted a new regime of accumulation, where a substantial part of profits were made through financial channels and speculation, rather than through trade and commodity production. In 2015, the added value of China's tertiary sector accounted for more than 50% of GDP. Since then, the proportion of financial growth in GDP reached 8.3%%. McKinsey and Company even estimated that the banking sector contributed 80% of Chinese economy's profit in 2016.

Meanwhile, the upgrading of Chinese real economy, where industrial firms were facing severe problems of declining export market and profitability, was overwhelmed by government spending in domestic infrastructure and bank lending to State-owned firms. Chinese economic gravity was deviated from export-manufacturing industries to monetary and finance-related sectors, including real properties and shadow banking. A new circle of accumulation emerged even before the techno-economic paradigm achieved to have substantial transformation based on new technologies:

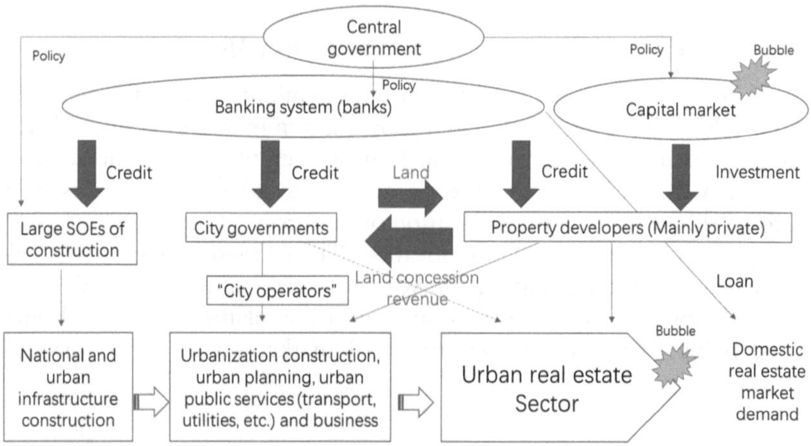

Fig. 3.2 Investment models of infrastructure and real estate in China. (Source: Author)

1. Externally, the decrease of export market needs due to world crisis slowed down the catch-up steps of Chinese manufacturing sectors in global value chain;
2. The Chinese central government reinforced its expansionary fiscal and monetary policy to inject excessive liquidity in the economy;
3. The manufacturing sectors became less and less attractive for investment, due to rising labor costs, insufficient domestic consumption demand, overcapacity, and diminishing profitability;
4. Thus, money supply flooded and was accumulated in property markets, then stock markets, and recently foreign exchange markets, creating several rounds of inflation of assets prices, financial instability, and permanent bad loans;
5. The Chinese central government had to allocate more attention and resources on fiscal and monetary policies to handle the newly added problems of financial system, somehow leaving behind its industrial system which had been decoupled from China's financial realm but faced of the persisting problem of sustaining and upgrading.

From a perspective of macroeconomic regulation, it can be roughly said that China's factor-driving development was primarily led by local governments with the permission and encouragement of central government who later, on the other hand, played a much more prominent role in pushing the economy into investment-driven stage. With China's growth story becoming a "miracle," the central government even expected the economy would soon rush into innovation-driven stage. By 2010s, while the Chinese industrial system built up basic capabilities, it was still in the stage in catch-up, neither operates at the world technological frontier nor can continue to profit from low, unskilled wages in the past. The 2008 world crisis and external demand shocks, just as Porter (1998) warned for investment-driven stage, interrupted this vision. Chinese government's reaction to the crisis, unfortunately, turned its development path from investment-driving to liquidity-injecting, and troubled itself to handle the derivative consequences. The injected liquidity circulated within the financial system aiming at speculating the "value-based" assets rather than being channeled to industrial sectors for forming "knowledge-based" assets, creating the decoupling of real economy from virtual economy. Table 3.1 summarizes the policies, accumulation regimes, and techno-economic paradigms of China through the different development stages over the last 40 years.

Table 3.1 China's staged steps to the "middle-income trap"

Development Stage	*Policy and Regulation*	*Accumulation Regime*	*Techno-economic Paradigm*
Factor-driven stage (Before 2008)	– Localized industrial policies – Contractionary macroeconomic policy – Export-promotion policy – Technology--importation and transformation policy – FDI attraction policy – Decentralized fiscal system – Loose regulation on labor (labor law revised in 2007)	– Industrialization through export-oriented manufacturing; – Industrial firms took use of China's surplus labor from rural areas and built up low-cost advantage; – The export to international markets and foreign direct investment in China brought in large amount of foreign exchange; – The Chinese foreign exchange regime increased simultaneously national foreign reserves and domestic currency supply; – Governments invested heavily in infrastructure and land development to support manufacturing;	– Industrial system based on imported or transferred technologies from abroad; – Specialized in process manufacturing and assembly line production; – Formulation a techno-economic paradigm with industrial system as its core part and relevant social system depressed; – Early and growth phases of the techno-industrial life cycle.

Investment-driven stage (2008–2015)	– Centralized macroeconomic management system – Manipulating macroeconomic variables such as trade, investment, and consumption – Expansionary monetary and fiscal policies – Economic re-launching package – Macroeconomic rebalancing (2008–2014) – Supply-side Structural Reform (2014–present)	– The decrease of export market slowed down the catch-up of manufacturing sectors in global value chain; – Government reacted by expansionary fiscal and monetary policy, and injected excessive liquidity in the economy; – Industrial system had become unattractive for investment, due to rising labor costs, insufficient domestic consumption demand, overcapacity, and diminishing profitability; – Excessive money supply flooded and accumulated in property markets, then stock markets, and recently foreign exchange markets, creating several rounds of inflation of assets prices, financial instability, and permanent bad loans; – Central government had to spend more energies and resources on fiscal and monetary policies to handle the newly added problems of financial system, somehow leaving aside its industrial system which had been decoupled from the financial realm but faced of the persisting problem of sustaining and upgrading.	– Globally diffused and standardized manufacturing technologies; – The necessary technical knowledge for mass production of most of the products are simplified and become common knowledge; – Evolution of engineering knowledge and process improvement around new products; – Entering the mature or even end phase of the techno-industrial life cycle; – Emergence of internet-based technical systems such as sharing business, e-commerce, and platform models, but not yet form a dominant new paradigm to replace the existing one.

(*continued*)

Table 3.1 (continued)

Development Stage	*Policy and Regulation*	*Accumulation Regime*	*Techno-economic Paradigm*
The “desired” innovation-driven stage (after 2016, not yet fully achieved)	– Innovation policy or Chinese innovation-driven development strategy, including: – Mid and Long Term Science & Technology Plan Outline – Industrial Transformation & Upgrading Plan – Massive entrepreneurship and crowd innovation strategy – Made in China 2025 – Innovation-driven development strategy outline	– The expected new growth regime will include: – World class exports; – High added-value activities; – Dynamics of entrepreneurship; – …	– High skilled jobs; – High-tech industries; – Industrial competitiveness based on strong science & technology development; – Technological development around internet and intelligent technologies: a totally new techno-economic paradigm.

Source: Zhao W. and J. Ruet (2020) “Managing the Chinese Economy in ‘Post-Miracle’ Era: Crisis of Growth Model and Policy Responses”, *Post-Communist Economies*, 33:7, 820–841

For China, the so-called "middle-income trap" was caused partially by the fact that the country's established techno-economic paradigm, which started 35 years ago and generated the "China miracle," entered its end phase of life cycle in terms of creating technological breakthrough and was exhausted in terms of generating high profits. But China being trapped was more because of financialization which progressively substituted industrialization as main accumulation regime of the economy before entering into innovation-driven stage: it speculated derivatives, bubbles of assets, and even less legitimate schemes, built extraordinary paper mountains of wealth, and increased leverages through shadow banking, local debts, and bank NPL. Lacking an appropriate accumulation regime based on a new robust techno-economic paradigm, Chinese economy stepped in structural crisis after 2015.

Policy Change: From Demand Side to Supply Side

Table 3.1 also shows that contrary to a free market economy where economic situations constrain government and policy, the different development stages in China were crafted by different dominant modes of macroeconomic policy and regulation of its government, especially the Central government. It would be fair to say that, before its investment-driven stage entering into a dead end, the Chinese government had envisaged to bring the growth model to a new innovation-driven level. The financial crisis of 2008 forced the Chinese central government to face a set of multiple goals: it promised to keep high growth track, at the same time wanted to restructure the economy in the long run; it could not abandon the export-led industrialization, but it also saw the big potential of domestic market; it would like to transform the economy weight to more service-focused sectors, meanwhile it had to upgrade the manufacturing firms. Among all these goals, keeping the growth "miracle" away from hard landing in the short term became the priority, and the fiscal and monetary policies were their main weapons. So, it resulted that the central government's macro policies were hijacked by property and other assets bubbles, and became path-dependent in using quantitative easing and fiscal stimulation to save the economy from the edge of peril during 2008 to 2013. The strategy was then labeled as "economic rebalancing," concentrating on the demand side.

Actually, rebalancing the Chinese economy had been already put in agenda even before the 2008 crisis. Macroeconomic imbalances in China implied that the country's economic growth over 30 years had been based on super elevated levels of investment and over emphasis on export and systematic suppression of domestic consumption. Net exports were unlikely to provide China much cushion after 2008 and expansion of investment led to diminishing returns. China's central government decided to rebalance the share of GDP contributed by consumption and investment, making in former Premier Wen's words: *"greater effort to enhance the role of domestic demand, especially final consumption."* The re-launch package was in accordance to such orientation to modify the demand side. To boost consumption growth in the context of a negative drag from declining investment, the Chinese policy makers had to pursue a pro-consumption policy, rather than a purely export-driven growth strategy. Related to such a priority, China also promoted massively the development of service sectors, the logistics and distribution system to countryside, and urbanization.

Nevertheless, the performance of this macroeconomic structural rebalancing was not as high as expected. Aggregate demand was kept high because of investment increase, not consumption; service sectors were developed, with a biased weight on financial service. In regard with domestic consumption, China was in fact not a typical export-led economy like South Korea, Taiwan, and even Japan were or used to be. The extent to which GDP growth in China was driven by domestic consumption had been under-estimated. In 2016, consumption contributed 70% of GDP growth. The real final consumption expenditure grew at an average of 8.5% annually over the period of 2002–2012, and real household consumption an average of 9.5% annually since 2007 to 2011 (Banett et al., 2012). Rebalancing strategy led the Chinese consumption to grow strongly at around 8% annually after 2008, while the problem was that the growth in consumer spending had been slower than that of the overall economy and the increase in gross fixed investment, an average annual growth of over 13% per annum. In 2014, the share of private consumption in GDP fell to around 35% from around 45–50%, and it stagnated.

The reasons why Chinese domestic consumption stagnated were more structural than technical. Shortage of pension funds, rising prices of healthcare, and the corresponding high saving rate of households due to weak social security protection, all had negative impact on domestic consumption. The after-2012 anti-corruption movement also reduced final consumption related to officials. But the more profound reason was inequality of income distribution in China. Social Science Survey Center of Pekin University reported that in 2012, the Gini coefficient of net assets of Chinese households was 0.73, meaning the richest 1% households owned more than 1/3 of national net assets, while the bottom 25% households only owned 1% of national net assets.[3] Boston Consulting Group estimated that in 2015, the 2 Million high net value families in China owned 41% of investable assets in the country. The overall Chinese Gini coefficient was 0.48. Though there was steady increase of disposable income, it was the decreasing growth rate of disposable income that led to the decreasing growth rate of domestic consumption.

By 2014, it was evident that the consumption was touching a ceiling and there was surplus of production capacity due to "over-investment." Both Consumer Product Index and average profitability of industrial firms fell to 2%, and production capacity utilization rate fell to 70% in main industrial sectors. External economic situation had evolved from export demand reduction to exit of foreign direct investment in China, due to the "re-industrialization" of some developed economies, especially the United States. The Chinese government had to put aside the standard macroeconomic framework and face the more urgent and realistic problems from the supply side: the deceleration of economic growth since 2014, the considerable drop in industrial production since 2012, the major stock market slide in mid-2015, and the accumulation of overcapacity and overindebtedness of firms.

In the end of 2015, the central government formally launched the so-called supply-side structural reform, aiming to restructure the Chinese economy through deleting overcapacity, deleting storage, deleting leverage, reducing costs, and making up shortcomings (the "three deletions, one reduction, and one making-up," in official terms). Different from the Western definition of supply-side economics, the Chinese supply-side reform did not put tax reduction in the central place. The supply-side reform was more technical than structural, since it hardly touched the very core and rigid institutions in the Chinese economic system, such as the SOE system, the banking system, the health and social welfare system, the education system, the housing system, and the rule of law in a market economy. For Chinese central government, there was not much marginal

[3] Social Science Survey Center of Pekin University (2014), *China People Livelihood Development Report*, Beijing, China.

room to carry out further reform in these institutional areas because any of them was closely linked to China's profound social and political system, and specific incumbent interested groups.

The Focus on Local-Level Innovation Policy

Different from macroeconomic policy, innovation-driven strategy was more on industrial level. Almost the same time when the supply-side reform was nominated as macroeconomic strategy under China's "new normal state," innovation-driven development was re-emphasized as another important strategy in parallel. After all, the macroeconomic measures, neither the demand side nor the supply side, seemed to bring the economy back to a healthy growth track. The government believed that innovation could help not only restructuring and transforming the economy, but also solving other challenges from green growth, to an aging society and the "middle-income trap." Also, compared to supply-side reform, innovation-driven development strategy (IDS) was less relevant to China's unchangeable social-institutional system, more on finding technical solutions within the industrial system.

In fact, the Chinese IDS could be traced back to a series of early strategic planning of science & technology development and manufacturing sector development at industrial level, mainly carried out by Ministry of Science & Technology, and Ministry of Industries and Information Technologies, etc. In 2006, Chinese government issued the Outline of Medium and Long Term Plan for National Science and Technology Development (2006–2020). To facilitate implementation of the Plan, government ministries designed policies to help build an enterprise-centered national innovation system: tax incentives for innovative enterprises, prioritizing of domestic high-tech enterprises for government procurement, encouragement of assimilation and re-innovation based on imported technology, stronger protection of intellectual property rights, etc. Since 2007, Chinese government made a series of plans to transform and upgrade the manufacturing sectors, including promoting high-tech sector, advanced manufacturing sector, and modern service sector. It also set up an expert group in State Council to identify industrial "champions" capable of concluding strategic partnerships with foreign multinationals.

In 2015, the Chinese Premier Minister advocated to create "millions of entrepreneurs and massive innovations," trying to inject new dynamics in China's development. The same year China published its industrial masterplan "Made in China 2025," targeting all high-tech industries that strongly contribute to economic growth: automotive, aviation, machinery, robotics, high-tech maritime and railway equipment, energy-saving vehicles, medical devices, information technology, etc. By upgrading the mostly backward industrial processes of manufacturing sector, the Chinese government hoped to enhance the competitiveness of its firms on domestic market and to propel their global expansion. In 2016, Chinese government issued the National Innovation-driven Development Strategy Outline, proposing a "three-step" strategic target: to become an innovative country by 2020, a forefront of innovation-oriented country by 2030, and world's top scientific and technological innovation powerhouse by 2050.

By 2020 just before the Covid pandemic, more and more relevant industrial policy, science & technology policy, foreign trade policy, financial policy, and educational policy were clustered under the macroeconomic strategy umbrella of "innovation-driven development," with the aim to upgrade the Chinese economy to a new techno-economic paradigm. Figure 3.3 summarizes China's main macroeconomic policies after 2008 and the shift of focus to industrial-level policies for promoting innovation.

In terms of policy implementation of innovation-driven development strategy, the traditional way of Chinese central government relied very

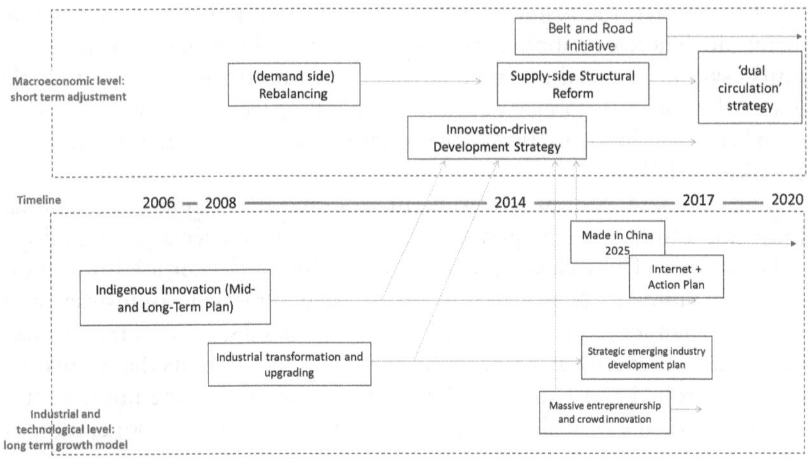

Fig. 3.3 Economic Policies of Chinese Central Government (Source: Author)

much on "top-level" design and centralized coordination. For example, to promote the implementation of Mid- and Long-Term Science and Technology Plan, the State Council proposed support policy incorporating 60 articles at first, then 79 detailed policy documents were proposed through inter-ministry cooperation involving 35 ministries including Ministry of Science & Technology, Ministry of Finance, and National Committee of Reform & Development. The policy documents later were diffused to local governments which worked out their corresponding implementation policy measures at different administrative levels. In this process, central government played a guiding role to direct the local governments to concentrate on specific key areas, while most of the concrete measures on how to upgrade with S&T progress and innovation, industrialize with core and key technologies, develop emerging industries, high-tech industries, and service sector are for local governments to elaborate, according to their local situation.

By nature, innovation policy is local and decentralized. It is different from fiscal and monetary policies which can normally have anticipated and immediate consequences at macro level. Innovation is the result of a complex interplay of factors and actors in a long process of chained activities in production, diffusion, and use of new and economically useful knowledge. And the local knowledge of development is hard to be found in existing textbooks, theories, or in the heads of central planners (Ruffier, 2010). Since the factors are numerous and the reactions of relevant actors are difficult to predict, the result of intended innovation policy is always highly uncertain. Therefore, innovation policy requires addressing such an "innovation system" instead of single factors or actors. It should be systematic under the form of "policy package" integrating actions in various functional areas—education, trade, investment, finance, and science (Vonortas & Aridi, 2012).

The Chinese central government adopted the frame of National Innovation System as the general principle for its science and technology policy design. The follow-up plans such as National Plan for Innovation Capacity Building, National Plan for Strategic emerging industries, and National Plan for S&T Development were all based on such a framework. But unlike other critical macroeconomic policy instruments that were centrally controlled and had immediate nationwide effects, the implementation of national innovation policy relied very much on the cooperation of local governments and the many thousands of local companies. Local governments soon found that the National Innovation System framework was too big, too vague, and too difficult to be operationalized in concrete policies, even though they had to label their policy framework as "regional innovation system" in order to follow the central government's guideline.

Meanwhile, at regional level, since innovations took place primarily in some concrete local milieu by entrepreneurs and firms who worked on new technology and new product, China's innovation policy was best set up at subnational government level targeting micro-level projects or local-level ecosystems. Locally well-defined innovation policy targeted to specific industries, sites, communities, or even firms and were articulated to move gradually from micro to macro levels. In a large-scale economy as China, changes often began with effective micro-changes, which then served as models or sources of motivation for building a critical mass of initiatives through a combination of top-down and bottom-up actions. As the intermediate level between micro-reforms and structured national policy reform, the meso- or local-level actors, including local governments and companies, thus became critical for scaling up these reforms because they created the base for major reforms in the end (World Bank, 2010).

Conclusion

In China, the most important technological prowess of most of its manufacturing firms was formed fundamentally during the factor-driven stage in local industrial clusters with frequent international connections, not during the investment-driven stage by central government policy push with a so-called national innovation system. Besides, innovation-driven development stage for China is still a prospection than a reality.

The growth model of China itself is composed of different capital accumulation regimes formed at different stages, such as export, domestic infrastructure investment, then financial market liberalization, and later the E-commerce platform economy, all based on manufacturing economy built up since 40 years. Each of these stages has specific policy implications and the Chinese central government now has to face the challenge of shifting to a new accumulation regime in the long run. After 2020, the growth dynamics has been diminishing and China had to upgrade its manufacturing economy to an innovation level, and build up new capital accumulation regime on it (Fig. 3.4).

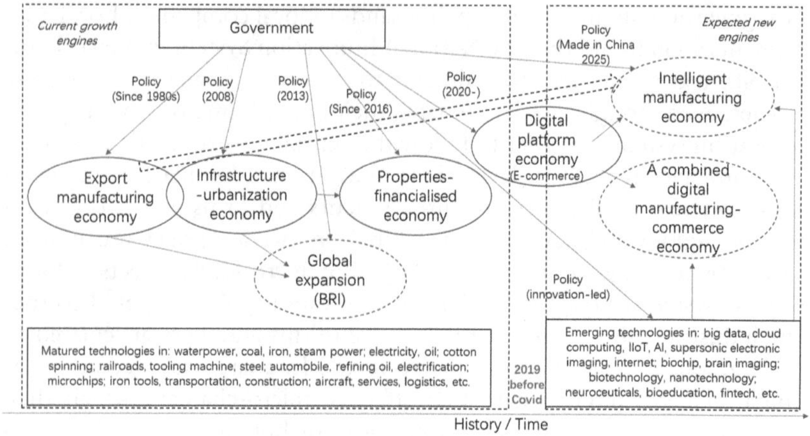

Fig. 3.4 China in search of New Growth Model. (Source: Author)

This chapter is in fact a background note on how China's macroeconomic transformation has driven the shift from traditional short-term monetary and fiscal policies to industrial and innovation policies. And the essence of innovation policies is that they can only be effectively implemented as regional innovation policies by local governments. The key of successful implementing China's innovation-driven development strategy was neither in central government's planning, nor in the laissez-faire market, but in the hands of Chinese local governments who interacted directly and daily with different territorial socio-economic actors.

Empirical observation of the Chinese economy has led us to argue that the problem of imitation-to-innovation transformation was and would be solved primarily by local governments and companies by a bottom-up approach, rather than by macroeconomic policies, national innovation system structure, or even formal R&D programs in a top-down approach. The Guangdong Province, its local governments, and business companies present a typical case of such a bottom-up innovation development. We now turn to check these proofs in more detail in Part II.

References

Banett, S., Myrvoda, A., & Nabat, M. (2012). Sino-Spending. *Finance and Development, 49*(3), 28–30.

Boyer, R. (2011). The Chinese growth regime and the world economy. In R. Boyer, H. Uemura, & A. Isogai (Eds.), *Diversity and transformations of Asian capitalisms* (pp. 184–205). Routledge. Chapter 10. (Routledge Studies in the Modern World Economy; No. 96).).

Boyer, R., & Saillard, Y. (2001). *Regulation theory: The state of art.* Routledge.

Freeman, C., & Perez, C. (1988). Structural crises of adjustment, business cycles and investment behavior. In Dosi et al. (Eds.), *Technical change and economic theory* (pp. 38–66). Pinter Publishers.

Oi, J. C. (1992). Fiscal reform and the economic foundations of local state corporatism in China. *World Politics, 45*(1), 99–126.

Perez, C. (2002). *Technological revolutions and financial capital: The dynamics of bubbles and global ages.* Elgar.

Perez, C., & Soete, L. (1988). Catching up in technology: entry barriers and windows of opportunity. In Dosi et al. (Eds.), *Technical change and economic theory* (pp. 458–479). Pinter Publishers.

Porter, M. E. (1998). *The competitive advantage of nations.* Macmillan Press Ltd.

Ruffier, J. (2010). The knowledge of industrial development. *Chinese Sociology and Anthropology, 42*(3, Spring), 74–86.

Vonortas, N. S., & Aridi, A. (2012). *Innovation Policy Handbook* (p. 202). Center for International Science and Technology Policy, The George Washington University.

World Bank. (2010). *Innovation policy: Guide for developing countries* (p. 408). The World Bank.

Zhao, W., & La Pira, F. (2013). Chinese entrepreneurship: Institutions, ecosystems and growth limits. *Advances in Economics and Business, 1*, 72–88. https://doi.org/10.13189/aeb.2013.010204

PART II

The Bottom-Up Innovation Model Of Guangdong

CHAPTER 4

Technological Learning: The Competitiveness from Shop-Floor

Introduction

The industrial geography of China was primarily the product of the States historical priorities: "Heavy" industry was concentrated in the North-East. Maoist's created a "fiefdom economy" that had meager success and the effect of dissipating the country's industrial effort (Gipouloux, 2005). The result was a territorial imbalance which has haunted Chinese planners ever since (Fan, 1997).

The policy of an open-economy after 1979 led to Chinese industrialization freeing itself from the commands of the State. Whereas the State invested heavily in the high-technology companies in Beijing and Shanghai,

---

This chapter is rewritten of several original papers of the author, including "The Innovation and Learning Capabilities of Chinese Firms," by ZHAO Wei, and Rigas ARVANITIS (2010), in *Chinese Sociology and Anthropology*, vol. 42, no. 3, Spring 2010, pp. 6–27. New York: M. E. Sharpe, Inc.; "L'apprentissage technologique dans les pays émergents, Au-delà de l'atelier et de l'entreprise," by Rigas ARVANITIS, Daniel VILLAVICENCIO, et Wei ZHAO (2014), dan la *Revue d'anthropologie des connaissances,* 2014/3, Vol. 8 No. 3, pp. 495–521; and "Technological Learning in Six Firms in South China : Success and Limits of an Industrialization Model," by Rigas ARVANITIS, Wei Zhao, Haixiong Qiu, and Jian-niu Xu (2006), in *International Journal of Technology Management*, 36 (1/2/3), pp. 108–125.

W. Zhao, *Remade in South China*, IPP Studies in the Frontiers of China's Public Policy,
https://doi.org/10.1007/978-981-95-7277-9_4

and built up technology development parks throughout the land and special economic zones on the coast, private capital was situated anywhere where the State had not undertaken any action, and where companies could sell to the local market. Thus, in the beginning, Beijing and especially Shanghai had very low levels of private capital in industrial production activities; conversely, the cities of Hangzhou (Zhejiang), Chongqing in the province of Sichuan, Guangzhou (capital of Guangdong), and Shenzhen (one of China's first special economic zones situated in Southern Guangdong, nearby Hong Kong) had the highest proportions of private companies before 2004 (Gipouloux, 2005).

These extremely dynamic provinces were where the strongest centers of industrial agglomeration were found in the 2000s. They were different from the government's economic zones. They operated in the low-technology and labor-intensive sectors with less central government support but numerous SMEs. Clusters of new firms financed mostly by private capital had come to superimpose on China's historical industrial geography of the past 40 years. The pattern of economic geography had changed under the power of the State's voluntarism planning policy. It broke free from the government sanction and long-established industrial sites.

From the late 1990s, the industrial development in the coastal zones brought not only the emergence of a light industrial areas, but also white goods manufacturing, where previously only small-scale mechanical sectors were in operation. The peculiarity of the growth of new industrial sectors was that they had been developed predominantly with private capital (Guiheux, 2002), including foreign and overseas investment, in creating local firms.

Guangdong and Latecomer Firms

Guangdong's rural industrialization corresponds to an initial phase of Chinese growth between 1983 and 1988. But at the end of the 1980s, overheating plus saturation of consumer demand for food and food-related products, clothing, and durable consumer goods pulled local companies into production overcapacity, a situation quite much like the overcapacity of Chinese industry later.

This phase was followed by foreign direct investments (FDI) in the early 1990s made by firms from industrialized world such as Japan, the United States, and the European countries, and SMEs operating in Taiwan and Hong Kong, as well as by Chinese living abroad. In 2001, investments from Taiwan and Hong Kong represented 47.5% of the foreign investments in Guangdong.

Chinese investors coming from abroad arrived not only with the capital but also with their links to global suppliers and clients. In addition, these "foreign-invested" firms had the advantage of close relations between the entrepreneurs involved, and those in power locally. The technological level of these firms was superior to that of the small town and village companies. They had brought, and continued to bring into Guangdong their network of customers and the marketing, which went with them. Often, they had placed themselves in domains where the international value chains were directed by contractors and buyers in the rich countries (Europe, the United States, and Japan). In this way they became indispensable intermediaries between low-cost suppliers or contractors in Guangdong, and the global buyers. The foreign investors of Taiwan and Hong Kong ensured both a continuous flow of finance and an integral place in the global market. There were many such firms[1] in Dongguan, a city between Shenzhen and Guangzhou in Guangdong. At the end of the 1990s, other regions of China where labor was cheaper were in competition with these firms, notably in the region of Zhejiang, near Shanghai and a large number of multinationals.

Backward to 40 years ago, nobody thought Guangdong would become "the factory of the world." Guangdong's initial development relied on the combination of two types of companies: productive units employing unskilled, mainly immigrant labor force funded by foreign capital (mainly from Hong Kong and Taiwan); and, small industrial units created by local entrepreneurs (Chan, 2003). This combination of local and overseas Chinese enterprises created an impressive web of industrial companies, making of Guangdong and, more specifically, the Pearl River Delta (PRD), a region that has achieved one of the fastest growth rates in the world. This "miracle" of South China industrialization was based on the creation of industrial private or privately managed enterprises, and mainly of small- and medium-sized entrepreneurial firms, with originally endogenous capital and technology.

[1] They were often called *sanlai yibu*, which signifies three resources and an obligation: "*the three resources are the raw materials, the parts and samples supplied by the foreign investor, and* yibu, *compensation provided by the local firm to the foreign investor in the form of finished products.*"

Guangdong's entrepreneurial companies emerged in small towns and villages at the beginning of the 1980s, and the distribution of new industries as a whole was almost entirely determined with the sprouting of small-town and village-based firms. They operated de facto according to the private mode, but ideologically they behaved as collective firms. They used raw materials, cheap labor and specialized in certain sectors (paper manufacture, food industry, plumbing, etc.). They first worked for the home market and then restructured to focus on the export market with the aim to gain access to new technology and new product demand from foreign customers (Arvanitis et al., 2006). For example, Galanz, a company manufacturing microwave ovens in Shunde of Guangdong, was initially a small company in a small town but later became the largest producer of microwave ovens in the world.

But not all these small-town and village firms became dynamic eventually. For example, Weili, a company known for producing washing machines in Zhongshan City of Guangdong, where new dynamic workshops coexisted alongside old workshops—from the industrialization era. These companies in small towns and villages were not run by collective entities, neither financed by the public institution nor governed by any centralized planning.

Like entrepreneurs everywhere, the local entrepreneurs of Guangdong were highly resourceful people who operated at the limits of legality—in the grey area where what was permitted was that which was not specifically prohibited (Ruffier, 2006). It was the period "blessed" by Deng Xiaoping himself when he declared that "*the colour of the cat didn't matter as long as it caught mice.*" These entrepreneurs shared similar characteristics that made them extremely atypical seen against the background of the country's social institutions. They were both Cantonese and non-Cantonese, mostly secondary school unfinished. They began with no money and got no money from banks nor from the State. With their experience of working with "foreign-invested" companies, they cheated, used surplus tools and material from State sectors to develop their own business.

Politically, if they joined the Communist Party, it was often for ensuring their economic success. Joining the Party was not the reason why they undertook entrepreneurial activities. They are self-made, highly independent with neither support from the State nor financial aid. They had to be on society's fringes to escape the communist ethic. They made money by bending the laws, but once this money was obtained, they invested the whole lot in their factory. In this sense, they made no difference from what

Max Weber or Joseph Schumpeter described as "capitalist" business owners who succeed function of creation.[2] These chiefs were really exceptional people (Ruffier et al., 2006, p. 7).

At origin, the local firms in Guangdong were typical "latecomers" because they were dislocated from international sources of technology, science, and R&D, or even dislocated from demanding users, international markets, advanced user-producer links, clusters, networks, industrial districts, etc. (Hobday, 1995). They were initially resource-poor, but driven by a strategy that searched for ways of capturing resources (Mathews, 2002). The strategy was exploiting the few advantages they had—such as linking with advanced firms in various kinds of contracting or licensing arrangements, and leveraging resources (knowledge, technology, and market access channels) from such linkages to enhance their capabilities and technological competences, in a process best described as technological learning.

Defining "Technological Learning"

Amsden (1989) and Amsden and Chu (2003) pointed that technological learning at shop-floor of firms is the original driving force of such an upgrading. She detailed the three aspects of technological learning as:

1. speed of learning (how rapidly foreign technology is borrowed, which depends on investment rate of firm, investing in foreign design, and arrangement of technology acquisition or transfer),
2. scale of learning (whether foreign technology is utilized at the appropriate scale, which depends on how fast the market is growing and whether firm is producing at an appropriate scale), and
3. efficiency of learning (how efficiently foreign technology is employed, which depends on firm's experience related to cumulative production and the effects of learning by doing on firm).

Very much in line with Amsden, Hobday (1994, 1995) showed how electronics companies in the four dragons of East Asia linked their

[2] It is true that Max Weber found in the protestant religion the moral basis that allowed the first generation of industrial leaders to emerge. Schumpeter preferred to try and define the moral ethos of the entrepreneur: and this moral ethos does not seem very different from that of the entrepreneurs in Guangdong.

technological learning to export markets; specifically, subcontracting and original equipment manufacturing (OEM) mechanisms acted as a training school for latecomers, enabling them to overcome entry barriers and to assimilate manufacturing and design technology. In contrast with R&D and design-led strategies, latecomer firms began with incremental improvements to manufacturing processes which led on to minor product innovations. Since the development of technological capabilities during catch-up was a learning process, firms' internal development and design capabilities grow as it moves between successive stages from OEM to ODM (original design manufacturing) and OBM (original brand manufacturing), but there was no role for research. On the basis of the East Asian experience, this sustaining perspective of innovation asserts that successful latecomer firms may go through a kind of "reverse product cycle." They begin with simple assembly processes but gradually and systematically accumulate the capability to modify, design, and build their own new product and process technologies progressively. Customers play a major part in this cycle, which proceeds through successively higher value-added forms of production.

Technological Learning in East Asia

Since the seminal work on technological learning in the developing world of Jorge Katz and Alice Amsden, a lot of the work has focused on East Asian economies, such as Japan, South Korea, and Taiwan, on the theory of late industrialization, the creation of international value chains, and the role of the State. Japan's reverse engineering was done by engineers to discover the technological principles of a device, object, or system through analysis of its structure, its features, and operation. Technically, this activity amounted to reproduce the original product. Some industrial know-how was set up with reverse engineering: it required detecting potential market needs, locating sources of technical and productive knowledge, and locating products in new markets. It also involved the search for relevant information, effective interaction between members inside and outside the group. Japanese firms were found to be in intensive interactions between manufacturing operators and maintenance technicians, between unions and management, and among suppliers, vendors, workshops, etc. Continuous experiments on the assembly line and dividing the workshops in self-contained units greatly impressed the Westerners who analyzed the

Japanese capitalism. Their engineering process never disconnected in workshops the production design from in-house R & D.

Similarly, in South Korea, informal transfer of technology had contributed to the development of capacities of large and small firms whose employees carefully and systematically imitated foreign technologies. In most cases, Korean firms manufactured products by imitating the style or design of the market leader but labeling the products with their own brands and defining unique specifications. When Korean firms had access to newer technologies, they were able to quickly position themselves in developing new products. This is what Linsu Kim called the transition from "duplicative imitation" to "creative imitation" (Kim, 2000). The famous Korean firm in semiconductor industry today had earlier experiences in mastering mass production of electronics goods in conceiving and executing major investments in plant and equipment, and most fundamentally of all in appraising a new business area and executing an entry strategy. These were well-honed skills when the Korean firm elected to enter the semiconductor sector.

As for Taiwan, some studies such as Gereffi (1999) and Ernst and Kim (2002) sought to understand the subcontracting effect in the creation of global chains of supply. One analysis of the Taiwanese electronics industry (Ernst, 2000, p. 224) emphasized the diversity of linkages between Taiwanese subcontractors, foreign clients, and providers of technology. International linkages included a variety of ties with sales, manufacturing, and engineering support from affiliates of foreign firms; they also included different forms and trajectories of integration into global production networks of American and Japanese electronics firms. Taiwanese firms typically relied on concurrent knowledge outsourcing: they pursued different approaches in parallel, rather than concentrating exclusively on one particular linkage. Observing the Taiwanese electronic industry, Hobday (1997) theorized a continuous upgrading path of latecomer firms from simple suppliers, original equipment manufacturers (OEM), through original design manufacturers (ODM), to own brand manufacturers (OBM).

This technological learning was also seen as a structural feature that went hand-in-hand with some special institutional arrangements (Kim, 1997). In 1990s, there had been an impressive number of studies centered on issues like national innovation system, institutions, and overall environmental conditions of industrialization (see, for instance, Lall, 1998; Chen & Sewell, 1996; Shin, 1996).Technological learning had been at the center of these discussions, so much so that some authors proposed to replace the concept of National System of Innovation by that of National System of Technological Learning (Mathews, 1999). In general, learning and educational achievements were seen as underlying features of Asian societies (Rowen, 1998).

An Alternative to Absorptive Capacity

Technological learning is a set of activities and not just investment in physical assets, which are more or less intensely experienced by latecomer firm regarding the way of production, product design, and various interventions on equipment. Some of these activities aim at strengthening the human potential of firms related to control of equipment, engineering, and R & D. Learning requires means assimilating knowledge for imitation but also means accumulating and creating new knowledge for innovation (Kim, 1998). By nature, technological learning is a cumulative process over time, very specific to each firm, and collective in the sense that it involves more than one person inside the firm (Arvanitis & Villavicencio, 1998; Figueiredo, 2002).

Economists have used the notions of "production capabilities" and "technological capabilities" to differentiate two resulting paths of technological learning, particularly in the developing countries (Bell & Pavitt, 1995). For large and developed economies, the equivalent concept to technological learning is "absorptive capacity," introduced already in the Chap. 2 (Cohen & Levinthal, 1990). Absorptive capacity is formally defined in terms of an organization's capability to capture, absorb, and exploit new information in a way that enhances its competitive and strategic options on R&D. The expenditures on R&D, in return, are seen to provide the firm with a greater capacity for absorbing technological and market "shocks," and thus enhancing its competitive prospects, rather than simply as a means of bringing new products to market.

From the perspective of technological learning, learning cannot be reduced to R&D, even if it is an essential component. Moreover, R&D is not linked to production or the market in a linear and simple way (Rosenberg et al., 1992). The existence of an R&D unit is not limited to some large R&D facilities with specific research projects; R&D's functions can be much wider, supporting the whole productive process, particularly in small and medium enterprises where it is frequently undercounted (Arvanitis & Vonortas, 2000; Acs & Audretsch, 1991; Kleinknecht &

Reijnen, 1991). Nevertheless, the leverage function of absorptive capacity among R&D, external technical information, and firm's internal technology knowledge is also the main function of technological learning. Latecomer firms are not concerned to generate "new technological knowledge," but to adapt existing technologies which are unlikely to be presented to latecomer firms in a discrete package. So, latecomer firms have to "absorb" and assemble existing technologies from a variety of external sources, then leverage them in their manufacturing, designing, and engineering activities. Their technological knowledge on product and process can be progressively increased, which in return, will enhance their absorptive capacity of additional technologies from external sources. Technological learning is a leveraged process of internal activities and external sources.

Internal Processes and External Linkages

An empirical description of technological learning would identify two types of activities: those that permit the enhancement of products and processes inside the enterprise (internal learning), and activities with the same purpose but in relation to clients, suppliers, and external sources of knowledge (external or interactive learning) (Pirela et al., 1993; Arvanitis, 2000). Internal learning includes activities such as: seeking technological information on alternative technological routes, adaptation of technology, development of better and new products, and adaptation and design of processes. Product and process innovations, strictly speaking, are part of this learning experience as well as R&D, design, engineering, maintenance, and quality management. Corporate R & D often plays an essential role of liaison between firms and outside world.

These activities which seem primarily responsible for technological learning can be explained in more detail (Arvanitis et al., 2014):

1. *Seeking information on technological alternatives.* This is an essential component of what Rosenberg described the selection of technologies. It is also a function of the R&D (but also of other departments: engineering, technology management, maintenance, management strategy …). In wider sense, it includes also poaching of experienced personnel from outside, extensive literature search, observation of technology in operation, and temporary hiring of foreign engineers. Identifying sources of foreign technology.

2. *The negotiation of technology.* Particularly important activity in the context of developing countries as it is to ensure that the firm negotiates better and knows what it needs during a transfer of technology. It is an activity of acquiring technology transfer, hiring foreign expatriates, overseas R&D, etc.
3. *The assimilation of technologies through the adaptation of parts and equipment.* This is the most basic activity of technological learning. The need to adapt technologies to local conditions, local raw materials, or the specific constraints of the market is actually a powerful means of probing technology. It also includes improvement of imported technologies and their application to other areas. It is termed as assimilation or application, largely through learning by doing and learning by using.
4. *Product development.* Whether new products or adapting existing products, these developments are essential in the corporate technology strategy. This may include formulating or reformulating all or part of a product, design of new or improved product, copying or reproduction with or without the consent of the original patent holders. Product innovations that fall into this category are, however, broader and would be recognized as part of product innovations by an engineer.
5. *The design of new or improved processes.* It may include all activities since the modification or adaptation of a simple design or an integral design of a completely new process. Process design activity is probably the most complex among those that constitute the process of technological learning.

Training can also be part of these activities even though in most firms, technical training is primarily restricted to managers or technicians for tasks of management and learning of foreign languages. However, a firm that incorporated relatively poorly trained staff at the start can be particularly efficient and innovative because of the collective construction of skills.

External or interactive learning activities can take a very wide variety of forms. Table 4.1 summarizes those external relations that are related to a foreign provider of technology, and their impact on the creation of technological capabilities. Innovation by nature is a process of interactive learning and in business it is generally rooted in technological learning activities at shop-floor level. Many of the "technical" activities force latecomer firms to build strong relationships with their environment. These

Table 4.1 Linkage effects on technological learning

Technology Linkages	*Learning Effects*
Purchase of equipment with technical documentation for installation	The interaction is a market relation. The technology provider offers little support, and there is no learning by interaction.
Technology transfer contract, with technology licensing, technical assistance, engineering assistance, production assessment, "turn-key" project	The relation is commercial or hierarchical relation. Depending on the nature of the contract, the technology provider can be active, and learning by interaction can happen. Many contracts prohibit explicitly certain types of learning procedures (no copying, no adaptation permitted, no enhancements).
Contracts with a client (less formal but long-term relationship)	The relation is market-based and unstable. No formal technology transfers, but the providers of technology are also final clients, transmitting quality specifications and productive procedures. Usually, clients' engineer or technical personnel installs and checks quality procedures.
Subcontracting, co-production, OEM or ODM	Mainly hierarchical relation between users and providers of technology. The longer the relation is, overtime, the more active providers of technology are in transmitting larger parts of their know-how. Specific mechanisms of learning ("learning by monitoring" and quality control procedures included) and the subcontractor is subject to the production standards of clients' orders. Users of technology can upgrade by interacting on a more permanent basis with technology providers. Non--exclusive contracts are a bonus for the user of technology. The relationship of OEM/ODM is over long time and brings better learning ability.
Foreign direct investment, including joint ventures, contractual common enterprises	Hierarchical relation between providers and users of technology (Internalized relation similar to that between a subsidiary and headquarters). Providers will be more active depending on the degree of their investment. The larger their financial investment, the more intense is their effort. Technological learning is a process controlled by the headquarters. If the mother firm is willing, the affiliates will learn a lot. Usually the local firm gives access to market and gets technology in exchange.
Technical alliances, strategic R&D consortiums	The relations are an organized market. Providers and users of technology are very closely linked and share competencies. Members are at same technology level and develop complementary abilities.

(*continued*)

Table 4.1 (continued)

Technology Linkages	*Learning Effects*
R & D cooperation with universities and public research centers (rare in developing countries in take-off stage)	Complementary relationships. Suppliers and users of research and technology must work together. Strong technological learning. Complementary capabilities.

Source: Arvanitis, R., W. Zhao et al. (2006)

are links with suppliers, customers, and immediate technology partners. These links form what Lundvall (1998) called the "micro-foundation of innovation system."

Technological Learning from Foreign Client

From 1990s to the mid-2000s, the stage of industrial take-off in Guangdong, local latecomer firms followed the above pattern of technological learning in terms of internal processes and external effects of interaction with their immediate environment.[3] The outstanding characteristic of these local latecomer firms in terms of learning was the relationship with external actors, especially with their foreign clients. Except for the joint venture, foreign clients were the main sources of knowledge for these latecomer firms, by inspecting their productive processes, giving them blueprints, and pushing them for higher quality. The client was, thus, their main provider of technology, though the frameworks of interaction with latecomer firms were somehow different: OEM, joint venture, subcontracting, and multiple linkages, etc.

[3]The firm cases in this part were based on empirical work conducted during 2000 to 2003 in Guangdong. Interviews were undertaken to have qualitative appreciation of the "typical" latecomer firms in that period. Large firms and high-tech firms were not included since they were rare. The in-depth interview sought to capture the history of the focus firm, its linkages with providers of technology and clients, its insertion into the local policy and economy, internal management of manpower and quality, and its general strategy. Each interview lasted around one-and-a-half hours. Some interviews were followed by a factory tour. Interviews were also made in eight innovation centers among the 38 industrial clusters in Guangdong on their management issues and relations with local firms (clusters were reported in detail in Arvanitis & Qiu, 2004).

Learning Through OEM

The company TL was a typical factory created by "overseas Chinese" from Taiwan. The OEM model made Taiwan famous and fit well for a globalized industry, where the international brand put the orders while the factory dealt with the local advantages. Taiwanese producers, already used to these OEM arrangements, understood the full advantage they could get from coming to Mainland China. Somehow differently, Hong Kong capitalists also came to Mainland China seeking low costs, transforming Hong Kong into an industrial desert. In early stage of industrial take-off, local firms in Guangdong had no access to foreign clients with the same facility.

Established in Nanhai, an industrial city near Guangzhou (capital city of Guangdong Province), where the shoe industry had been supported by local government, TL was a large sport shoemaker inserted in the global value chain. In fact, TL group was a shoe-producing company quite strong in Taiwan, having already 15 factories in the Mainland China, all based on the production of sports shoes exclusively for foreign clients. Employing about 3000 workers, it produced sports shoes for Italian and North American brands. No foreign client had exclusive production in this factory. The factory was fit for the international market; it was able to produce for any large brand of sports shoes in the world. Containers were loaded inside the factory and shipped to the port of Nanhai.

TL had OEM arrangements with its principal clients and very stable contracts over time. The clients had permanent representatives located inside the factory for quality checks and production procedures supervision. The firm had a testing and experimental so-called "R&D unit," which proposed new models to clients, mostly variations of original models. In fact, the multinational brands relied more and more on these OEM providers for low-end changes in design. The cost of design was normally lower because designers had low wages. The factory had a good competence in testing quality, an essential feature for international trade. Feasibility study of new designs was part of the package for technological learning.

The local firm of TL group publicized its regular contacts with the international brand. In every office the "ethical rules" of the multinational were shown, particularly as to how labor and human resources should be managed by the multinational group. The factory seemed to work as a subsidiary of a multinational company. This was, however, a false picture:

management of labor and local resources was not controlled by the foreign partner. Clients only checked for quality and timing.

TL factory was a typical example of the "triangle manufacturing" depicted by Gereffi (1999, p. 60) in the apparel and textile industry where: "The US buyers place their orders with the (Taiwan or Hong Kong) manufacturers they have sourced from in the past, who in turn shift some or all of the requested production to affiliated offshore factories in low-wage countries (e.g., China, Indonesia or Vietnam)." TL had regular and long-term commitment to its clients. It accumulated progressively strong production and design capabilities, but had no original design; no capacity to innovate in original models since only their clients, the brand holders, could decide on innovation.

Learning in Joint Venture (JV)

The situation of TL can be contrasted to CB, a medium-sized packaging joint venture of a Guangdong city authority and a French multinational firm which was one of the largest packaging producers in the world. The multinational set up a joint venture with a company owned by a local government in early 1990s, the only legal form for foreign investment at that time. The Joint Venture (JV) model was once thought to be the panacea of technology transfers. China had provided legislative effort in order to promote FDI and JVs. Foreigners were usually uncomfortable with the figure of the JV, and most foreign companies wanted to become wholly owned foreign enterprises, when the law was authorizing the new possibility. In CB, the partnership was a forced one, not a chosen one, and whatever the benefits, it was always seen with suspicion. Inside the JV, there was an important input of technological know-how, as would be the case for the subsidiary of a transnational firm. The technical relation between local subsidiary and parent company was normally stable. Learning technologies was regarded as an internal process for the French multinational. But all final decisions depended on the internal structure and strategy of the transnational or foreign partner.

On entering the Chinese market, CB's French parent company was looking for immediate profitability, which arose from fully exploiting the market of the already existing local firm with which it formed the JV, and a strong and growing local market. A totally new investment was done in CB to serve exclusively a US multinational as client, leader of cosmetics, soaps, and detergents, by installing high-end equipment, using exclusive design for the molds, and maintaining close relationships with the equipment producers. This new production line coexisted with two older lines, serving different market segments.

For the French multinational, the existing Chinese local firm needed little reorganization when it was transformed into a JV. Technological reordering and financial cleanup were the two priorities of the new management. CB was small with around 280 workers and had always been earning money. The JV had benefited from the management experience of the French multinational, but on the whole, production management and personnel had been in the hands of the Chinese managers with long-time experience. Some technical personnel in highly technical areas such as molds had benefited from long stays in factories located in France.

In domestic market, competition with Chinese firms was quite fierce. Having a famous French brand was not sufficient to gain new clients. The only stable market for CB was its US transnational client. The French multinational had offered many times to buy the shares of the Chinese partner, but the city authority didn't want to lose a business that was earning money.

Learning as Contracted Supplier

Different from CB, WG is a local collective enterprise, that was, a firm that formally belonged partly to a collective body (the municipality). In the 1980s and early 1990s, most collective enterprises have been at the forefront of the Chinese industrialization, later becoming famous brands (like Haier or Lenovo). The particular ownership status didn't deter the dynamism of WG. Before the reform, it was once the only company in the town of Shuikou of Guangdong, an industrial cluster of small- and medium-sized enterprises (SMEs) in traditional sector which were main force of China's industrial growth in the factor-driven stage (Lemoine & Unal-Kesenci, 2004).

Like other firms in the cluster, WG was dedicated to producing simple faucets made from cast iron. With the reform policy during the 1980s the company was challenged: some of its workers, who had been working there for more than 20 years, created private enterprises. Faucets and plumbing in general was a good business when there was a construction boom in China. Soon many more firms were created by former workers of WG, which was called the "mother of all companies" in the town of Shuikou. But WG remained the largest company in town. Among other things, WG was the only one that had a metal-plating facility, a highly polluting activity that was nonetheless an obligatory passage point in producing faucets. Collectively owned, in fact, didn't mean "state-owned" and WG was managed very much in the same way as in other firms in the town of Shuikou. The technology was not so much better in WG than that in other firms. Additionally, WG produced along the standards that were offered by their foreign clients; for the local market, the company provided models for merchants.

HY and CZ were both private firms created by former workers of WG. Oriented mainly toward the national market, HY was a young firm (eight years old) in the faucets and plumbing business with 300 workers, all immigrants from other regions in China, like all workers in the other factories around. HY was quite well ordered, and managed as a family business, i.e., the woman looking at the accounts, her husband managing the production and public relations. It was considered one of the best companies in the city, although the owner did not seem willing to share any friendship toward the authorities: "public authority means taxes," as he said.

HY emphasized on quality control and productive processes. It was a better and stronger learner than many other firms in the region. Nonetheless, the whole productive process was mainly manual. What made the difference was its stronger quality control, a better division of production tasks, and a more efficient layout of the factory. More importantly, the firm benefited from one big contract with a Spanish client. After two years, the client proposed a joint venture, but the Chinese entrepreneur refused. Following pressure from local authorities, a joint venture had been set up, but the foreign client was a minor shareholder (only 20%), a rare situation at that time since most JVs were set up in a manner that benefiting more openly the foreign partner. HY's entrepreneur never wished to lose the diversity of clients and had no exclusive contracts with any client. Visits of foreign technical personnel were quite frequent, and the quality control was not local.

CZ, another private company in Shuikou, was exclusively oriented toward export. Created in early 1990s, it produced mainly for the German market. With 200 to 250 employees, CZ was a "real" ISO 9000 company. It had invested strongly in the ISO process, and the owner and general manager used the ISO system as a lever to maintain high quality. This firm had introduced many new products and made considerable adaptations to the production processes. The owner had visited professional fairs in

Germany and always brought with him faucets which were to be "reversed-engineered." Technicians coming from client-firms inspected CZ. In Europe, its production was considered of middle-range quality, and in order to produce higher quality, important investments would be made.

WG, HY, and CZ, all these local firms in Shuikou shared something in common: they were aching for foreign clients. "Our clients are our teachers," said one manager. All the best quality producers were linked one way or another to international clients who gave them new blueprints and proposed improvements in quality, even they had unstable relation to clients. They became contracted suppliers of foreign clients because they had to face strong local competition. They also knew that the local market was unable to sustain large quantity of producers and sooner or later only the best ones would survive in a more competitive market. So it was better to learn faster from clients.

Learning from Diversified Linkages

Meanwhile, when local latecomer firms grew bigger, they began to become both OEM producers and contracted suppliers, and expand the external linkages for learning. This was the case of JL, a larger-sized collective enterprise owned by local government of Jiangmen City, producing washing machines since 1979. JL started with a production of 200 machines per year, and till 2001 it had a capacity above one million. In the beginning of 2000, it produced among the highest quality washing machines in China (sales of two billion Yuans per year, around 250 million USD, and exported for eight million USD). It was the fifth biggest producer and the third biggest exporter of washing machines in China. In 2001, JL entered a JV with Mitsubishi for the production of air-conditioners, and was considering a partnership with General Electric in the washing machines business.

The production of washing machines in the 1990s exemplified the evolution of the Chinese market. The sector had been dominated rapidly by companies that later either disappeared or had lost their rank. A famous case was Weili, a collective company based in Zhongshan City, well known as the main producer in China. But by 2002, Weili only produced less than 20,000 cheap and obsolete units per year.

Managers of JL explained their success by the fact that they were a relatively small company that did not attract the envy and greed of provincial authorities. Apart from this political aspect, a constant strategy based on technological learning was perhaps a better explanation. JL had developed good processes, high quality products, created an R&D unit, and kept a continuous training for its personnel. Workers were mainly local people, not immigrants from other regions, and were rather well paid. JL searched actively to create production unit outside China: Brazil would probably be its next destination. JL was also an OEM producer for many large firms in China, such as Konka and TCL. These well-known brands produced other types of equipment like televisions, computers, and telephones. Washing machines under their brands were in fact produced by JL.

JL developed competencies in product design, training of human resources, and process capabilities. It benefited from the help of the city office of science and technology for developing partnerships with a local engineering school, and developing its R&D unit. It focused on Computer-Aided Design (CAD), a priority in Guangdong and also installed a GIS for sales management. Its research focused on a highly automated system of electronic commands of washing machines. It also designed specific molds for equipment. Cooperation with of Department of Engineering Tsinghua University in Beijing (among the most famous universities in China) was established, as well as with the Normal University of Beijing, the Industrial University of Harbin, and the Polytechnic University of South China in Guangzhou. Some of these collaborations were supported by the National Programme of Science and Technology. Its investment in R&D had always been quite high: 4.1% in 1998 and 5.9% of its sales in 2001. JL also entered in a partnership with General Electric (GE). Although the company did not show this as being of paramount importance, it was in fact a decisive step. JL then became a supplier of GE for washing machines sold in Latin America. The technical level of the machines attracted the attention of GE. Thus, entirely automatic machines were produced as an OEM arrangement with GE. The aim of JL was to have a strategic alliance with GE.

Having the cooperation with GE, JL updated its strategy to constantly produce new washing machines: new products represented 30% of their sales. "We want to export and be famous because of the quality of our products and our technological innovation," said the general manager. JL worked out a patent policy, a portfolio of 20 patents (of which seven were technical patents) and an intellectual property office, a rather unusual feature. Some patents were extended abroad. The firm also learned how to manage efficiently its network of suppliers. For example, the motors were produced outside JL and attained a 90% rate of acceptance. Then JL created an affiliate JV with Mitsubishi for the production of air-conditioners. "For Mitsubishi, the air-conditioning is a small division; for us, it means a lot. They have among the best technology, and we will learn a lot from their management. Our own development will benefit from this unit of JV." The JV was entirely Japanese-managed. The objective was to see how the Japanese managed their company.

JL represented a higher level of technological learning for latecomer firms. It emphasized not only on quality control and productive processes, but also on innovative products and organizational management. Other larger firms in China, such as Haier, TCL, Konka, or Legend (then Lenovo in 2004) had similar situation: having a more explicit learning strategy based on technological development and high standards in production; developing collaborative R&D with outside sources of knowledge. At the same time, these firms also seek to become, at least partially, OEM providers. OEM allowed for lower cost in entering the foreign markets, and permitted to get a grip on the technology as well as marketing in foreign countries. As an outcome, they also tried to set up facilities in foreign countries, a growing tendency for Chinese enterprises.

Technological Learning as Business Strategy

Learning, not solely relying on so-called comparative advantage, was the key of Guangdong's rising up as super export machine of China or the real "world workshop" in China. As illustrated in Table 4.2, which summarizes the main facts of examples mentioned in this part, the latecomer firms in Guangdong were quick learners under huge market competition. The capability of learning how to economically use technologies to meet client needs was the foundation of Guangdong firms' competitiveness.

First, they became very flexible and proactive in terms of commercial conditions in order to keep and satisfy foreign clients, often integrating their businesses in a network of subcontractors and even selling to bigger clients. Through the initial commercial contacts, they engaged actively in looking abroad for sources of technology and seek actively to cooperate with foreign clients in order to have access to better technology, as well as export channel.

They seek these contacts through varied forms and channels, always maintaining the variety of foreign clients and arrangements. In the absence of previous experiences, local firms relied on their foreign clients, rather than some public knowledge provider, or other external sources of

Table 4.2 Strategies of Guangdong latecomer firms with foreign clients

	TL (Nanhai)	*WG (Shuikou)*	*HY (Shuikou)*	*CZ (Shuikou)*	*CB (Zhongshan)*	*JL (Jiangmen)*
Products	Sporting shoes	Faucets	Faucets	Faucets	Packaging	Washing machines
Range of products	Small (large variety of design details)	Large	Large	Large	Small	Large
Ownership	JV Taiwan	Collective	Private	Private	JV France	Collective
Main client/main market	Foreign transnational (OEM)	Foreign clients and buyers (partial OEM), and national wholesalers	National and foreign wholesalers and foreign producers	Export 90% to foreign wholesalers	National industrial clients, large transnational client in China	National wholesalers and retailers
Needs of clients	Client's specifications + proposals of variants to the client	Client's specifications + own models	Client's specifications + own models	Client's specifications + own models	Client's specifications + own models	Client specifications + own models
Size (employees)	Approximately 3000, Mother Company owns 15 other factories.	Approximately 200	Approximately 400	Approximately 200–250	Approximately 1000	Approximately 2000
Presence of client	Control office inside factory	Technical inspections by client	Technical inspections by client	Technical inspections by client	Internal adaptations	Technical inspections by clients
Regularity of contacts with foreign clients	Permanently on-site, OEM arrangement	By orders + regular inspections	By orders + regular inspections	By orders (regular clients) + regular inspections	Regular clients	Regular clients, company seeks to provide OEM

Type of production	Large mass production	Medium-sized production	Medium-sized mass production	Medium-sized production	Large mass production	Large mass production
Type of productive process	Batch, semi manual	Batch, semi manual + automated metal plating	Batch, semi manual	Batch, semi manual	Continuous process, automated	Continuous process, semi manual
Initial investment	Medium	Medium	Low	Low	Low + High	Medium
Difficulty of accessing the foreign market	Easy	Medium	Difficult	Difficult	Easy	Medium
Exclusivity of production for one client	No, but exclusive models	No	No	No	Yes (one product)	Yes, some products
Subcontractors	Few	Few	Few	Few	Few	Many
Origin of inputs	Imported	National	National	National	National and imported	Imported/some national
Origin of owner/manager	Taiwan	Local, ex-worker of a local factory	Local, ex-worker of the collective factory WG	Local, ex-worker of the collective factory WG	Expatriate managers + Chinese manager	Local, engineer
Industrial cluster	Yes	Yes	Yes	Yes	No	No
Authorities support	Strong	Medium	Low	Low	Medium	Strong
ISO 9000	Yes	No	No	Yes	Yes	Yes
R&D	Yes, design and test	No	No	No	No formal unit of R&D, technology development team	Yes, strong R&D and collaborative links with universities

Source: ARVANITIS, R., W. Zhao et al. (2006)

technical advice. For example, many firms kept their subcontracted manufacturing activity (parts production in short term and simultaneous cooperation with client), even after they became OEM producers (whole product manufacturing and long-term cooperation with client). This multiple-channel "copy and fabrication" strategy opened possibilities for larger production scale, better knowledge, and wider markets. The association with a foreign client was thus strategic to practically all latecomer firms that wanted to go up the value chain, to approach the technological frontier and to access the more lucrative markets.

Even firms advancing more rapidly toward an innovation frontier were in this pragmatic, down-to-earth learning strategy, upgrading cumulatively productive and control knowledge. These firms introduced new models as long as their foreign clients provided them new blueprints. The firm JL seemed to enter in a transitional stage in upgrading from a basic productive learning to more sophisticated technological learning. But it maintained the same diversified portfolio of clients and products, aggregating more sources of knowledge and trying to keep a multiplicity of external sources. It accepted purposefully to be both OEM producer for some products and an autonomous brand for others, depending on the market.

Conclusion: Competitiveness Source of Shop-Floor

This learning strategy, to some degree, is what has been employed by firms in other Asian economies, especially those in Taiwan and South Korea; it nonetheless was the actual early-stage industrialization process in China: technological learning took place in a large variety of medium-sized firms (collective-owned, private, overseas Chinese investment, etc.), not so much through technology transfers from foreign multinationals that invested in China (inward FDI) or through some other providers such as universities, technical canters or consultants, but through their foreign clients. Local latecomer firms acquired most of technological knowledge they needed from clients, then accumulated and created more and more knowledge by themselves. Guangdong's ascendance to become China's "world factory" originated from its local firms' technological learning, not based on any planned national industrial or technological programs.

Maybe what is surprising is how such an ordinary firm-level technological learning could lead to an extraordinary fast industrialization at the macro level, the so-called "China Miracle" (Lin et al., 2000). The answer might rely on the size of this common-type learning. When an ordinary learning behavior spread through thousands of all kinds of firms in an economy like the Chinese, the result would be like the consequences of a typical Chinese social movement, i.e., a mass outcome or a "miracle." China, from 1990s to 2000s, had been carrying out a massive technological learning movement throughout its industrial firms. It laid down its industrial competitiveness today.

But the real competitiveness of latecomer firms came firstly from factories or workshops within each firm, not from firms at corporate level (Arvanitis et al., 2014). The process of learning is observable at the micro level of production workshops and is difficult to extrapolate to the whole enterprise. The reason is that firm is generally not mono- or mono-production workshop but often a sum of workshops. Thus, one firm probably has equipment that operates with workshops that are unrelated to each other. This heterogeneity of workshops, production processes, and their technologies is persistent in latecomer firms.

For example, a JV company near the city of Guangzhou was a leader in detergents market. It produced detergent powders for mass market and later ventured into the production of detergents for dishwashing liquids of multinationals' brand names. Production of new detergents required less bulky equipment, very different from those for clothes washing powders. As the bottles were small, bottling equipment was automatic, faster, and expensive for installation. The equipment depreciation was possible only by large scale of sales and strong growth. Since the dishwashing market was just at the beginning in that period, the JV had to keep old, polluting, and highly labor-intensive manual and semi-automated production lines alongside the highly capital intensive ultra-modern workshop with advanced equipment.

The heterogeneity of production technologies was due to the heterogeneity of customers and clients. Since their multinational clients were the primary input channel of new production technologies and products, technological learning was undertaken primarily in the new workshop, rather than across the whole firm. The JV was regarded by multinationals as just a workshop which entered into direct relationship with the clients, their designated suppliers, and other actors who could provide the knowledge that the workshop was not able to generate internally.

Learning at workshop floor constantly increased the labor productivity, which was very low at the beginning. But the challenge was still how to synchronize different workshops or different business units using different levels of technologies and establish more linkages with broader business environment. Many of such things went beyond the capability of the latecomer firms' management and became barriers to their further growth. It was the local government in Guangdong which created some favorable conditions for the shop-floor learning by playing of role of corporate management and coordination. For example, one key capability of latecomer firms in Guangzhou was that they could quickly increase or decrease the volume of production. This ability was largely due to the fact that they could obtain easily more land from local governments. Besides, local governments invested heavily in infrastructures and actively promoted the development of industrial clusters, which eventually helped local firms to catch the early opportunities to grow, a topic that the next chapter will treat.

References

Acs, Z., & Audretsch, D. (Eds.). (1991). *R&D, firm size and innovative activity.* Innovation and Technological Change.

Amsden, A. H. (1989). *Asia's next Giant. South Korea and the late industrialization.* Oxford University Press.

Amsden, A. H., & Chu, W.-w. (2003). *Beyond late development: Taiwan's upgrading policies* (p. 224). The MIT Press.

Arvanitis, R., D. Villavicencio, & W. Zhao (2014) L'apprentissage technologique dans les pays émergents, Au-delà de l'atelier et de l'entreprise, *Revue d'anthropologie des connaissances,* 2014/3, Vol.8 No. 3, pp. 495-521

Arvanitis, R., & Qiu, H. (2004). R&D in universities and different institutional settings in South China: Research for policy, final research report for IDRC, research Institute for Guangdong Development (ZURIGud), Zhongshan (sun Yat-sen) university, Guangzhou and IRD, Paris, November.

Arvanitis, R., & Villavicencio, D. (Eds.). (1998). Comparative perspectives on technological learning. Special Issue *Science, Technology and Society.* Sage, Vol. 3, No. 1.

Arvanitis, R., & Vonortas, N. (2000). Apprentissage et coopération à travers la Recherche-Développement. *Technologie, Idéologie, Pratiques (TIP), 14*(1), 225–246.

Arvanitis, R., Zhao, W., Qiu, H., & Xu, J.-n. (2006). Technological learning in six firms in South China: Success and limits of an industrialization model. *International Journal of Technology Management, 36*(1/2/3), 108–125.

Arvanitis, R., Villavicencio, D., & Zhao, W. (2014). L'apprentissage technologique dans les pays émergents, Au-delà de l'atelier et de l'entreprise. *Revue d'anthropologie des connaissances, 8*(3), 495–521.

Bell, M., & Pavitt, K. (1995). Technological accumulation and industrial growth: Contrasts between developed and developing countries. *Industrial and Corporate Change, 2*(2), 157–210.

Chan, A. (2003) Les effets de la mondialisation sur les conditions de travail en Chine. *Perspectives Chinoises*, Janvier–Février, 75, 43–52.

Chen, C.-F., & Sewell, G. (1996). Strategies for technological development in South Korea and Taiwan: The case of semiconductors. *Research Policy, 25*, 759–783.

Cohen, W., & Levinthal, D. (1990). Absorptive capacity: A new perspective on learning and innovation. *Administrative Science Quarterly, 35*(1), 128–152.

Ernst, D. (2000). Inter-organizational knowledge outsourcing: What permits small Taiwanese firms to compete in computer industry. *Asia-Pacific Journal of Management, 17*(2), 223–255.

Ernst, D., & Kim, L. (2002). Global production networks, knowledge diffusion, and local capability formation. *Research Policy, 31*(8–9), 1417–1429.

Fan, C. C. (1997). Uneven development and beyond: Regional development theory in post-Mao China. *International Journal of Urban and Regional Research,* 21, 620–639. https://doi.org/10.1111/1468-2427.00105

Figueiredo, P. N. (2002). Does technological learning pay off? Inter-firm differences in technological capability-accumulation paths and operational performance improvement. *Research Policy, 31*(1), 73–94.

Gereffi, G. (1999). International trade and industrial upgrading in the apparel commodity chain. *Journal of International Economics, 48*(1), 37–70.

Gipouloux, F. (2005). *La Chine du XXIe siècle Une nouvelle superpuissance?* (322 p.). Armand Colin.

Guiheux, G. (2002, May–June). The incomplete crystallization of the private sector. China Perspectives, 42, 24–35.

Hobday, M. (1994). Export-led technology development in the four dragons: The case of electronics. *Development and Change, 25*, 333–361.

Hobday, M. (1995). *Innovation in East Asia: The challenge to Japan*. Edward Elgar.

Hobday, M. (1997). Latecomer catch-up strategies in electronics: Samsung of Korea and ACER of Taiwan. *Asia Pacific Business Review, 4*(2–3), 48–83.

Kim, L. (1997). *Imitation to innovation: The dynamics of Korea's technological learning*. Harvard Business School Press.

Kim, L. (1998, July–August). Crisis construction and organizational learning: Capability building in catching-up at Hyundai motor. *Organization Science, 9*(4), 506–521.

Kim, L. (2000). The dynamics of technological learning in industrialization. *INTECH*.

Kleinknecht, A., & Reijnen, J. (1991). More evidence on the undercounting of small firm R&D. *Research Policy, 20*(6), 579–587.

Lall, S. (1998). Technology and human capital in maturing Asian countries. *Science, Technology and Society, 3*(1), 11–48.
Lemoine, F., & Unal-Kesenci, D. (2004). Assembly trade and technology transfer: The case of China. *World Development, 32*(5), 829–850.
Lin, Y. J., Cai, F., & Li, Z. (2000). *Le Miracle Chinois. Stratégie de Développement et Réforme Economique (The China Miracle, 1996)*. Economica.
Lundvall, B. A. (1998). Why study national systems and national styles of innovation? , *Technology Analysis & Strategic Management, 10*(4), 407–421.
Mathews, J. A. (1999). From national innovation systems to national systems of economic learning: The case of technology diffusion management in East Asia. In DRUID Summer Conference National Innovation Systems, Industrial Dynamics and Innovation Policy, Rebild, Denmark, 9–12 June.
Mathews, J. A. (2002). Competitive advantages of the latecomer firm: A resource-based account of industrial catch-up strategies. *Asia Pacific Journal of Management, 19*, 467–488.
Pirela, A., Rengifo, R., Arvanitis, R., & Mercado, A. (1993). Technological learning and entrepreneurial behaviour: A taxonomy of the chemical industry in Venezuela. *Research Policy, 22*(5–6), 431–454.
Rosenberg, N., Landau, R., & Mowery, D. (1992). *Technology and the wealth of nations*. Stanford University Press.
Rowen, H. S. (1998). *Behind east Asian growth. The Political and Social Foundations of Prosperity*. Routledge.
Ruffier, J. (2006). *Faut-il avoir peur des usines chinoises?* Editions L'Harmattan.
Ruffier, J., Arvanitis, R., & Zhao, W. (2006). Patrons privés et patrons publics au Guangdong: quelques éléments de différentiation des stratégies et des comportements. In P. Béraud, G. Olivier Faure, & J.-L. Perrault (Eds.), *Négociation internationale et processus des affaires en Chine* (pp. 145–156). Maison Neuve & Larose.
Shin, J.-S. (1996). *The economics of the latecomers. Catching-up, technology transfer and institutions in Germany, Japan and South Korea*. Routledge.

CHAPTER 5

Innovation Policy and Local Cluster of Entrepreneurs

Introduction

The previous chapter analyzed the technology learning strategies of local enterprises during the industrial take-off phase. The real micro level was not the firm but the workshop. The experiences of emerging countries, more or less successful, show that the economic catch-up is primarily related to certain classes of stock of technological learning in workshops, those that ensure the link between the workshop and actors in its immediate productive environment. Therefore, in practice, the implementation of technological learning strategies requires a particularly suitable local environment that provides various supports and resources. To a large extent, the local environment depends on government policies. While central government policies can provide a contextual framework, the policies

This chapter is based on an original paper "Innovation policy and local cluster of entrepreneurs in South China," by ZHAO Wei, Arvanitis, R. and La Pira, F. (2011), published in *International Journal of Management and Enterprise Development*, Vol. 11, Nos. 2/3/4, pp. 109–126. The chapter also adapts some materials from an original paper "Chinese Entrepreneurship: Institutions, Ecosystems and Growth Limits," by ZHAO Wei, Frank La Pira (2013), published in *Advances in Economics and Business*, Vol. 1, 72–88. https://doi.org/10.13189/aeb.2013.010204

W. Zhao, *Remade in South China*, IPP Studies in the Frontiers of China's Public Policy,
https://doi.org/10.1007/978-981-95-7277-9_5

adopted by local governments have a more significant impact on corporate strategies and behaviors.

It was in Guangdong Province that the first special economic zones in China were created. It was also the arena where businesses flourished, financed with capital from Hong Kong and subsequently from Taiwan (Vogel (1989). When firms improving quickly in climbing the ladder of technologies, with a strong entrepreneurial spirit and business-oriented style, Guangdong local governments created many favorable conditions for such pragmatic and rapid technological learning. By 2007, Guangdong's competitiveness was constructed on these grass root learning dynamics and pragmatism of government policies. From late 1990s, a multitude of "product-based" towns and villages agglomerating hundreds, sometimes thousands of firms of a single type of product emerged. These industrial cities, teeming with private-public mixed companies proliferated and even became the symbols of success in China.

Yet, the industrial clusters in Guangdong had not been created by the policy of the State. If Guangdong's spectacular industrialization movement spontaneously emerged, it was legitimate to question the role of local authorities in this process of emergence, and whether the role of the State had been important in the economic development of this region. The Chinese central government had an industrial policy that focused on the promotion of innovative big business and generally in promoting the transfer of technology. Furthermore, the State encouraged foreign partners to joint venture with large state enterprises (Zhao, 2013). The same vision presided over the forced privatization of state-owned enterprises (Huchet, 2000). But in the province of Guangdong things didn't eventuate, as the state would've expected.

In fact, there existed the contradictions between the macro policy which would allocate resources to state-owned firms, and the evolution of not formally sanctioned private entrepreneurs in Guangdong. The innovative implementation of industrial policy at local level was the major driving force behind China's rapid industrialization and emergence of private entrepreneurs. The peculiarity of the clusters in Guangdong was the symbiotic relationship between business, entrepreneurs, and local governments, which has slowly shaped a specific model of industrialization. The unique aspect of this region is that it was neither planned nor even predictable, but what has appeared is entrepreneurial firms grouping together by product and economic sectors.

Entrepreneurship and Context

Entrepreneurship research has traditionally focused on individuals—the founder/s, and given less attention to the temporal or geographical externalities that affect entrepreneurial activities (Shane, 2003; Scott & Venkataraman, 2000). However, entrepreneurship or innovative development of new business depends on specific economic, social, legal, technological, and cultural contexts, emphasized by (Schumpeter, 1934), in the entrepreneur's relationship with bankers and real resource providers. Schumpeter's diagnosis of the social division between entrepreneur, banker, and owner, with the state as facilitator and night-watchman securing the property rights of the individuals in the capitalist mode of production, can be taken as the basic model of the entrepreneurial context. He distinguishes three roles in the process of innovative entrepreneurship: the inventor, who invents a new idea; the entrepreneur who commercializes this new idea; the capitalist, who provides the financial resources to the entrepreneur and bears the risk of the innovation project. The Schumpeterian entrepreneur is the economic agent who has innovative ideas for the new combinations of factors of production. Thus, entrepreneurship always involves more than just the entrepreneur, and it must take account of groups and individuals whose cooperation is needed for a successful business, and who have claims, rights, and interests at stake with the firm's activities: shareholders and investors, employees, consumers/clients, suppliers, and the various socio-political communities which provide the infrastructures, laws, regulation, and legitimacy.

The contemporary idea of the context of entrepreneurship elaborates on the effects of the institutional environment on opportunity exploitation. Shane (2003) discusses a variety of variables from the economic environment to the rule of law, and the socio-cultural environment. Also, business historians have revealed how historical contexts shape the structure of entrepreneurial activity, and how new opportunities in a specific period of time are pursued and found, and the wide variation in organizational form of entrepreneurial behavior (Jones & Wadhwani, 2007). For example, when formal institutions of a country condemn the exploitation of a set of opportunities by deeming them illegal, a realm of opportunities will exist for entrepreneurs willing to operate outside formal institutional boundaries. These entrepreneurs rely on cooperative groups or social communities for survival as entrepreneurs (Webb et al., 2009). Empirical research on the shadow economies of Southern Europe (Italy and Greece) shows how their specific contexts, characterized by government's level of corruption and immigration policies led to a boom in entrepreneurship of illegal immigrants (La Pira & Zhao, 2011). Comparative studies on entrepreneurial context in 12 emerging economies in Asia finds that the major problems entrepreneurs face are the rapidly changing environment, inefficient infrastructures, and unstable policies. The intersection of formal and informal institutions creates four basic entrepreneurial contexts and each provides its own specific opportunities: the bazaar economy, the State-controlled economy, the liberal economy, and the shadow economy (Dana et al., 2009).

The institutional and social aspects on entrepreneurial context, when combined with more micro-network and cluster backgrounds, become very powerful driving forces of systemic emerging or geographic clustering of entrepreneurial activities. There are many examples of highly innovative regions concentrated around entrepreneurs, with a wide variety of linkages with each other. Patton and Kenny (2003) provide an example arguing that the reason many successful entrepreneurs emerge in the same region is often due to the context of local and regional entrepreneurial networks, such as in Silicon Valley and the Cambridge Technopole. In fact, network context of entrepreneurship impacts on the innovation process of entrepreneurs. A particular mix of strong and weak links and a particular position in the network structure is preferable when it comes to discovering and realizing innovative projects. Research has also found that among other things, contingencies play an important role on innovation (Hulsink et al., 2008).

The Chinese Context of Entrepreneurship

Chinese culture and ethnic networks have been long an area of inquiry of entrepreneurial context in China. The key elements responsible for Chinese entrepreneurial success rest in the cultural and ethnic characteristics, such as Confucian value, collective discipline, familism, community norms, Chinese traditions, etc. (Liu, 2006). *Guanxi* or a particular sense of "social connections" is particularly important mechanism used to improve Chinese entrepreneur's business and overcome some of the underdeveloped legal and financial infrastructure in the environment. For example, a study of Chinese immigrant entrepreneurs in Canada found that they draw support in their work from members of their social group including the educated elite of the Chinese/Canadian immigrant community.

A survey of 158 venture capital investment decisions in Beijing and Shanghai in China found that a social relationship is an important factor for investment once a venture has been selected for funding (Liu, 2006; Batjargal & Mannie, 2002). Case studies also have shown that *Guanxi* networks commonly connect private entrepreneurs with actors in the political sphere (McNally et al., 2007).

Eesley (2009) argues that economic liberalization and relevant institutional and political reforms offer unique entrepreneurial opportunities in China. During the post-2000 period, the institutional environment can be characterized as one that more directly supports the growth of high-tech startups. With its active involvement of state actors in guiding transactions at the firm level, the Chinese economy is also labeled "politicized capitalism" (Nee & Sonja, 2006).

Although the state continues to favor state-owned and controlled firms, it has cumulatively accommodated robust bottom-up entrepreneurial action through macroeconomic policies and legal reforms to legitimize the private enterprise economy and secure property rights. Revenue maximization motivates the government's accommodation with entrepreneurs (Nee, 2009). The empirical work done by Krug (2000) found that individual behavior of Chinese entrepreneurs reflects a systematic response to the situational constraint all would-be entrepreneurs face, namely a high level of uncertainty and weak institutions. In this situation a weak organizational identity allows a flexible response to new opportunities, while accountability is achieved by a mix of reviving old economic institutions, hijacking social organizations, and building new business practices (Krug, 2000). Also, for Chinese entrepreneurs, the local government matters more than the state, based on three core elements of China's institutional architecture: local regulatory autonomy, informal enforcement of property rights, and networks between state organizations and entrepreneurs (Krug & Hendrischke, 2006).

This results in grass root entrepreneurship, which is similar to the Schumpeterian entrepreneur, state entrepreneurship, which is a new administrative behavior, and institutional entrepreneurship that is leverage between market and planned systems (Zhao, 2009). Specifically, an institutional entrepreneur's ultimate objective is the success of his business venture. However, in order to make his business venture a success, he has to overcome institutional obstacles. Thus, the innovation is external and contextual, not just within his firm (Li et al., 2005).

Many researchers have already highlighted the contribution of special economic zones and industrial clusters in China to its economic growth (Zeng, 2011), as well as its importance to boost entrepreneurial activities, e.g., Huang et al. (2008); Ruan and Xiaobo (2009); Fleishera et al. (2010). We now need to trace the diversified systems of Chinese entrepreneurs, by looking at broader institutional and policy contexts, and reveal the driving forces behind the entrepreneurial clusters in China.

The Systems of Entrepreneurship in China

In China, during 1998 and 2007, the number of above-scale industrial firms increased from 165 thousand to 302 thousand, with an increase by 5.8 times of manufacturing sales. In fact, the entrepreneurship in China had a background of dual economic emergence of the private sector and the renascent state sector, and co-evolution between new market players and former planning players. After the economic opening and reform, China developed a very special socialist market economy, characterized by the dominance of government control, but with emergence of a private sector composed by Chinese local firms, Chinese overseas firms, and foreign firms. In parallel to the emerging private sector, China also sustained and even reinforced its state sector, transforming itself from the old planned style to a new Keynesian system. Private enterprises were permitted to compete and operate in a free market environment, but the State grasps most of the benefits and redistribute to state-owned sectors.

Renascent Entrepreneurship Within State Sector

Many wrongly believed that after the Soviet-style planned economy, reform for 40 years led China toward a capitalist market economy, in which private individuals and corporations owned the means of production and, motivated by the desire for profit, competed in free markets under conditions of limited restraint by government. Many forgot that China's fundamental economic institutions were ruled by socialist principles, deeply rooted in its political system. State sectors included State-owned enterprises (SOE) which was the core part. SOE were diversified firms under government control established by and around administrative bureaus during the 1980s.

With the gradual opening of China in 1978, China's political authorities fostered connections between Chinese SOE subsequently leading to the creation of these business groups. In 1995, the official numbers given was 20, 000 business groups in the country when it was also reported that they accounted for approximately one quarter of the total state-owned assets. In 1997, the State Council selected industries while incorporating small and underperforming state companies at the same time. Along with making China the "world factory" in the 1990s, resources, especially financial resources, were drawn back to the State sectors. Even today, the share of SOE in business is estimated still over 50%; some of them are large enough such as Sinopec, State Grid, and China National Petroleum. Some of them are in the process of internationalization.

It was true that in the beginning there were only reductions in the planned sector and business changes, and there was no emergence. But gradually the State sector learnt to react to the pressure from private sector. China was eventually able to develop a new State sector that renewed their activities by adopting new technologies and management systems, with funding from the profits channeled through the State-controlled financial institutions (banks, stock market, insurance companies, investment funds, or direct payments to local governments, particularly through their tax offices, etc.). The emerged State-owned firms dominated the most important infrastructure sectors, such as telecommunications, petroleum, and chemicals, even in automobiles and some electronics. It should be noted that the state sector also included other organizations supporting the SOE: public health institutions, education, science and technology, finance, labor, etc.

The firms created or renewed in the course of this State sector reemergence were mostly orthodox firms in the eyes of government and their growth was due mainly to subsidization from government. In China, there was a bias in favor of large State-owned enterprises in the design of policy instruments for innovation. This bias appeared to influence the choice of policy instruments. For instance, programs for private-public partnerships for innovation, which emerged in OECD countries as instruments to foster long-term industry-science linkages, found their place in China to promote SOE and universities cooperation in the 2010s. In fact, Chinese policy mix was characterized by the strong legacy of the planned economy, as the programs—literally "plans" in Chinese—were the main instruments for addressing policy priorities. The operation of national innovation system was very centralized, and the relation between State and SOEs was much closer. Chinese central government purposefully followed the catch-up trajectory of Japan and South Korea, constructing national system specifically in service of state-owned enterprises. These firms continued to obtain State's support and took use easily resources in the national system of innovation.

Grass roots Private Entrepreneurship

But originally there was one kind of entrepreneurship in China: the private sector, or non-State sector, since private sector did not exist before, it emerged itself as an island in the sea, which is sometimes described as bamboo capitalism (Economist, 2011). This pattern of entrepreneurship included firms under different forms: red-hat enterprise, FDI from Hong Kong, Taiwan, and Macau, the late-comers business, etc. The private firms originated from the better exploitation of the residual resources in State sector. These resources were circulated outside the State sector system. The strength of these companies was very uncertain. They needed to live and survive to create a clean-living space, a specific knowledge, a learning exercise for both organizational and technological aspects, which could make them stronger. All other phenomena were logical consequences that flow from this first and only entrepreneurship in China. These new enterprises took the share of manufacturing in the global value chains, in exploiting the abundant and low-cost labor resources in China. Most of them exported to foreign markets and earned foreign exchange. Most of them were also in nature local FDI. From the late 1990s, there begun to have more and more real Chinese private firms participating in global value chains. This export-oriented non-State sector constituted the main growth engine of Chinese economy.

These Chinese entrepreneurs did not depend on support from China's national innovation system constructed by the central government. They could be called "grass roots," because in their creation and growth process they got little attention and support from government. They were almost outside the sight of government. Their emergence was due to the combination of Chinese comparative advantageous domestic endowments, such as cheap labor, huge internal market space, abundant natural resources (Lin, 2012), and the globalization of value chain and the recent formulation of international innovation system. The learning pattern of this entrepreneurship consisted of a double process: one was taking part of the global value chain of industrial production; the other was taking use of

Chinese comparative advantages in industrial production. The double process was nothing mysterious than just a normal industrialization process.

The disruption between 1980s and the before was the worldwide separation of functions of a value chain of production. Industrial production included a series of functions from design of product to selling to client, sometimes until service after sales. Some steps implied production or transformation of manufactured goods; other steps consisted of providing services or information. Along this process, ownership linkages were replaced by the contractual relations between independent firms. These firms might be located in different places in the planet but were linked around a value chain (Berger, 2006). From 1990s, most of functions of production and components were moved to China. The movement was not at firm level, but at industrial level, meaning all industries moved their production and components sections to China. The globalization of value chain didn't industrialize some specific firms in China, but the whole country and its whole industries. This de-localization of industries to China gave a golden opportunity to whichever Chinese firms, but specifically small- and medium-sized non-State firms, to absorb and develop production capacity. Learning started from production and component functions, but later some firms extended to distribution, product design, even marketing, and after-sales service. It was a typical routine of Southeast Asian firms from OEM to ODM to OBM.

On the other side, grass roots Chinese entrepreneurship also benefited from the boom of huge domestic market. By leveraging technologies that they got from foreign clients to the domestic market, these Chinese firms began to master all the functions in the value chain, from product development, through production, to marketing. They set up big vertically integrated organization to coordinate their activities, just as big firms for mass production in the United States in the nineteenth century. The fast growth began with cost advantages that large scale and broad scope provided in relatively technologically advanced and capital-intensive industries in China. It continued with heavy investments in manufacturing, marketing, and distribution. Geographic expansion and moves into related product markets both led to economies of scale, and economies of scope in Chinese market. These firms, when big enough, also tried to take use of the former reserve of scientific and technological competence leaked out by former science and technology system in China, to industrialize the design and technology to mass production. But this linkage was always difficult to be inserted into formal plan of the State.

Thus, most firms in this pattern of entrepreneurship, even those active in R&D now, had both limited capabilities and a low propensity to innovate. The private sectors included only business firms, with little support from other sectors. In fact, many of the grass roots firms' innovation depended upon the various forms of public support granted by the different levels of government to tenants of science and technology parks. But the period also witnessed the emergence of clusters of small firms in some regions, notably Zhejiang, Jiangsu and Guangdong provinces.

Quasi-Private Entrepreneurship

The dual emergence of private enterprises and the renewed State sector created a bias of access to certain strategic resources (technological, human, financial and even organizational) for entrepreneurship. The type of ownership (property rights) of an entrepreneurial course determined its possibilities to get the support from outside the firm (education institutions, university research, public technology centers, banks loans, information sharing, etc.). Grass root entrepreneurs encountered major obstacles to the development of innovation (funding, control of strategic products, inability to recruit top level personnel, impossibility to get support in technical activity when it was not part of public companies or public or quasi-public bodies), even from the very start-up phase. Most grass root entrepreneurs had to find cooperation with state sectors, and entered into partnership with the State, in order to gain the needed resources. The solution was often to mix the private entrepreneurship with that in State sector and found a new institutional arrangement (red-hat of firm, subcontracting from SOE, fake joint venture with SOE, subordinating to a non-profit public organization, etc.).

All these ways could be called "institutional" entrepreneurship in China. Most firms in this pattern had a hybrid institutional form of ownership from the beginning. They were often semi-public and semi-private firms, or the collective firms with vague ownership classification, or the mixture of State-assets and private investments. The State-owned aspects of firms allowed them to have very specific insertion within the national innovation system and created a firm-specific context different from that of industrialization pattern. But their private or non-state aspects made these firms adopt industrialization-type learning pattern. The uniqueness of this pattern was that entrepreneurs should have institutional access to resources provided by national policy and innovation system, benefited the equivalent regulation environment as the SOEs; at the same time, their firms' operation adopted totally the model of grass roots firms (mass production, cheap labor force exploitation, assimilating technologies from foreign clients, competing by price advantage and quantity, etc.). Moreover, entrepreneurship of this pattern skillfully combined the strong points from both State and market, brokering between State-controlled resources and market power. For example, a firm of this pattern could well integrate its R&D projects into national planning and get governmental subsidies, even direct investment in development; at the same time, it might use its huge production capacity to push its foreign clients to give more technologies, or to acquire foreign surplus production capacity and move it back to China. The quasi-private entrepreneurs took advantage of the former immobilized technological reserves in planned innovation system and new technological knowledge of foreign clients and partners (Lu, 1997). They in fact created an economic and technological convention between different systems, and their success depended on the brokerage capability of entrepreneurs.

The Entrepreneurship-Based Economy in China

Since 40 years, the double emergence of State entrepreneurship (State-owned firm reform, attracting foreign direct investment, export-led strategy) and private or quasi-private entrepreneurship (informal privatization of state-assets, township and village enterprises, and private firms) continuously created a variety of business firms in China, though the life-cycle of each specific firm was often short. Most of entrepreneurs' resources and creation were contributed to Chinese unique institutional contexts to make the so-called "institutional innovation." For Chinese entrepreneurs, firm was a cognitive focusing device or dominant logic device for collective action. The institutional identity of the firm served to give a social and legal basis for the coordination, production, and collaboration of resources.

Institutional arrangement of ownership rights was absolutely needed to establish to control resources, and a generalized labor contract to coordinate resources. In China, this institutional arrangement of ownership would subsequently determine more or less the firm's internal relationships and activities (organizational form, quality management, human development efforts, and compensation systems) and specific external linkages with suppliers, customers, and knowledge institutions. Thus it became the close focus and dominant logic of entrepreneurs in China. But the innovation required collaboration with outside and other organization, and focus on market, not institution itself. So, the Schumpeterian-type innovation mainly lied outside the focal scope of Chinese entrepreneurship.

However, the whole Chinese economy without Schumpeterian entrepreneurship and innovation achieved to gain consecutive growth thanks to the established specific macro monetary circular overflowing its various systems of entrepreneurial activities. China's whole process of economic functioning and monetary circular can be shown by Fig. 5.1.

Above all, China's unique monetary, banking, and financial system was in fact a State-owned sector. Chinese Government had full control over

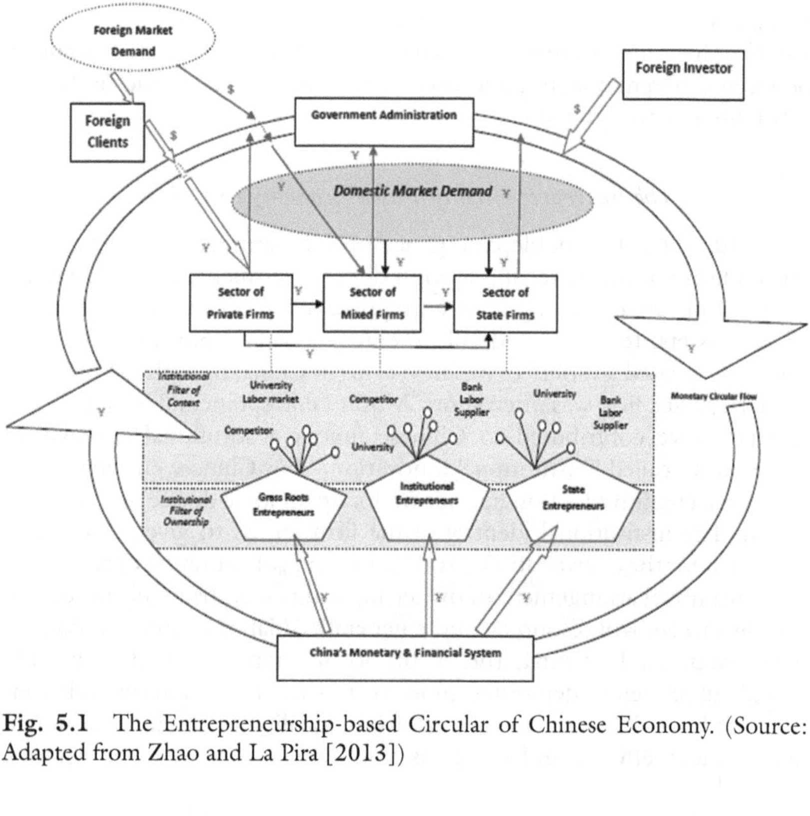

Fig. 5.1 The Entrepreneurship-based Circular of Chinese Economy. (Source: Adapted from Zhao and La Pira [2013])

money circulation process and uses the whole financial system (including its stock markets) as a huge financing machine for its economic expansion. In China, the use of interest rate as monetary policy tool was only recent. Government managed the quantity of money through banks and financial institutions.

The Chinese macro monetary and financial system had several characteristics. First, China's banks and financial institutions could effectively absorb the economy's monetary savings. Even if the interest rate is zero, China's savings would be still very high. This was because the whole financial sector was government-owned; households were not worried about the risk of bank failure and expected that the financial sector would always exist. These savings were mainly transformed to industrial investments in large firms through Chinese financial system. State-owned and large firms continued to expand their productive capacity. While small and medium-sized enterprises, which employed 80 percent of workers, had minimal access to financial services because that sector was dominated by four large banks that primarily serve large companies.

In addition to savings, the Government absorbed money through taxes and fees from firms and households. China's foreign exchange system absorbed most of the foreign exchange earnings of Chinese exports firms and foreign currency brought by foreign investors (for direct investment or financial investment). Besides, Chinese government set up a floating exchange rate system with reference to a basket of currencies.

Under the Government's command, the key function of Chinese State-owned financial system was "investment transfusion," meaning channeling and allocating the savings and financial resources to investment projects in the real economy. The result of these continuous waves of investment was the "piling up" of different types of productive ecosystems in China (Arvanitis et al., 2003). Entrepreneurial firms, especially new ventures, were receivers of these investments.

But entrepreneurship in China had to go through the institutional filters which clarify the ownership of new firm. Most banks in China were large banks and had no internal process adapted to give credits to small private entrepreneurs. They were used to finance the key projects within planned frameworks. "Investment transfusion" was biased to entrepreneurship within State-owned sector. Through the financial system, China used private accumulations and foreign financial resources to feed its State-owned sector entrepreneurship.

On the other side, the real increase of consumption of Chinese goods met more or less the expectations of Chinese entrepreneurs, and made it possible that Chinese Government continue its investment push strategy. In fact, during the years, internal consumption had increased rapidly, though comparing with the even more rapid increase of supply and production capacity in China.

The continual creation of a wide variety of entrepreneurship systems imposed a kind of race to increase production quantity and size of enterprises.The mixture of firms from different origins plus the enduring structure of State enterprises and institutions over a long time prevented not only the dynamics of new Chinese firms and the private sector (*siying qiye*),[1] but also, the linkages between the local authorities and business entrepreneurs. The changes in the late 1990s were what explained the emergence of the industrial agglomerations along the Chinese coast (Arvanitis & Qiu, 2004).

As we have known from the previous chapter, technological learning was subject to such expansion but unlike the case of Korea and Japan, the Chinese private companies voluntarily placed themselves in a subordinate position compared to clients. To continue with our vocabulary: it seemed that the technological learning of companies was entirely dictated by the operating system and not very productively handled by firms (that is to say, actors with strategic capacity). This was also true in the type of knowledge that Chinese private companies handled: essentially knowledge production techniques, the know-how, and knowledge of workshop, but little knowledge of markets, channels of information distribution, or technological capabilities of suppliers. Did China come out with any policy that matched this pain point of the grass root entrepreneurs?

The Insufficiency of National Innovation Policy

Except for some successful reorganization of old State enterprises China's national industrial and innovation policies hardly promoted entrepreneurial clusters. At national level, Chinese industrial policy from early 1990s could be summarized as the following (Huchet, 2000, 2006):

[1] For example, some critics think that the policy of support for the FDI was less beneficial than it appeared to be because it held back the emergence of a true local capitalism (Huang, 2002).

1. Create or select "national champions." But this policy was difficult to implement (Huchet, 2000, 2006).[2] Curiously, it appeared more straightforward to create champions from new enterprises than by conversion of old industries. Practically all the globally known Chinese companies at that time, such as Haier, Lenovo, or Huawei, were linked to former public-sector enterprises (more precisely "collective" firms, belonging to municipal councils—*Zhen*—which changed and developed under private management regimes).
2. Reform, modernize, or privatize public-sector firms. This question was at the core of all industrial and financial decisions insofar as the State sector ensured employment in the North-East regions and the production of strategic products. It was still a fundamental question which cannot be just limited to financial reform.[3]
3. Concentrate certain activities around large firms or around certain technologies that the State declared to be priority or strategic. The avowed objective was to obtain technologies from abroad; in fields like the automotive industry, satellites, and transport, and then incorporated them into national industry. This form of localization worked on the basis of founding joint ventures where the State remained majority shareholder. The State aimed to maintain economic control of the firms so as to ensure that the technologies that the foreign partner brought could be assimilated into the Chinese production complex (INIDET, 2002).

Above all, there was a constant aim the Chinese authorities sustained in their industrial policy: "ensure exports of whatever the country produces." This was a pragmatic decision[4] as China could not increase revenues through Chinese consumers alone. Only foreign companies working in joint ventures could approve of this policy, which consisted of "filling containers" and seeing that the utmost was done to facilitate exports to more lucrative markets abroad. For as long as the Chinese economy was pulled

[2] The extensive analysis by JF Huchet was based at the same time on the forms of "governance" of firms and on the structural aspects of the Chinese economy. It is noteworthy to see how some authors (Nolan, 2001; Nolan & Zhang, 2002) put these aspects aside and advocate the setting-up of really large firms.

[3] On this subject, it is worth reading the article by Fernandez-Stembridge and Huchet (2006).

[4] Which we have heard expressed by leaders in local government councils in the South of China: "Our aim is to ensure the exportation of the products of S."

along by investment and not by demand, this strategy had little chance of changing.

As early from 1999, a national innovation promotion policy was also formulated in Beijing at the highest state level. Several publications were written with the aim of deciphering this innovation policy (Gu, 1999; Suttmeier & Cao, 1999; Liu & White, 2001; Cao, 2004; Huang et al., 2004). The targets of this innovation policy were mainly national institutions relevant to science and technology. This constant effort to ferment the available technology and encourage high quality research aimed to create a "new technological landscape" in China (Sigurdson, 2002). In this new industrial landscape, promoted by massive investment by the Chinese State, was the R&D investment of foreign companies (OECD, 2006), as mentioned in Chap. 2.

However, two aspects at least raise doubts about this somewhat optimistic vision.[5]

1. First of all, the innovation policy at national level was derived from the policy on science and technology[6] and for many years this was tied up by some highly cumbersome institutional processes: the reorganization of the R&D centers of public-sector enterprises (Gu, 1999), the merchandizing of centers of research, and the elimination of a great number of technology development centers of applied research, originating from the old communist organization.
2. The second aspect was that although the Chinese government had multiplied the means for consolidating this technological supply, the main weakness lied in the demand for technology, by firms. The structure of the Chinese economy allowed a dualism to persist in the system of innovation. The system of innovation the government maintained and supported was geared to public-sector firms and research centers in the public system. A whole array of institutions was set up over a period of many years, which, even after the economic deregulation policy still had the duty to sustain these State enterprises and these institutions, which gravitated around them.

[5] For an overall assessment of the innovation policy in China, see Arvanitis (2004 a, b).

[6] The analysis by Gu and Lundvall is a good example in this respect. These authors adopt the political vocabulary of the Chinese government whenever they have to set out the main orientations and objectives of national policy on innovation.

These institutions and firms formed a social system of regulation. Alongside this appears a set of institutions and firms made up largely of non-State firms and driven principally by the acquisition of resources and technologies from foreign markets. The great difference between the two systems was in the way in which technology was obtained. State enterprises and the centers of applied research were supposed to create some autonomy for China in technology development. Conversely, non-State firms were entirely dependent on imported technologies. Joint ventures and Chinese-owned private firms should ensure their business customers satisfactory production to meet the quality criteria imposed from outside, and conduct R&D only inasmuch as the technical properties of the given product required it in order to guarantee an exportable production.[7]

Therefore, simply implementing the Chinese national innovation policy was not effective. This was illustrated by the example of technological parks. The creation of technological parks had been progressing since the beginning of the 1980s, as had that of scientific incubators and technological development zones. A detailed examination of these zones in China (Hong et al., 2004) noted 85 in China, plus 58 academic science parks of smaller size. However, the economic and technological development zones (*jingji jishu kaifa qu*) were geographically and physically very different: it could involve a small urban neighborhood (a few buildings, especially in the case of the software industry) or really extensive geographical areas, like the Guangzhou technology development zone which occupied practically the whole eastern side of the municipality's urban area. The promotion of these zones was in line with an overall strategic plan devised in Beijing since the launch of the Torch programme (1988). Later measures were adopted to reduce the number of industrial parks, in order to stop wasting arable land and return the sites back to agriculture.

[7] For more details on the constituent elements of this "system" of production and innovation, or again a system of regulation, see the thesis by Zhao Wei (2013), in particular Chap. 4. The terminology evidently makes reference to vocabulary made popular by Gibbons et al. (1994) who talk of the appearance of new modes of knowledge production. Their description, strongly criticized by sociologists and science policy specialists concerning Western countries, seems to reflect well the socio-economic situation of China.

Local Cluster and Innovation Policy of Guangdong

Like all national policies in China, the national innovation policy was fortunately devolved and translated progressively at province level, by some local governments, into a "regional innovation policy." The provincial authorities found themselves confronted with the formidable task of having to define the exact limits of their involvement. Formidable, because for most "industrial agencies" in the provinces and in municipal councils, their involvement was always pragmatic according to the demands laid down by local firms. In most cases, the local civil servants drew up urban development plans that met the satisfaction of "foreign" investors and ensured the greatest possible visibility of the town or area of production.

The province of Guangdong rapidly responded to the prescription emanating from the national policy on innovation (Cheng, 2003).[8] The local government became aware of the importance of industrial activity. Contrary to the taxation or social policies which seemed to be imposed on the provincial government, industrial policy was a matter for a voluntarism approach.

Under the banner of national innovation policy, Guangdong provincial and township governments deployed a whole range of measures in favor of development of "industrial clusters"—or local production system specialized in specific products or sectors—as concrete support to business creation of entrepreneurs. The cluster policy resulted in a regional innovation system in gestation with a dynamic process of entrepreneurship, and which made the South of China one of the biggest workshops in the " World Factory" (Arvanitis & Jastrabsky, 2005). In 2007, 228 clusters in Guangdong, with a GDP of RMB 765 billion (about 95 billion US dollars), accounted for 25 percent of the total provincial GDP and about 8 percent of the total employment (Zeng, 2011); these clusters then became the main economic driver of the provincial economy.[9] We now turn to

[8] Note nevertheless that, politically, the post-1999 period was distinctly less profitable for Guangdong province than was previously the case: Shanghai became principal target for central government support and Guangdong had to make amends for its inability to anticipate and manage the monumental financial crisis that hit at the end of the 1990s.

[9] The exact number of officially recognized "clusters" implanted in the province is an uncertain figure. At the beginning of the twenty-first century, a quarter of the 404 administrative towns in the Pearl River Delta in Guangdong made up some 100 clusters of specialized activity.

details of this regional cluster policy and its impact on entrepreneurial opportunities.

Creating Technological and Organizational Opportunities

The most important part of Guangdong's policy of clusters was setting-up of centers of technology (called innovation center in official terms), hubs of competence implanted in local areas, which provided support for the generation of technical skills in firms. These centers of technology, located at the core of officially initiated industrial "clusters" were mainly geared to SMEs. They often started off by working as suppliers of basic services (concerning testing, standards, computerization, and so on). Some of these centers of innovation succeeded in becoming suppliers of models and prototypes.

Xiqiao Town was an example in the cotton-based textile industry. There were 1670 textile firms in the town. Xiqiao had a complement of 2600 weaving machines. Factory size was small and disparate and the level of technology used was low. In May 1999, the government decided to set up a center for innovation with emphasis on CAD techniques. The center produced more than 8000 CAD-assisted textile patterns, most of which were used by the various firms. There was a very strong link between the center and the firms involved, owing notably to the center's role as intermediary for all that concerns computerization of industrial firms. The center's clientele existed beyond the industrial cluster, into Zhejiang, Hunan, and Taiwan. It was set up with an investment of 7 million RMB Yuans, and later became self-sufficient financially, living solely by selling its services.

This example of innovation center showed two particularities of cluster policy. First of all, only by selling services could innovation centers guarantee certain longevity. The local government was trying to rid itself of the responsibility of financing the center; while it's easy to justify an investment for the setup it was practically impossible to cover the center's running costs.

The second point was that cluster policies also promoted the emergence of a network of suppliers around medium-sized or large firms in the assembly sectors. This was the most important key to the success of entrepreneurial innovation, since it encouraged firms to adopt unique organizational forms and develop various external linkages. For example, in Guangdong, the motorcycle company Dachangjiang was the main driving force behind the creation of a concentrated network of suppliers. In the

District of Pengjiang (Jiangmen City), three motorcycle assembly firms (Dachangjiang, Dihao, and Yunbao) and about 30 component-manufacturing firms generated an active motorcycle economy. Japanese manufacturers actively supported their technological development.

As a contrast, Weili, was for nine years the largest producer of washing machines in China. It sold basic washing machines, which met the needs of the first great surge of growth in the 1980s. However, as soon as it became necessary to introduce more sophisticated models—a superior level of training and technology, Weili lost its way. It was extremely inadequate in meeting its challenges, and the leaders of Weili didn't actively search for external linkages and subsequently failed.

The above-mentioned policy, with private initiatives encouraging resource pooling, was primarily one of non-financial support for firms within "clusters." The Guangdong local governments seek to support the industrial upgrading of thousands of independent firms that set up without any State help because Chinese firms were not necessarily innovative and to avoid a fight between Chinese firms as occurred in the television manufacturing sector (Cao, 2004; Zhao, 2006). The negative image of that industry left in Chinese people's memory was often interpreted in terms of insufficient quality, inadequate technology, which resulted in a cost-cutting strategy. These price-based fights for survival produced victims in many other sectors. What the local governments attempted to do is to provide firms with more effective means to compete.

Creating Market Opportunities

In Guangdong, once local authorities attracted new arrivals that had strategic potential and provided some technological resources, they had relatively little power over the linkages firms may make with the outside world. The dynamics at work in economic regions were not driven by the public authorities' efforts, but by the movement that the firms implanted there stimulated and fed. In some cases, a strong structure-building effect was created by a large company in an assembly sector, which organized its network of suppliers, as is the case for the automobile and motorcycle industry. But other foreign investors did not create linkages. For example, the Chinese policy focusing on electronics did not seem to have generated subcontractor networks. A company like INTEL in China, for example, did not seek so much to bring its subcontractors closer together geographically as to reduce them in number and arranged it so that there were as few entries and exits of components as possible.[10]

The local governments' implementation of convergent measures of support for clusters not only brought technological resources to new firms, but also promoted their market access and social reputation, thus creating a context rich with opportunities for local entrepreneurs. Close observation of enterprise development in the agglomerations showed the operating strategy of firms stemming from the wave of industrialization.

Entrepreneurs obtained contracts with foreign clients who not only guaranteed outlets for the production, but ensured the acquisition of the product and the productive technology that went with it. Entrepreneurs then combined the technology from client with cheap labor to produce products for their clients. The whole process became very smooth when the local context was supportive and friendly. Regardless of the sector; new firms obtained productive technology not through formal technology transfer contracts, but by means of direct support from their clients (Arvanitis et al., 2006). Furthermore, firms were always on the lookout to expand their customer base and varied forms of contract, as Ernst and Kim (2002, p. 3) reported:

> *International linkages include a variety of ties with sales, manufacturing, and engineering support affiliates of foreign firms; they also include different forms and trajectories of integration into global production networks of American and Japanese electronics firms. Taiwanese firms typically have relied on concurrent knowledge outsourcing: they have pursued different approaches in parallel, rather than concentrating exclusively on one particular linkage.*

Therefore, grouping together on one geographical site brought a priori advantages for firms, which thus gained visits from numerous market prospectors or future customers attracted by the concentration of firms involved in the same products. This pattern was reproduced systematically in all the industrial towns of the Pearl River Delta. It was not the fruit of the design of any industrial development plan from the central government, it is a matter of local governments' accompanying firms in their growth by seeking to impede them as little as possible. And the policy of naming industrial clusters was in reality a way for local authorities to acquire legitimacy for their firms support. It became a way for the local

[10] Interview Dawn INTEL, Pers. comm. February 2006.

authorities to obtain greater publicity for already established agglomerations of factories, as well as to encourage entrepreneurship.

The Chinese central government tried to control the economy and businesses, while local governments, by contrast, seek to promote economic activity. These differing attitudes of local authorities were due to the fact that local governments depended on business tax revenues and local GDP to evaluate its political performance: which was measured by the wealth of local governments and by the number of firms created locally.

Local Cluster Policy: Context of Entrepreneurship and Innovation

Normally regional innovation system and policy are regarded as proactive context of entrepreneurship. At practical level, many "clusters success stories" from Asia and the enthusiasm for them has left little room for examination of the effects of agglomeration and notably of the role of the States policy. But our observations in this chapter bring into questions the kind of concrete policy that can boost local entrepreneurship.

In developing economies, when creating new ventures and catch-up SMEs, the situation often requires entrepreneurs to address the technological choices they have difficulty in financing or formulating. So a major part of cluster policy in the beginning deals more with technological rather than economic development, quite similar to the firm strategy focus. But the desire of entrepreneurs to succeed pushes officials to attract foreign customers and gain market access and resources for the whole cluster. In return, the strong dependency of entrepreneurs on their foreign customers for acquiring technology will force local officials to ask the centers of innovation within cluster to develop more technologies adapted to entrepreneurs' needs.

Innovation centers, established by local government in the cluster, normally start by providing new products and innovation services, as well as information and technology consulting; intellectual property rights (IPR) protection; and professional training, testing, and certification. Progressively, they become a platform for cooperation among government, business, and research institutes—a facilitator for entrepreneurial innovation. While banks finance is notoriously difficult to access, entrepreneurs also need to gain immediate access to: labor, production techniques with foreign customers, natural resources, and market information on products, etc. Local governments can provide these resources in their own way, which facilitates the creation of new firms. Cluster policies in Guangdong were also very substantial and not all under financial form.

The case of Guangdong provided some good explanation on the emergence of private entrepreneurs in clusters. Innovation system and cluster policy were important context of entrepreneurship. But more precisely, the major driving force of cluster-based entrepreneurship was not central government policy but the pragmatic cluster promotion policies deployed by local governments. By establishing the so-called innovation centers, coordinating business linkages with outside world, and organizing activities to attract foreign customers, local governments eventually created a quasi-regional innovation system and policy which provided rich institutional, technological, and market opportunities to local entrepreneurs.

At the stage of factor-driven development in Guangdong, the local cluster policy was very suitable to incubate entrepreneurship and upgrade the new firms' innovation capabilities. Under the banner of "entrepreneurship clusters," cluster policy operationally promoted and combined the market and technological changes around specific firm projects. In fact, the local governments performed the strategic integration function of innovation management in firms. To some extent, the innovativeness of Guangdong's industrialization model was first of all the entrepreneurial behavior of policy deployment by local authorities, which constituted the key linkage between China's macroeconomic development and private business initiatives.

Conclusion

Major activities of entrepreneurship in China were cluster-based, concentrated in the coastal regions, especially in Zhejiang, Guangdong, Fujian, and Jiangsu provinces. By banding together small businesses of the same industry in the same region and specialized in one narrowly defined stage of production, private Chinese entrepreneurs overcome the barriers to running a business in an economy still dominated by state sectors, and become the engine of China's rapid export-led growth.

For entrepreneurship to flourish, they need a pertinent and favorable context in which to start. Chinese entrepreneurs were not motivated by the permission to join the Party, but cultivated and encouraged by local clusters. As "babies born in cluster," they did not necessarily share the same enthusiasm over the clusters as officials. They may even disagree with officials as long as their firms tried to adopt the strategies of external growth, high specialization, upscale, or closer integration into international value chains that made them highly dependent on their foreign principals/clients. For example, many entrepreneurs in Guangdong were strongly against the new industrial upgrading policy later implemented by the Provincial Government after 2007, which would force the closure of low-value industries in the region. In years to follow, strategies for upgrading industry would be at the core of Chinese government political and economic policy. The cluster conditions in which Chinese private firms kicked off and developed later would become useful foundations to both officials and entrepreneurs, bringing them to the front door of further innovation.

References

Arvanitis, R. (2004a). L'émergence d'un Bourg industriel du Delta de la Rivière des Perles. *L'exemple de Shuikou*. IRD et Centre franco-chinois de sociologie de l'industrie et des technologies.

Arvanitis, R. (2004b). La politique d'innovation en China - un essai d'interprétation, *La Lettre de l'Antenne* (Antenne expérimentale franco-chinois de sciences humaines et sociales à Pékin http://www.antenne-pekin.com), no° 3, mai 2004.

Arvanitis, R., & Jastrabsky, E. (2005). Un système d'innovation régional en gestation: l'exemple du Guangdong. *Perspectives Chinoises, 92*(Novembre–décembre), 14–28.

Arvanitis, R., Miège, P., & Zhao, W. (2003). Regard(s) sur l'émergence d'une économie de marché en China. *Perspectives Chinoises, 77*, 53–65.

Arvanitis, R., & Qiu, H. (2004, November). R&D in universities and different institutional settings in South China: Research for policy. In *Final research report for IDRC*. Research Institute for Guangdong Development (ZURIGud), Zhongshan (Sun Yat-sen) University. Research report for IDRC.

Arvanitis, R., Zhao, W., Qiu, H., & Xu, J. N. (2006). Technological learning in six firms in South China: Success and limits of an industrialization model. *International Journal of Technology Management, 36*(1/2/3), 108–125.

Batjargal, B., & Mannie, M. L. (2002). Entrepreneurs' access to private equity in China. *The role of social capital,* William Davidson Working Paper Number 453, 48 pages.

Berger, S. (2006). *Made in monde*. Editions du Seuil.

Cao, C. (2004). Challenges for China's industrial development: A technological assessment. *China Perspectives, 54*, 4–16.

Cheng, J. Y. S. (Ed.). (2003). *Guangdong: Preparing for the WTO challenge*. The Chinese University Press.

Dana, L. P., Annabelle, J., & Frank, L. (2009, Fall). Comprendre le contexte entrepreneurial dans les pays émergents d'Asie: une étude comparative. *Journal of Small Business and Entrepreneurship, 22*(4), 53–73.

Economist. (2011, March 10). *Bamboo Capitalism.*

Eesley, C. E. (2009). Entrepreneurship and China: History of policy reforms and institutional development. *MS&E Working Paper,* Stanford University, 57 pages.

Ernst, D., & Kim, L. (2002). Global production networks, knowledge diffusion, and local capability formation. *Research Policy, 31*(8–9), 1417–1429.

Fernandez-Stembridge, L., & Huchet, J. F. (2006). What's next for China's SOEs. *Far Eastern Economic Review, 169*(5), 32–36.

Fleishera, B., Dinghuan, H., McGuiree, W., & Xiaobo, Z. (2010, September). The evolution of an industrial cluster in China. *China Economic Review, 21*(3), 456–469.

Gibbons, M., Limoges, C., & Nowotny, H. (1994). *The new production of knowledge. The dynamics of science and research in contemporary society.* Sage.

Gu, S. (1999). China's industrial technology: Market reform and Organisational change. Routledge in association with UNU Press.

Hong, S. B. H., Yim, D. S. Y., & Kim, K. K. (2004). *Characteristics and types of Chinese innovation clusters in comparison with Korean cases.* STEPI.

Huang, C., Amorim, C., & Spinoglio, M. (2004). Organization, programme and structure: An analysis of the Chinese innovation policy framework. *R&D Management, 34*(4), 367–387.

Huang, Y. (2002). *Selling China: The institutional Foundation of Foreign Direct Investment during the reform era.* Cambridge University Press.

Huang, Z., Xiaobo, Z., & Yunwei, Z. (2008, September). The role of clustering in rural industrialization: A case study of the footwear industry in Wenzhou. *China Economic Review, 19*(3), 409–420.

Huchet, J. F. (2000). La face cachée des réformes du secteur public en China. *Perspectives Chinoises, 60*(mars-avril), 41–52.

Huchet, J. F. (2006, juillet). Privatisation et restructuration des PME d'État en Chine. *Critique Internationale,* 32, 173–187.

Hulsink, W., Elfring, T., & Stam, W. (2008). The locus of innovation in small and medium-sized firms: The importance of social capital and networking in innovative entrepreneurship. *ERIM report series research in management*, 47 pages, http://hdl.handle.net/1765/12873

INIDET. (éd.) (2002). Transferts de technologie et efficience productive dans les country émergents (en Français et chinois). Université Sun Yatsen et INIDET.

Jones, G., & Wadhwani, R. D. (2007). Entrepreneurship and business history: Renewing the research agenda. Harvard Business School Working Paper 07-007, 51 pages.

Krug, B. (2000). Ties that bind: The emergence of entrepreneurs in China. *ERIM report series research in management*, ERS-2000-44-ORG, 30 pages.

Krug, B., & Hendrischke, H. (2006). China's institutional architecture: A new institutional economics and organization theory, perspective on the links between local governance and local enterprises, paper presented at the *"Shifts in Governance" conference, Hangzhou, July 2006*, 32 pages.

La Pira, F., & Zhao, W. (2011). Entrepreneurship and the shadow economies of southern Europe, *unpublished manuscript,* ESC Saint-Etienne, 23 pages.

Li, D. D., Junxin, F., & Hongping, J. (2005). Institutional entrepreneurs. *Working Paper HKUST6224/02H,* Hong Kong University of Science and Technology, 10 pages.

Lin, J. Y. (2012). *New structural economics: A framework for rethinking development.* World Bank.

Liu, H. (2006). Paradigm shift in overseas Chinese entrepreneurship? Preliminary observations and critiques, *working paper of Centre for Chinese Studies,* University of Manchester, 29 pages.

Liu, X., & White, S. (2001). Comparing innovation systems: A framework and application to China's transitional context. *Research Policy, 30*, 1091–1114.

Lu, Q. (1997). *Learning and innovation in economic transition: The rise of science and technology enterprises in Chinese information technology industry, printed paper presented to the International Conference on Knowledge.* Economy and Society, Montreal, Canada.

McNally, C. A., Hong, G., & Guangwei, H. (2007). Entrepreneurship and political Guanxi networks in China's private sector. *East-West Center working papers, no. 19*, august 2007, 23 pages.

Nee, V. (2009). Endogenous institutional change and capitalism in China. *Conference paper on "1989": Twenty years after*, Laguna Beach, CA November 5–8, 2009, 19 pages.

Nee, V., & Sonja, O. (2006). China's politicized capitalism. *Working Paper*, Department of Sociology, Cornell University, 65 pages.

Nolan, P. (2001). *China and the global economy: National champions, industrial policy, and the big business revolution.* Palgrave.

Nolan, P., & Zhang, J. (2002). The challenge of globalization for large Chinese firms. *World Development, 30*(12), 2089–2107.

OECD. (2006). Reviews of innovation policy: China. Synthesis Report, Paris, 68 pages.

Patton, D., & Kenny, M. (2003). Innovation and social capital in silicon valley. *BRIE (the Berkeley roundtable on the international economy) working paper*, 28 pages.

Ruan, J., & Xiaobo, Z. (2009, October). Finance and cluster-based industrial development in China. *Economic Development and Cultural Change, 58*(1), 143–164.

Schumpeter, J. A. (1934). *The theory of economic development.* Harvard University Press.

Scott, S., & Venkataraman, S. (2000). The promise of entrepreneurship as a field of research. *Academy of Management Review, 25*, 217–226.

Sigurdson, J. (2002). A new technological landscape in China. *China Perspectives, 42*, 37–54.

Shane, S. (2003). *A General theory of entrepreneurship: The individual-opportunity nexus*. Edward Elgar Publishing https://doi.org/10.4337/9781781007990

Suttmeier, R. P., & Cao, C. (1999). China faces the new industrial revolution : Achievement and uncertainty in the search for research and innovation strategies. *Asian Perspective, 23*(3), 153–200.

Vogel, E. (1989). *One step ahead. Guangdong Under Economic Reform*. Cambridge University Press.

Webb, J. W., Laszlo, T. R., Duane, I., & David, G. S. (2009). You Say Illegal, I Say Legitimate: Entrepreneurship in the Informal Economy. *Academy of Management Review, 34*(3), 492–510.

Zeng, D Z 2011 How do special economic zones and industrial clusters drive China's rapid development? *Policy Research Working Paper 5583, The World Bank*, Washington, 51 pages.

Zhao, W. (2006). *Economie de l'innovation et développement des capacités technologiques en Chine: l'apprentissage technologique dans les industries automobile et électronique en Chine*. thèse doctorale de l'Université Paris 3, Paris.

Zhao, W. (2009). How China competes? Global challenges to the Chinese firms, communication to 2nd Asia management and entrepreneurship workshop, Brussels, Belgium, November 30–December 1st, 2009, 34 pages.

Zhao, W. (2013). La capacité d'innovation chinoise. *Apprentissage technologique dans les industries automobiles et électroniques*, Saarbrücken : PAF Presses académique francophones, Catégorie : Économie, 2013, 540 p.

Zhao, W., & La Pira, F. (2013). Chinese Entrepreneurship: Institutions, Ecosystems and Growth Limits. *Advances in Economics and Business, 1*, 72–88. https://doi.org/10.13189/aeb.2013.010204

CHAPTER 6

Dynamic Capabilities: The Imperative for Innovation Management

Introduction

As described in Chaps. 4 and 5, the Chinese industrialization during the 1990s and 2000s was a rapid integration of SMEs in global networks of contractors, for example in electronics and clothing, and the development of an important domestic light industry which provided parts and sometimes equipment to foreign companies as clients. Then, in the end of 2000s, the challenge to the Chinese firms was to find ways to "move up the global value chain," that is to say, to produce more sophisticated products and be less dependent on international outsourcers (Bironneau et al., 2012). In reality, there were many Chinese firms beginning to move from being simply assemblers or providers to have access to the final consumption market. They wanted to choose their markets rather than to be chosen by their foreign clients. Beyond strong production experience and technology accumulated in business, these Chinese firms try to combine new technologies from different sources in order to adapt to market conditions. Overall, after 2008, it appeared that China was struggling to build

The original version of this chapter "How Do Chinese Firms Manage Innovation? A Perspective of Dynamic Capabilities" was published in *Asian Research Policy*, 7 (2016) 33–55.

W. Zhao, *Remade in South China*, IPP Studies in the Frontiers of China's Public Policy,
https://doi.org/10.1007/978-981-95-7277-9_6

a real innovation capacity of industry (Zhao & Arvanitis, 2010; Zhao, 2015).

Theoretically, this firm-level technological learning in China brings nothing new to the existing model of catch-up in East Asian economies. The Chinese firms followed a mixed pattern of interactive learning, maintaining a variety of sources of technology, keeping a large portfolio of clients and products, accepting to be at the same time manufacturing subcontractors, OEM providers for some products, and autonomous brand makers for others, depending on the market. They introduced new models as long as their foreign clients provided them new blueprints. Even firms advancing more rapidly toward an innovation frontier are in this pragmatic, down-to-earth catching-up model, upgrading cumulatively productive and control knowledge. These catch-up firms, who entered in a transitional stage in upgrading from a basic production to more sophisticated technology development, maintained the same diversified types of contacts with their clients, simply aggregating more sources of knowledge and trying to keep a multiplicity of external sources (Arvanitis et al., 2006).

As mentioned in Chap. 4, companies in developing economies are often called "latecomers" firms (Hobday, 1995). When they learn over time to accumulate technological capabilities and progressively carry out some innovative activities, they become "catch-up" firms, because they begin to compete with firms at the international frontier in advanced industrial countries (Mathews, 2006). Many catch-up firms have experienced substantial difficulty during this process of transformation from imitators or followers to real innovators. In Guangdong, after local firms successfully emerged through active technological learning, they found it difficult to upgrade to innovation level. Continuing the previous way could not level them up to a new stage: being best student could not be converted to being a teacher.

By the time of the 2008 crisis, Chinese firms had already very well taken use of the double trends of globalization of industrial production and standardization of complex technologies. But it was also during this period of time that the weakness of Chinese innovation capacity became evident, i.e., most of Chinese firms begun to touch an "invisible ceiling" of forging ahead to innovate in global competition. They knew much better how to use the "common" process and engineering know-how supplied by Western firms to power the global value chains than how to manage the whole company to transform from imitators or followers to true innovators. For these catch-up firms, there was no simple and automatic progression from the early stage of accumulation of technological capabilities to high-level stage of building up of management capabilities of integrating skillfully the complex change processes of innovation, while the dynamic capabilities are in fact an imperative to manage innovation in the invest-driven stage of development.

The Strategy of Innovation Management

Managing the Transition from Imitation to Innovation

The traditional literature of catch-up firms emphasizes on their technological learning process and knowledge acquisition practice while inadequate attention has been paid to their strategic management aspects. There is no simple linear progression from the early stage of accumulation of the minimum levels of innovative capability to the management of knowledge as a strategic asset and the deployment of core capabilities (Dutrénit, 2000, 2004). The transition process is complex and while catch-up firms make the breakthrough in innovation, they have to build deeper and broader specialized knowledge and develop new ways of strategic integration. The innovation capability can be reached only through a specific kind of "spontaneous" actions rather than a succession of different stages of formation of technological capabilities.

Similarly, based on South Korea's experience from imitation to innovation, Linsu Kim (1997, 1998) argues that cumulative learning of firms takes place through learning-by-doing, but discontinuous learning takes place only in crisis. Effective learning firms (such as Hyundai) construct a crisis by setting ambitious targets intentionally to develop organizational systems and manage their processes to make the crises truly creative. Although creative imitation (producing knockoffs and clones) through reverse-engineering is still important, it is the continuous increase in in--house R&D investment that plays the key role in leap from coping imitation to indigenous innovation. He suggests that catch-up firms shall intensify dramatically their formal R&D activities to engage in independent product innovation and participate actively in global alliances.

Also, innovation capacity of firms depends largely on relationships with suppliers and customers, with organizations and institutions that can supply technologies, and with the immediate environment that allows firms to consolidate R & D and engineering activities. This systemic nature of innovation requires not only learning and using of advanced technologies, but also more sophisticated approaches and specialized competencies of "innovation management." Firms never come out with new products or improved processes in isolation. For innovation, they have to manage simultaneously the changes in technologies, organizations, and markets, and integrate them timely (Tidd et al., 1997).

The continuing debate over whether the technological learning, or the production mode, or the market linkages, or the knowledge management, or the R&D management is the key for catch-up firms to move onto innovation stage calls for more attention to basic theories on management of innovation in Western advanced firms. Indeed, innovators can inspire the followers on which way to take. Similarly, there is a large amount of literature on management of innovation and the role of dynamic capabilities in Western innovative firms, which can be a heuristic to explore the managerial aspects of catch-up firms.

Managing the Innovation as a Process

At general level, innovation can be regarded as a series of industrial activities translating new technologies and knowledge into products and services in the market. These activities of firms are technical, commercial, and economic by nature and consist essentially of interactive learning between individuals and organizations related to implementing new technologies. In a broader sense, innovation involves institutional, organizational, and psychological changes in doing business. According to Dosi (1988), innovation as a process is an adventure of searching and problem-solving. It needs to mobilize and combine public and private (individual-specific and firm-specific) knowledge, general scientific principles, and unique experience. It also needs appropriate procedures of communication among knowledge and implicit capabilities.

In management practice, it is more pertinent to take "innovation" as a complex process or processes than just as results of process. As shown by the linked-chain model (Kline, 1985), the key activities include:

1. "research and knowledge creation,"
2. "market exploration and discovering,"
3. "invention and analytical design,"
4. "details design and test,"
5. "re-design and manufacturing," and
6. "distribution and marketing," etc.

They are linked with each other and constitute different feedback loops with different types of innovation.

Pavitt (2003) identified three overlapping processes of innovation: the production of knowledge; the translation of knowledge into products, systems, processes, and services; and the continuous matching of the product of innovation to market demand. The difficulty of managing innovation process lies in the fact that with the increasing specialization of knowledge production and the sophistication of products and contained knowledge, it is more and more difficult to integrate technological opportunities, market demand, and organizational arrangements just rightly to produce the expected new outcome. To innovate, firms have to coordinate and integrate various specialized knowledge, and carry out learning under conditions of uncertainty. The formal management approach proposed by Tidd et al. (1997) emphasizes on supporting the innovation development project through coordinating four strategic aspects:

1. elaborating an innovation strategy,
2. building an organization for innovation,
3. setting up implementation mechanisms of project, and
4. exploiting external links with market and alliance.

Similarly, Trott (2005) defined innovation management as the practice of integrating activities of strategic planning, technology research and development, marketing, and organizing, all based on firm's accumulated knowledge. Thus, the nature of innovation management is not managing the processes of technological change, market change, and organizational change separately, but coordinating and integrating all these changes.

In practice, the management of technological change emphasizes on new technology forecasting and evaluation (Christensen, 1997), new product development (Henderson & Clark, 1990), R&D investment (Cohen & Levinthal, 1990), and innovative design (Le Masson et al., 2010). These activities reach beyond efforts to improve the efficiency of production or research and development, to include the effectiveness of technological development, which is the translation of technology into successful products and services.

Based on the classic model of "innovation diffusion" (Rogers, 1983), the management of market change had a shift from depending on crude market segmentation and analysis of consumer behavior, to relationship and networked marketing that demands fine targeting of product development and closer linkages with lead customers (von Hippel, 1989; Moore, 2014). The management of organizational change has shifted from an emphasis on change management of structure and culture, to the design and improvement of new mechanism for project implementation and internal work processes, such as knowledge management (Nonaka & Teukeuchi, 1995), corporate venturing (Burgelman & Sayles, 1986), and external linkages and networks to profit from innovation (Teece, 1986).

However, the knotty part of innovation management is still at firm's strategic level. Since the processes of technological, market, and organizational change interact with each other, the management of innovation is inherently interdisciplinary and multifunctional. It compasses the management of R&D, production and operations management, marketing management, product development or organizational development. Strategic managers should match organizational structures and processes which support innovation, and opportunities for, and constraints on, innovation in specific technological and market environments. The key task of managing innovation is how to integrate simultaneously these changes of market, technology, and organization (Tidd et al., 1997).

Schumpeter's economics definition of innovation is long overdue for the realization of new combinations of factors of production. But the strategic management focus is more on combination of various change processes. Taking the project management of a radical innovation as example, the first step should be selecting the right disruptive technology. There are two criteria for a disruptive technology: it never exceeds the existing technical performance but exceeds the performance requirements of the market; and it is improving rapidly its own technical performance. Once managers decide to pick up technology for its disruptive nature, the next step is to position the initial market for the technology. Because the technological change implies an emergence of new market, managers can only detect the new segment relying on weak signals generated from interacting directly with experts, scholars, venture capitalists and potential distributors, and other unconventional channels. Managers can get market information such as who the customers are, which product features they want, and what price they would pay, by fast experimental marketing or market tests through a related or unrelated start-up organization. At the same time, the created start-up organization shall undertake the business development with disruptive technology. Even when the emerging market becomes bigger and stable, this organization's independence in design, production, sales, and distribution shall be maintained, instead of being assimilated back into its parent company (Bower & Christensen, 1995).

Dynamic Capabilities: Strategic Integration of Changes

The strategic dimensions of managing innovation by top managers can be characterized as a main part of the "dynamic capabilities," which enable firms to create, deploy, and protect the intangible assets that support superior long-run business performance (Teece, 2007). Originally, the concept refers to firms' ability to adapt to and exploit changes in their business environment and even to provoke change. According to perceptions of stability or dynamism in the environment, some authors decompose dynamic capabilities into three levels: incremental, renewing, and regenerating capabilities of firm (Ambrosini et al., 2009).

More precisely, all along the activities of enhancing, combining, protecting, and, when necessary, reconfiguring the firms' intangible and tangible assets, dynamic capabilities can be disaggregated into three specific capacities:

1. to sense and shape opportunities and threats,
2. to seize attractive market possibilities, and
3. to transform the organization to maintain good fit with the business environment (Teece, 2007).

Sensing means firms actively predict the future, study, search, scan, and explore all the development possibilities. Seizing means firms make choice among opportunities, invest to exploit the potentials, and allocate resources to realize development. Transforming means firms fix resources in assets, institutionalize the activities, create new structures, and change routines to keep the development trend.

Dynamic capabilities are the fruits of entrepreneurial management of managers. Entrepreneurship is about sensing and understanding opportunities, getting things started, and finding new and better ways of putting things together. It is about creatively coordinating the assembly of disparate and usually specialized elements, getting "approvals" for non-routine activities, and sensing business opportunities. Entrepreneurial management has little to do with analyzing and optimizing. It is more about sensing and seizing—figuring out the next big opportunity and how to address it (Teece, 2012).

The very entrepreneurial and forward-looking nature of dynamic capabilities is exactly what management needs for innovation. Though dynamic capabilities are firm-specific and different firms may need expertise in different areas, they are generally manifested by firm's competency of integrating activities of different natures: the exploration of strategic options and certain opportunities, the exploitation of technological endowment and unique intellectual property, as well as its customer base and upstream relations with suppliers, and the organizational "routines" or common aspects of practice in the firm that allow it to adjust to a user needs to get a customer, and to establish a price for products / services without too much regard for competition.

This strategic management competence to overview and combine different change processes is a unique asset to firms in innovation-based competition. In large multi-technology multi-market corporations, headquarters management staff has to develop such dynamic capabilities because they are able to mobilize and allocate resources to innovation project. In capital market and financial institutions, some venture capitalists and investment bankers also build up their visions over innovative projects and use financial tools (portfolio management, option-pricing method, etc.) and corporate governance restructuring power (alliance, merger and acquisition, spin-off, etc.) to combine various processes of changes (Teece & Pisano, 1994; Teece et al., 1997).

The decomposition of dynamic capabilities into concrete actions of sensing, seizing, and transforming has significant implication to innovation management. In fact, strategic integration of technological change, market change, and organizational change requires all these concrete actions in each change process. Therefore, developing and coordinating the dynamic capabilities in every change process constitute the key roadmap of innovation management. As demonstrated by literature, managing firms with some accumulated technological capabilities from developing economies to forge ahead to compete with world-class enterprises at innovation frontier is not an easy job. The combination of detailed breakdowns of dynamic capabilities and innovation process provides a fresh framework to assess and manage the innovation practice of catch-up firms.

Assessing the Innovation Strategy of Chinese Companies

How did the Chinese companies develop innovation in technology or business model? What were exactly their strengths and weaknesses in management? Were they able to build and use some integration capabilities for innovation management? And how did they exploit the resources inside or outside the firm, the government, and from elsewhere?

In the following sections, we will use some cases and examples of Chinese industrial firms to illuminate how they seek to establish innovation capacity in terms of strategic management. The cases of Chinese firms vary in terms of ownership, size, and fame. The textile industry was mainly represented by private small and medium sized local firms who were export-oriented, but at the same time supplied domestic market. In electronic industry, larger State-owned firms with higher technological level could be found. Similarly, the automobile firms in this chapter were large State-owned firms. The limited numbers of the most internationalized Chinese firms were all large joint-stock companies. Nevertheless, all these firms had a more or less similar history of technological capability development starting from OEM (Original Equipment Manufacturing) or subcontracting production for foreign companies as their "clients" or "customers." In terms of developing innovation capacity, these Chinese industrial firms eventually confronted the similar or even same problematic of catching-up and forging ahead, once they had already accumulated certain amount of technological capability.

The firm cases in textile and electronic industries are all based on primary information collected through visits and in-depth interviews. The main fieldwork in China was carried out between March of 2007 and April of 2009 through the research program "Innovation Potential of Chinese Industries," financed by the Hong Kong–based French Research Center on China (CEFC) in cooperation with the Research Institute of Guangdong Development (Sun Yat-sen University in China). Thanks to the official nature of the research program, most of our firm visits were recommended, arranged and accompanied by local government officials. At each firm visit, in-depth interviews lasting 1–2 hours with senior managers or company owners were undertaken, followed by factory or site visit.[1] The information of Bluestar Company in France was also based on our field visit in 2013.

The sampling of firms for field interviews was principally done by local governments, with their preferences and standards to select "well-established, large sized, relatively well performed and technologically sophisticated local firms and entrepreneurial activities." Many of case firms were located in Guangdong Province, which was often called the "world factory" due to its lion share of China's foreign trade value (25.1% in 2011). These firms, with even the most famous Chinese corporations like Lenovo or Huawei, all experienced the early development stage of OEM or subcontract manufacturing. So they were all typical Chinese catch-up firms, with better or worse performance.

The period from 2008 to 2012 was very important for these quantitatively large enough but qualitatively still less innovative firms, because they truly began to reach the limits of their long catching-up process and met difficulty in upgrading to innovation level. The 2008 world economic crisis imposed in fact a "window of threat" or "moment of truth" on Chinese industrial firms and exposed them intensively to main problems of innovation management. At that moment, it was a big question whether Chinese firms were able to "make the crisis truly creative" and take it as an opportunity to innovate, just like South Korean firms (Kim, 1998). With the analysis framework drawn from the theories discussed earlier, we assess each firm's dynamic management (sensing, seizing, and transforming) of each innovation process (technological change, market change, and organizational change). Based on these detailed assessments of cases, we can identify the key areas of problems in their innovation management, such as integration, coordination, dynamism, and forward-looking, etc.

[1]A list of visited firms during these two years contains mainly: Fenghua High-Tech Corporation (Zhaoqing), TCL Joint-stock Corporation (Huizhou), Huaiji Auto Accessories Company (Huaiji), Zhaoqing Auto Parts & Accessories Company (Huaiji), Dachangjiang Motorcycle Group (Jiangmen), Shuopu Motorcycle Technology Company (Jiangmen), Hedy Group (Guangzhou), Delica Plumbing Equipment Company (Shuikou), Shuikou Technological Innovation Center (Shuikou), Yishion Group (Humen), Humen Textile Innovation Center (Humen), Fumin Fashion City Company (Humen), Xiaiqo Textile Innovation Center (Xiqiao), Dachong Furniture Technology Center (Dachong), Zhengda Pharmaceutical Company (Wuhan), Balance Pharmaceutical Company (Wuhan), Mike Bio-Pharmaceutical Company (Xiamen), North-East Pharmaceutical Company (Changchun), Geely Group (Ningbo), Beijing Oriental Electronics Group (Beijing), Delphi Shanghai Ltd. (Shanghai), Desano Bio-Pharmaceutical Company (Shanghai), and Shanghai-Volkswagen Company (Shanghai).

Companies in Textile Industry

As OEM producers, textile firms in Guangdong became specialized in manufacturing products according to the specifications given by the foreign clients. For local firms in Dachong Town of Zhongshan, a textile cluster in the Western part of Pearl River Delta, the possibility of innovating in product or process depended very much on their relations with foreign clients. Since 1993, Dachong cluster has became one of the biggest Chinese producers specialized in jeans for export under foreign brands. In terms of technological change, the firms were on a typical path of incremental technological accumulation. They learnt mature process technologies from foreign clients by using imported equipment and doing production jobs on the shop-floor. The product designs were given by foreign firms to exploit the economies of scale in these firms who adopted industrialization-age factory structures. To them, the "market" was the foreign firms who place orders, with which they had very little contact. These local firms had no knowledge in fact on the final customers of their products, since access to final foreign markets was extremely difficult to them.

Foreign orders were decreased enormously during the 2008 economic crisis and the owners of the biggest factories in the cluster collectively attempted to sell directly abroad, with the support from local authority. But they found that the distribution channels to final customers were all controlled by their foreign clients, without them they were unable to interact with the real market. The strength of firms in Dachong included cheap labor, large scale, and low costs in production. Their weakness was their dependence on foreign clients and the eventual distance from end-market. This weakness in market linkage could be fatal because even with good manufacturing expertise and facilities, the firms were far from the true sources of technology—the users.

The factories made improvement in efficiency of using standardized technologies, but the purchasing prices given by clients were so low that their production capacity was very vulnerable to fluctuations in world markets and they had no additional resources to invest in R&D or market detection. As private firms, it was impossible for them to get loans for investing in any new business development activities from banks, who only lend to large State firms.

Yet the low margin in textiles was not unavoidable. On the Eastern side of Pearl River Delta, the clothing firms in Humen district of Dongguan

City were more successful. In this specialized industrial district, local government established a public technical center, whose duties ranged from fashion designing to copy Western models and marketing to export. This technical center created its own market—a building accommodating hundreds of small business who opened their stands of clothes exhibition. Each year the district held a competition of young Chinese designers and sends the winners to follow training in an English school of design. The result was that it was easier for firms in Humen to develop and promote their own brands and business networks. Later, the technical center was acquired by a local private garment group Yishion, which had a business of 3 billion Yuan yearly. The technical center thus became a profit center and opened to foreign design companies.

Yishion was founded in 1997 as an OEM manufacturer of garments. Later it entered in wholesale business and became an apparel trader specialized in import/export of clothes, which brought it a lot of contacts with retailers in and outside China. Then Yishion discovered a very buoyant market in China—the children's clothing—and created its own brand "Yishion." In 2000, it sold its wholesale business and established its own brand stores by developing a franchise network in China. Until 2008, it had a network of 2000 stores all across the country and became the 9th biggest apparel group in China. Yishion was no longer a manufacturer under other companies' brands because its franchise stores only sold its own brand products. It even expanded its marketing network in neighboring countries of Southeast Asia.

The big shift from exports to domestic or regional markets of Yishion happened in the beginning of 2007, when it restructured the whole organization in group form and kept its headquarters in Dongguan to focus on developing new activities: new products, fashion design of clothes but also franchise concept stores, and improvement of quality management system. Other than its product line for children, Yishion re-segmented the clothes market and launched four new product lines: leisure clothes series, sport clothes series, fashion clothes series, and business clothes series. After transforming the acquired public technical center to its own platform of design, Yishion recruited new designers and collaborated with overseas design firms to develop new series of products.

Every year, Yishion launched 10 thousand new clothes models in the market. At its site of headquarters, initiated by Mr. GUO Donglin, the CEO and his management team, Yishion constructed a giant "show center" composed of all kinds of concept boutiques and stores designed specially to sell its own brand clothes. Franchisees were solicited to visit the boutiques and select the collections of clothes. Yishion changed its business model from selling clothes to retailers to selling design services, boutique systems, and clothes to the franchisees. In upstream activities, Yishion integrated all suppliers in its new IT system and the terminals in the boutiques of its Show Center were also connected with suppliers. In 2002, Yishion already invested to establish a Quality Examination & Test Center (QETC). In 2005, it invested 40 million Yuan to build up a Specialized Quality Examination & Test Laboratory (SQETL) which was the biggest test lab in clothes chemical elements in China. Till 2007, Yishion finally built up a complete QETC with a total investment of 120 million Yuan and more than 1000 employees working on clothes quality. The QETC was able to monitor and test all textile elements from its material inputs to finished clothes. A hot-line service center was also created to receive and treat the complaints and requirements of clients and franchise stores.

Certainly, the firms like Yishion were still far from being innovatively competitive in Western markets. But the key element of Yishion's bigger innovation potential than firms in Dachong lied not merely on its stronger dynamics of technology development through privatization of a public technical center, but also on its investment in market research, sales system, and brand building in Chinese market. The participation in domestic consumption growth generated more comfortable margins to Yishion so that it could continue to invest in design and technical progress. The relative success of Yishion in managing innovation was due to its technological sourcing from Western clients, at the same time its learning actively and directly from final customers and new market segments. This management strategy of parallel learning from both technological providers and final customers in market in fact should suit most of the small-and medium-sized firms in local clusters of Dachong and Humen. It was also the main lesson which was drawn from the experience of some State-owned firms in "strategic" industries. These State-owned firms often had the most advanced machines, good work organization, better paid employees, and bigger power over suppliers. Contrary to private firms, they had R&D activities supported by public programs of technology development and easier access to universities and technical centers for cooperation. Moreover, several of these firms were themselves originated from public research centers that are "commoditized" (Bironneau, 2012). They also had arranged partnerships with banks to ensure their investment. But in terms of managing market change, they were not as good as their private counterparts.

Companies in Electronic Industry

Fenghua Hi-Tech Corporation, located in the Northern part of Pearl River Delta, was a State-owned company benefiting from innovation policy of national and local governments. Founded in 1984, Fenghua was ever the number one producer of electronic components in China and ranked number 8 in the world. Fenghua produced various electronic components, including resistors, capacitors and transistors, with its 16 production lines. It diversified in artificial silica for components used in printed circuit boards and motherboards. From 1999, its business experienced a spectacular growth: in the late of 2000s, Fenghua occupied in the domestic market a quarter of China's production of components and exported to the world (USA, Japan, France, Germany, and Poland). About 70% of their production was for very large customers (Motorola, Thomson, etc. …).

Fenghua's production of electronic materials (binders and powders) was also one of the biggest in China. In 1985, it imported a line of production of silica layers whose technology was "multi layers ceramic capacitor" (MLCC technology) from the United States. At that time, sixteen lines of the same technology were imported into China but only the line of Fenghua was installed and kept. From 1991, Fenghua increased its production capacity and gradually extended its production sites to Shenzhen, Suzhou, and Jilin Province. In 1993, it reached to have another capacity of 100 million units of aluminum capacitors. In 1995, it reached to produce 5 billion units of resistors. In 1997, it reached the production of 360 million units of transistors. In 2001, Fenghua set up a production line of MLCC which became its main product, and a production line of magnetic cores with a capacity of 4000 tons a year. In 2002, it had reached the capacity of 80 billion units of electronic components. With the increase of productive capability, the staff number grew from more than 100 to 10,000 employees: 500 employees in the production of powder materials, 9000 in components, and 500 in equipment manufacturing.

Indeed, from early enough Fenghua extended its production from components to artificial silica, an essential raw material for all electronic components, and attempted to become technological leader in this field in China. Fenghua decided to focus on materials because it found that that the key process technology could only be identified in material: It also took long time to integrate process technology into the component production. Fenghua, as other component producers, would not leave this key issue in MLCC production controlled by other firms.

The organizational change of Fenghua was rather exogenous. Arranged by Central Government, the company jointly developed local-produced ceramic materials of MLCC with Qinghua University in 1995. In 1996, Fenghua was publicly traded, with 20% of the capital owned by the city government of Zhaoqing, 20% by the State, and the rest floating in the market. With government as major shareholder, Fenghua's development projects of electronic powders and binders were integrated in the National Torch Programme and enjoyed financing from Ministry of Science and Technology. In 2000, Fenghua was approved by Central government to increase its A share stocks and collected 1.1 billion Yuan to invest in its project of "National Base of Large-scale Components" approved also by the government. To support the technology development of Fenghua, the government established 3 technology centers at national level and one research institute inside the firm. Government allocated to it more than 1000 experts in electronic technology. Fenghua was selected as one of the 36 pilot stations of post-doctoral research in firms at national level. To assure the sales of its products, the government designated Fenghua as the key national supplier of localized components for mobile telecommunication products.

With such huge financial support, technological aid, and market access from State, Fenghua built up technological competences in material technology, equipment technology, transformation technology, painting technology, and some design and test technology. However, during 2001–2004, the whole electronic components market fell down. During 2001 to 2003, high frequency PCs had rigid exigencies of the components and that required technological breakthroughs of component producers. At the same time, small scale products such as mobile phones needed also new components. Therefore, the old products were in end of their life cycle, and the market demands of traditional components were in decrease. In Chinese and international markets, there were increasing demands for new products, smaller but with higher quality. Fenghua, with 5% of sales allocated to R&D, responded by investing additional 30 million Yuan for R & D to modify its product lines. Its Research Institute successfully developed new resistor in MLCC (capacitor) in replacing silver and BAI metal by NIE metal. During 2000 to 2006, Fenghua developed 140 new technologies: 20% of them were inventions and others were practical new designs. In 2006, Fenghua recovered its sales with 1.2 billion Yuan revenues.

It was also during this period of time, that Fenghua's R&D was directed to high added value materials (binders and powders), mainly for MLCC. Before 2001, 60–80% of MLCC cost was of materials; but after 2001, only 30–40% of MLCC cost was of materials, and high-valued components only had 20% cost of materials. Besides, conventional products had 40–50% of cost for manufacturing, but high-valued products contained 80% of cost for manufacturing process, mainly for equipment investment. Therefore, Fenghua turned its R&D focus from materials to specific equipment. As a first step, Fenghua developed test equipment, such as Auto Optical Inspection Equipment. With own-produced equipment, Fenghua could economize 200–300 million Yuan in capital budgeting. Yet most of its equipment was still imported. Fenghua emerged as a main player in high and middle voltage products. With lots of investment in equipment, it reached the economy of scale very easily. But for products of same capacity, it had gaps with Japanese companies and competitors in the world market.

From 2005 to 2006, Fenghua found that there was a big change on the demand side from its clients. Before, the clients purchased electronic components one by one. So Fenghua sold its components by piece and had to negotiate every year with its downstream clients on prices of every component. But suddenly, clients turned to competitors to purchase the integrated-set of components to save money. It brought a big reduction of prices in the market. Fenghua didn't predict the market change, but had to plan producing integrated-sets to serve its clients. Once again, Fenghua found itself in a very disadvantageous position in face of upstream IC designers. Once the IC design finished, Fenghua could only accept and produce according to the architectural design of IC. Fenghua would like to have designers integrate their components in IC design in early phase. So it negotiated with some IC designers, and even created a joint research laboratory with a Taiwanese IC firm of mobile phones who had strong ties to a US institute and foreign companies. Nevertheless, for Fenghua, becoming a system integrator in mobile telecommunications represented another technological path beyond Fenghua's core competency, and the dominant position of IC designers in the value chain seemed very difficult to be broken down.

It was also during this critical period of time that Fenghua lost its key clients, in face of fierce competition in electronic components from foreign and Taiwanese companies such as Chuntian, Guoju, TDK, and Taiuyotai, etc. One key client lost was INTEL, the leading company of micro-processor in the world. The multinational had identified Fenghua as a qualified supplier and even created joint R & D programs with it. However, Intel had nearly 150 Chinese suppliers. In the beginning of 2008, INTEL made an internal decision to break the contract with Fenghua. This loss of relationship with a key customer was fatal for the firm, because the pulling force of its particular MLCC technology, whose technical performance ranked far behind the Japanese and Korean competitors, suddenly disappeared. The break-up with INTEL imposed a dead end on Fenghua's MLCC technology. In fact, to attain a global level and approach the technological frontier as Samsung, Fenghua should have invested much more in R & D, and continuously improved the method of manufacturing. Its relationship with INTEL was particular, because INTEL was Fenghua's key client and key technology source at the same time. Staying in an ecosystem is vital if a firm wants to maintain and improve the high-level technological capabilities.

Fenghua, despite of its significant internal technology efforts, ongoing State support, and good financial and credit conditions, was eventually not able to insert itself into such a small and closed circle composed of global producers of multilayer components. The loss of key market relations left Fenghua perplexed in overall development direction. It hesitated between the ideas of integrating in a system integrator and finding a comfortable place in the new industrial chain, or localizing the production to strengthen its industrial structure of transistor, capacitor, and resistor production, or implementing own brand strategy through investing more in indigenous R&D. In 2007, Fenghua started searching for strategic investors since the financial support from the State was almost exhausted. The government's plan was also selling Fenghua to foreign groups. In 2008, it decided to stop production abruptly.

The rise of Fenghua was due to its enormous inputs in R&D with the government's supportive corporatization reform of organization. The technologies developed through R&D were innovative for Fenghua, but in the electronic components industry they were mostly catching-up to the technology frontier. Fenghua could sense the technological opportunities and invest in developing them. But it had difficulty in transforming and exploiting the developed technologies to attain and maintain competitive advantage in the market. Every time it worked out a new technology closer to the frontier, the technology became obsolete quickly. This difficulty of building up market competitiveness seems to be due to the weakness in technological capabilities—Fenghua was always one step lagged behind the most advanced technology.

But the real cause is the absence of dynamic capabilities to manage the market change. Fenghua was not able to project market trends and sense threat from market. Its over-dependence on a limited number of clients seriously reduced their power to negotiate technology change process with its clients in the market (who were its key technology sources). In terms of market linkages, Fenghua was in the same situation as the Chinese private OEM producers of jeans or garments, whose relationship with foreign customers was essential because these customers were also technology providers. This situation was very different from those of Taiwanese companies or Japanese and Korean companies some twenty to thirty years ago. These East Asian companies strategically leveraged their technologies and production capacities to diversify customers and markets. They actively searched for new market opportunities, invested in market development, and maintained strong customer relations. In turn, they negotiated better commercial and technological cooperation conditions with their foreign clients (Ernst & Kim, 2002). Their good mastering of market change supported the technological change process with strength. With no capability on market change, Fenghua was not able to articulate between technological progress and market development, despite its significant investment in technology and production. And the reason why Fenghua was lack of "feeling and sense" of market change may be due to the heavy intervention of government: on one hand, Fenghua's market was almost "guaranteed" by the government; on the other, Fenghua's management team had only limited control over the organizational change process. The corporate governance, project financing structure, and even personnel allocation were all arranged by the government: the dynamic capabilities of making organizational change were weak in Fenghua. Without strong supports from active market management and effective organizational change, its technological adventure eventually fell to a dead end.

The Companies of TCL and BOE

The problem of integrating effectively changes of market and customer needed to lead choice of technological paths can be found in other electronic firms. For example, the television producer TCL launched its overseas expansion after strong growth in the domestic market. In 2002, TCL bought the television division of Schneider, but stopped the production in 2004. TCL also bought the mobile phone business unit of Alcatel and the colors TVs division of Thomson. At that time, TCL was already the world leader of cathode television, occupying 11% of the global market. It planned to reduce the selling price of TVs by controlling Thomson's manufacturing technologies and supply chains through acquiring the weak Western brand. However, there was a sharp decline of demands in market, especially in Europe. TCL underestimated the speed of market changes and the fastness of technological change. When TCL Thomson launched its new LCD product in 2005, TCL found itself fall behind its competitors in the European market, in terms of knowledge of LCD technology. Its organization and collective expertise exclusively in cathode technologies were of little help to meet the new demand of flat screens TVs. Though TCL finally didn't miss the technological transition to LCD,[2] its way of managing innovation was problematic. TCL's aggressive international acquisition represented a dynamic organizational development triggered by the needs of exploiting existing technologies, but its relative inactive market change management made TCL difficult sense and seize the technologies a step ahead of market. It followed passively emerging technologies in the market. Like many other reputed Chinese firms (Lenovo, Galanz, Medea, etc.), TCL became eventually important market player, thanks more to its productive capacity of large scale, than to the dynamic capabilities of orchestrating technologies, markets and organizations to make innovation.

If the problem of dynamic capabilities in Fenghua and TCL was on managing of market change in relation to technological change, the problem of most Chinese firms' efforts to upgrade to innovation was still more related to absence of appropriate management of imported technology itself. Beijing Oriental Electronic Company (BOE), a factory of CRT (CRT) in Beijing, was such an example. In the eighties, BOE established a joint venture with Matsushita to produce electronic tubes for color TVs, but the technology was still managed and controlled by Japanese companies. BOE wanted to change from the cathode technology (CRT) to liquid crystal display (LCD) monitors. So BOE chose to acquire

[2] In 2009, it was the 3rd biggest brand of LCD TV in China and the 7th biggest worldwide. It was a bigger LCD TV exporter than any of its Chinese rivals.

technology through organizational acquisition of foreign companies. It bought the STN-LCD divisions of Hyundai Group (Hynix) and the business unit producing TFT-LCD. Then BOE bought the distribution company of Hynix liquid crystals and invested in constructing production lines of the fifth-generation TFT-LCD in its own factories in China. To get the key technology, BOE singed turn-key contract with Hyundai Group for constructing three complete production lines of TFT-LCD, including the patents of the TFT-LCD of second and third generation, buildings, workshops, fixed assets, and the entire global distribution network. In short, BOE's acquisition covered all the operations necessary for the acquisition of hardware technologies, access to information sources and methods of commercial distribution: it bought everything that was tangible and believed in this way it mastered the complete technology and, more important, could become the market leader. However, after the accomplishment of turn-key contract, when BOE began producing liquid crystals displays (LCD), managers discovered that the manufacturing process needed a lot of tacit knowledge and know-how. For example, the production of screens actually depended on the temperature and humidity. But this tacit knowledge, only based on the experience of workers on the production line, was not included in the purchase contract and obviously not transferred to BOE.

BOE had to invest more for acquiring the tacit knowledge on LCD technology, such as training and exchanges with workers in Korean and Japanese firms. When it finally mastered the whole process, the imported technology had already become obsolete in the market. Moreover, operating costs were too high compared to competitors because of the additional investment required for technology transfer. To catch up with technological change, BOE decided to import the fifth-generation TFT-LCD. However, after losing a lot of money in the acquisition of Korean production chains, it had not enough resources to ensure the new technological leap forward. BOE eventually lost control of upstream suppliers, as well as its downstream distributors, due to the increased costs of production.

Companies in Automotive Industry

Similar to BOE, many Chinese State-owned automobile firms also tried to move closer to innovation frontier through transferring and absorbing foreign technologies, supported by the national policy which encouraged large Chinese corporations to invest directly in foreign companies. A typical case was the acquisition of the car company MG Rover by two Chinese groups: SAIC (Shanghai Automotive Industrial Corporation), China's largest auto company, and Nanjing Automobile Corporation (NAC). The process of acquisition of MG Rover Group was complicated and two very different Chinese companies were put together without a successful dialogue. The technologies of MG Rover were split into two packages: SAIC spent 67 million British pounds to purchase the technologies of two patented car models (Rover 25 and 75) and two patented engine models (KV4 and KV6). SAIC acquired no assembly line or physical production assets, neither the brand of Rover. NAC, on its side, spent 53 million British pounds to buy MG and Austin brands, the technologies of four patented car models (MGZR, MGZS, MGZT, MGTF) and three engine models, as well as all assembly lines for manufacturing those car models and motors. When the deals were completed, the two Chinese firms started to compete with each other in the Chinese market, instead of cooperating.

In late 2005, SAIC created an imitated Chinese brand "Roewe" in domestic market by using the technologies it had acquired from MG Rover. It was virtually a legal copy of the Rover 75. Three years later, SAIC sold totally 5300 cars under the brand "Roewe 750." With no equipment and no production line, SAIC encountered difficulty in reproducing exactly the Rover car model. For example, the engine manufacturing required advanced equipment. SAIC produced some engines by itself, most of engines were still bought from its traditional Chinese suppliers. SAIC sensed the coming opportunities in Chinese automobile market and would like to catch it as soon as possible. But it would not wait for a high quality Roewe to launch. NAC has the same attitude of rush into the domestic market, except that the initial situation was a little different: NAC bought the MG brand, so it has all the legality of using this brand. Owning the properties of the brand, technology, production equipment, and assembly lines, NAC also decided to launch as quickly as possible the car production and marketing it on the domestic market. NAC dismantled all the engine production lines and the most important car production lines of Rover, and transported them from United Kingdom to China. As a result, NAC spent more than four months to re-install all the lines on their production site in China. The dislocated lines, mainly for manufacturing more than 40 key engine components, were composed of more than 600 equipment. In July 2007, without R & D activities on the imported lines, NAC launched its car model MG ZT, the Chinese version of MG7. Later, NAC used these lines to reproduce other MG car models for the Chinese market.

The above three State-owned firms, BOE, SAIC and NAC, like many other Chinese State firms, identified the emerging Chinese market opportunity and intended to catch it by imported foreign technologies. After overseas M&A deals, they all dismantled the tangible assets, relocated them to China, and sell products to domestic market, instead of continuing the operations abroad or re-export to foreign markets. They couldn't fully absorb, assimilate, and transform the bought technologies because there was no dynamics to create new internal and external organizational arrangements to carry on further technological change, such as JV or alliance which could facilitate transfer of tacit knowledge. The purchase of high technology and advanced equipment cannot assure upgrading to innovation of firms. As a result, these firms counted on their old tactics of large production scale, low sales pricing, and short lead time to market, to survive the competition in domestic Chinese market.

Chinese Emerging Multinational Companies

Nevertheless, better innovation management practice with stronger dynamic capabilities could be found in Chinese automobile industry. The acquisition of Volvo by Geely, a private car maker only entering the automobile industry in 1997, was an example. Geely kept almost all the organizational structures of Volvo outside China and triggered further development of Chinese market for Volvo cars. Two new Volvo factories were constructed in Chengdu and Daqing to produce new models for Chinese market. Geely established a joint R&D platform with Volvo to develop CMA models, but the program was dominated by Volvo R&D team. Geely integrated the procurement systems of the two companies and reduced enormously the production cost of Volvo for both Chinese and international markets.

A similar example was Chinese Bluestar Company, a subsidiary of largest Chinese national chemical group ChemChina. In 2007, after acquiring the French Rhoda Silicon, Bluestar kept the French R&D center with 130 researchers in Lyon almost intact. Over years, Bluestar continued to invest in the R&D projects in France but also created internal training and personnel exchange programs with manufacturing factories in China. Bluestar later bought upstream activities through acquiring Elkem, a Norway chemical company, and downstream activities through acquiring Adisséo, a French animal nutrition and sulfur producer, whose business were linked to former Rhodia Silicon. By these organizational and managerial arrangements, Bluestar progressively assimilated the core technologies as well as the know-hows of Rhodia Silicon and diffused them across the whole group.

Generally, those few Chinese firms that succeed in internationalization development were those that deviate from strategy of large quantity and lower prices. The management characteristics of their more successful innovative activities appeared again and again: firstly, by learning and absorbing foreign technology, they established close interactions with customers in domestic market, as well as the branded foreign clients; they became more and more sensitive to market demands; then, through creation of new organizational frameworks such as overseas R & D centers, alliances, or mergers & acquisitions, they approached further foreign sources of knowledge; normally they will restructure the internal and external organizations, and leverage the Chinese production capacity with newly acquired technological capabilities for global markets (Zahra et al., 2000).

Huawei may be the most typical case of such dynamic management. It tested its production capacity and management of wireless networks in China's Xinjiang region first before seeking to export to developing markets such as Zimbabwe, Kenya, and Thailand. It then established R&D centers in Europe (Stockholm), Texas, and Silicon Valley, and recently in India and Russia to detect the most advanced technologies. Note that Huawei created its first R & D centers abroad very early, well before its production line of server network was fully finished and when it was under legal attack of CISCO who accused Huawei of plagiarizing its server technology. Of course, overseas R&D Centers of Huawei were not for adapting its research already conducted in China, but for learning, acquiring, and repatriating foreign technologies, to both overseas market and later Chinese market.

As for the appliance manufacturer Haier, when it established operations in the United States, it smartly targeted the specific market segments in North America, such as dormitory refrigerators, wine refrigerators, and TV sets in children's room, etc., things they were able to produce easily in mass with their standard technologies. Based on market feedbacks, Haier launched more sophisticated R&D projects to further develop the North American market.

But not all Chinese emerging multinational firms managed well the innovation dynamics all the time. Lenovo, which had made a series of international acquisitions, might be an example of problematic dynamic capabilities. The acquisition of PC business from IBM reinforced Lenovo's technological progress in laptop computers, but Lenovo didn't reconfigure and transform the emerging market of mobile phones, even it is already sensed it early and try to seize it by investing in production in 2002. Lenovo bought out Motorola Mobile in 2014, but this seizing action was too late. Lenovo neither seized the opportunity of internet business, even it was fully aware of the transformation of IBM. After acquisition of IBM, Lenovo spent huge energies and resources to transform the internal organization to focus on embedding IBM's market sales system and PC technologies in the group, while neglecting to large extent the market dynamics. It had world-class production scale, cost control and supply chain system, but its R&D budget was below 1.9% during 2006–2014. The firm seemed to stop sensing.

The Dynamic Capabilities of Chinese Companies

From 2000s to 2010s, with government support, there were signs of development of innovation capacity through firm R&D as well as creation of R&D centers by multinationals in China. Some iconic companies made seriously investment in R&D, such as Huawei and Lenovo. The result was in an increase in both labor productivity (value added per head) and total factor productivity in the manufacturing sector. Chinese industry was more innovative than is generally acknowledged. Chinese firms established strong positions in two types of innovation—developing new products and services that address consumer needs, and process innovations that made manufacturing more efficient.

The exceptional growth attracted some argument that Chinese firms already developed a new model of "cost innovation," i.e., making innovations by exploiting low cost labor and materials (Zeng & Williamson, 2007). A McKinsey report also concludes that China had the potential to meet its "innovation imperative" and to emerge as a driving force in innovation globally (McKinsey & Company, 2015). For Hout and Michael (2014), the speed with which Chinese firms developed new products from existing technologies and ramp up large-scale production was quite impressive. They learned how to produce swiftly to meet buyers' demand for quick turnaround; to adapt designs to use different materials when the original materials were too expensive or unavailable; to modify equipment so that they could make different products; and, above all, to keep costs down. All these skills were based on their early experience of technological learning.

Though Chinese firms didn't involve the upstream creation of technology, original designs, selection of materials, and design of equipment, or customer knowledge and marketing savvy, their strong points were mainly downstream industrial competencies. The practices of Chinese firms in managing innovation were characterized by the following ways (Hout & Michael, 2014):

1. Chinese firms generally keep engineering and manufacturing close, often co-locating them.
2. Chinese firms tend to acquire new technologies either through formal licensing deals or by reverse-engineering them, but they keep the physical work of experimentation and production in-house.
3. Chinese firms hire more midlevel engineering and manufacturing people, even though they're getting expensive. The added engineering and manufacturing bandwidth gives the Chinese firms possibility of solving difficult problems in product industrialization. When Apple had to redesign the screen of its first iPhone at the last minute, its Shenzhen supplier roused its engineers out of bed, developed a better screen, and overhauled the production line—in just four days' time.

The firm cases in previous section also show that Chinese firms were technology learners. In terms of linking market needs with commoditized technologies, most of Chinese firms had huge potential of growth and improvement, which was under-utilized and could be exploited through more investments in in-house R & D and partnering with external research institutions. In terms of dynamic capabilities, we synthesize the analysis of each firm's innovation management practice in Table 6.1.

Table 6.1 illustrates some main problems of innovation management in Chinese firms during the 2010s. At the most basic level, many Chinese firms confused "innovation" with "invention" and replaced innovation by technological breakthrough, patent registration, or R&D investment. Innovation management was thus heavily biased to technology management and was regarded as technical matters to be handled by product designers, engineers, and technicians. Even in terms of managing

Table 6.1 Assessment of Innovation Management of the Chinese Firms

	Sensing, seizing, and transforming of technological change	*Sensing, seizing, and transforming of market change*	*Sensing, seizing, and transforming of organizational change*	*"Orchestration" skills of strategic integration*
Firms in Dachong (private SMEs)	– Weak in sensing (technologies were brought in by foreign clients) – Strong in seizing and transforming (mass production capacity)	– Very weak (no access to final market)	– Very weak (keeping the simple factory structure)	– Weak (owners were not able to leverage technological capabilities to change market positioning and business models.) – Weak technology sensing due to absence of market access
Yishion (large private firm)	– Strong (buying the public center and pursuing fashion designs)	– Very strong (recognizing children's clothes and segments; local brand building; franchising)	– Very strong (creating the franchising system; upgrading IT system; improving QC system, etc.)	– Very strong (integrating design, suppliers, franchise stores, etc. in its show center system)
Fenghua (large state-owned firm)	– Weak in sensing the most advanced technologies – Strong in seizing (investing in technology development) – Medium in transforming (technology became obsolete before fully exploited)	– Very weak (depending on a few foreign clients; government endorsement)	– Weak (most of organizational change was arranged and directed by government)	– Very weak (since there was no market prediction, there was always technological "surprise" to the firm. No market input in technological change.) – No organizational motivation to trigger market development

(*continued*)

Table 6.1 (continued)

	Sensing, seizing, and transforming of technological change	*Sensing, seizing, and transforming of market change*	*Sensing, seizing, and transforming of organizational change*	*"Orchestration" skills of strategic integration*
TCL (large joint-stock company)	– Weak in sensing the most advanced technologies – Strong in seizing and investing – Strong in transforming and exploiting acquired technologies through manufacturing system	– Strong in Chinese market but weak in European market	– Strong in sensing and seizing (overseas mergers and acquisitions of Thomson) – Medium in transforming (difficulty in cultural integration)	– Problematic (didn't take maximum use of foreign acquisition to trigger market change process in Europe and then the technological change process)
BOE (large state-owned firm)	– Medium in sensing the most advanced technologies in the world – Strong in seizing, investing in and exploiting acquired technologies	– Strong in Chinese market but very weak in foreign market	– Very weak (problems of managing personnel and employees)	– Very weak (only concentrating on managing technologies as tangible commodities)

(*continued*)

Table 6.1 (continued)

	Sensing, seizing, and transforming of technological change	*Sensing, seizing, and transforming of market change*	*Sensing, seizing, and transforming of organizational change*	*"Orchestration" skills of strategic integration*
SAIC & NAV (large state-owned firms)	– Strong in sensing foreign advanced technologies – Medium in seizing and transforming (buying the equipment and technologies without further development and investment)	– Strong in sensing and seizing the Chinese market – Very weak in foreign market	– Very weak (no organizational change since only the acquired assets were moved to China)	– Medium (somehow combing the Chinese market opportunities with imported technologies through overseas assets take-over)
Geely, Bluestar, Haier, Huawei (emerging Chinese MNCs)	– Strong or every strong in detecting foreign technologies – Very strong in investing in overseas R&D – Very strong in exploiting the developed technologies	– Strong in exploring and developing foreign markets – Medium in transforming and reconfiguring foreign markets	– Very strong in sensing and seizing organizational change through aggressive M&A – Strong in transforming overseas organizations and structure (relative successful cultural integration)	– Strong (managing the market, technology and organization changes simultaneously to create positive feedbacks among them; leveraging Chinese production capacities with foreign technologies in both foreign and domestic markets)

(*continued*)

Table 6.1 (continued)

	Sensing, seizing, and transforming of technological change	*Sensing, seizing, and transforming of market change*	*Sensing, seizing, and transforming of organizational change*	*"Orchestration" skills of strategic integration*
Lenovo (emerging Chinese MNC)	– Weak in sensing (mobile and internet technologies) – Medium in seizing (investment in mobile was light and then late) – Strong in transforming and reconfiguring (for matured PC technologies)	– Strong in sensing (having a strong tradition of selling and customer service) – Medium in seizing the new market trends – Strong in transforming (setting and managing distribution system; branding)	– Strong in sensing and seizing (buying IBM PC business; moving head-office to the United States, etc.) – Weak in transforming (not creative in organizational change; difficulty in cultural integration)	– Problematic (strong in sustaining the existing business but weak in orchestrating in creating new business; typical incumbent syndrome.)

Source: Author

technological change itself, Chinese firms, especially large State-owned firms, gave more importance to hardware and information of technology than to knowledge and human skills in technology acquisition, as the cases of BOE, SAIC and NAC demonstrated. Some others just focused on technical advancement rather than changing market and competition situation, as the case of TCL.

For those who built up large productive capacity through strong technological learning and accumulation with customers, including foreigners as their technology providers, either they were kept too distant from the final consumers (as the firms in Dachong Cluster), or they became too much dependent on key foreign client in technology (as Fenghua). Sensing, seizing, and transforming the market was absent in their innovation management. The counter-example was Yishion, which began to forge ahead in innovation thanks to its development in domestic market and avoided too much technological path dependency on foreign clients.

Merely managing R&D or marketing was not enough for innovation. The dynamics of technological, market, and organizational changes were inter-linked and reinforced each other. Theories on innovation management, particularly the approach of dynamic capabilities, emphasize the importance of integrating strategically the technological, market, and organizational changes to successful innovation. As shown by the cases, the integration, articulation, or "orchestration" skills were often the weak points for managing innovation in Chinese firms. Firms like Geely, Huawei, Haier, and Bluestar were skillful in integrating and articulating simultaneously and appropriately the different dimensions of change in innovation, but the firms having this type of dynamic capabilities were still rare to find in China.

In this respect, China differed dramatically from the competitive challenge to Western companies that Japan presented many years ago. Japan's secret sauce was management; but that is China's weakness (Lieberthal & Lieberthal, 2003). Maybe it would take decades for them to overcome the ingrained management weaknesses that prevent them from mastering the dynamics of innovation. Knowing the importance of management to innovation, Chinese managers could start by asking some basic questions when facing a potential innovation project:

1. How do we choose the technology? Do we have a clear technology strategy and a suitable roadmap for technological capability development? Is technological innovation the core part of project?
2. Do we have a corresponding market strategy for the technological innovation? What relations and interactions with customers or clients should we have to support the coming technological change? How will we change the market with the innovation?
3. Should we change correspondingly our internal and external organizations of people and business to meet the technological innovation? What way of organizing people and activities is suitable to achieve the innovation goal of project?
4. Most importantly, how can we coordinate and integrate the above changes in three domains? Can we articulate and leverage these three processes to create sustainable dynamics of innovation of the firm? Do we have such dynamic capabilities in management?

By nature, the rampant problem of weak dynamic capabilities in managing innovation in China was the shortage of high-level human resources of managers. China needed a whole new generation of managers to upgrade. In fact, innovation management as a specialized major could be found in several top business schools in China. Entrepreneurial and forward-looking managers were difficult to find in existing corporations, since the strategic development divisions of large firms or strategy consultants were mainly oriented to financial strategies or IT operations. Some innovation managers may be employed in financial sectors (policy-leading funds, industrial investment funds, venture capital firms, specialized technology banks, and business angels, etc.). Chinese government understood the importance of these intangible assets and capabilities and began to reform its education and training system to form a new generation of managers. On the other side, they also began to free the firms to find their own strategies and cultivate their endogenous capabilities of managing innovation.

Conclusion

When Chinese firms, like catch-up firms in other developing countries, tried to innovate closer to the frontier, specific management skills became be vital, among others factors. The company cases in this chapter highlights how Chinese firms manage the technological, market, and organizational changes for innovation activities in terms of sensing, seizing, and transforming them. If the Chinese firms were more or less strong in managing technologies, markets or organizational changes separately, the most innovative firms were also strong in a kind of dynamic capabilities: management skills of strategically orchestrating and integrating the change processes in different fields. In this sense, the weak capability of strategic integration was the main problem of innovation management in China.

In the beginning of 2010s, Chinese companies reached at a critical moment of transition from imitation to innovation. They already accumulated rich production capacity through technological learning, but were also more problematic in terms of innovation management. In the following years, many of the case firms in the chapter and the other emerging E-commerce companies in China would evolve quickly in their way of managing innovation and achieve tremendous business performance.

Their successful transformation was largely due to the very supportive strategic industrial policy of upgrading from central and local governments.

References

Ambrosini, V., Bowman, C., & Collier, N. (2009). Dynamic capabilities: An exploration of how firms renew their resource base. *British Journal of Management, 20*(S1), 9–24.

Arvanitis, R., Zhao, W., Qiu, H., & Xu, J. N. (2006). Technological learning in six firms in South China: Success and limits of an industrialization model. *International Journal of Technology Management, 36*(1/2/3), 108–125.

Bironneau, R. (2012). Le système d'innovation chinois. In R. Bironneau, R. Arvanitis, F. Bafoil, & B. Kahane (Eds.), *China Innovation Inc. Des politiques industrielles aux entreprises innovantes.* Presses de Sciences Po.

Bironneau, R., Arvanitis, R., Bafoil, F., & Kahane, B. (Eds.). (2012). *China innovation Inc.* Presses de Sciences Po.

Bower, J. L., & Christensen, C. M. (1995). Disruptive technologies: Catching the wave. *Harvard Business Review*, 43–53.

Burgelman, K. A., & Sayles, L. R. (1986). *Inside Corporate Innovation.* Macmillan.

Christensen, C. M. (1997). *The innovator's dilemma: When new technologies cause great firms to fail.* Harvard Business School Press.

Cohen, W., & Levinthal, D. A. (1990). Absorptive capacity: A new perspective on learning and innovation. *Administrative Science Quarterly, 35*(1), 128–152.

Dosi, G. (1988). The nature of the innovative process. In G. Dosi, C. Freeman, R. Nelson, G. Silverberg, & L. Soete (Eds.), *Technical change and economic theory.* Pinter Publishers.

Dutrénit, G. (2000). Learning and knowledge management in the firm. In *From knowledge accumulation to strategic capabilities.* Edward Elgar.

Dutrénit, G. (2004). Building technological capabilities in latecomer firms: A review essay. *Science, Technology & Society, 9*(2), 209–241.

Ernst, D., & Kim, L. (2002). Global production networks, knowledge diffusion, and local capability formation. *Research Policy, 31*(8–9), 1417–1429.

Henderson, R. M., & Clark, K. B. (1990). Architectural innovation: The reconfiguration of existing product technologies and the failure of established firms. *Administrative Science Quarterly, 35*(1), 9–30.

Hobday, M. (1995). *Innovation in East Asia: The challenge to Japan.* Edward Elgar.

Hout, T., & Michael, D. (2014, September). A Chinese approach to management. *Harvard Business Review.*

Kim, L. (1997). *Imitation to innovation* (p. 303). Harvard Business School Press.

Kim, L. (1998). Crisis construction and organizational learning: Capability building in catching-up at Hyundai motor. *Organization Science, 9*(4), 506–521.

Kline, S. (1985). Innovation is not a linear process. *Research Management, 28,* 36–45.

Le Masson, P., Weil, B., & Hatchuel, A. (2010). *Strategic Management of Innovation and Design*. Cambridge University Press.

Lieberthal, K., & Lieberthal, G. (2003, October). The great transition. *Harvard Business Review*.

Mathews, J. A. (2006). Catch-up strategies and the latecomer effect in industrial development. *New Political Economy, 11*(3), 313–335.

McKinsey & Company. (2015). *The China effect on global innovation* (p. 136). McKinsey Global Institute.

Moore, G. A. (2014). *Crossing the chasm: Marketing and selling high-tech products to mainstream customers* (3rd ed.). Harper Collins Publishers.

Nonaka, I., & Teukeuchi, H. (1995). *The knowledge-creating company: How Japanese companies create the dynamics of innovation*. Oxford University Press.

Pavitt, K. (2003). The process of innovation. In J. Fagerberg, D. Mowery, & R. Nelson (Eds.), *Handbook on innovation*. Oxford University Press.

Rogers, E. M. (1983). *Diffusion of innovations* (3rd ed.). Free Press of Glencoe.

Teece, D. (1986). profiting from technological innovation: Implications for integration, collaboration, licensing and public policy. *Research Policy, 15*(6).

Teece, D. (2007). Explicating dynamic capabilities: The nature and microfoundations of (sustainable) Enterprise performance. *Strategic Management Journal, 28*(13), 1319–1350.

Teece, D. (2012). Dynamic Capabilities: Routines versus Entrepreneurial Action. *Journal of Management Studies, 49*(8), 1395–1401.

Teece, D., & Pisano, G. (1994). The dynamic capabilities of firms: An introduction. *Industrial and Corporate Change, 3*, 537–556.

Teece, D., Pisano, G., & Shuen, A. (1997). Dynamic capabilities and strategic management. *Strategic Management Journal, 18*, 509–533.

Tidd, J., Bessant, J., & Pavitt, K. (1997). Managing innovation: Integrating technological. In *Market and organizational change*. Wiley.

Trott, P. (2005). *Innovation management and new product development*. Prentice Hall.

von Hippel, E. (1989). *The sources of innovation*. Oxford University Press.

Zahra, S. A., Ireland, R. D., & Hitt, M. A. (2000). International expansion by new venture firms: International diversity, mode of market entry, technological learning, and performance. *Academy of Management Journal, 43*(5), 925–950.

Zeng, M., & Williamson, P. J. (2007). Dragons at your door. In *How Chinese cost innovation is disrupting global competition*. Harvard Business School Press.

Zhao, W. (2015). Is R&D upgrading China from imitation to innovation? An institutional analysis of absorptive capacity. *Journal Transition Studies Review, 22*(2), 81–110.

Zhao, W., & Arvanitis, R. (2010). The innovation and learning capabilities of Chinese firms, technological development in the automobile and electronics industries. *Chinese Sociology and Anthropology, 42*(3), 6–27.

CHAPTER 7

The Strategic Industrial Policy of Upgrading and Transformation

Introduction

After the global crisis of 2008, China found that its entire economic structure is unbalanced. Externally it depended too much on export growth and internally it faced deep problems of sustainable supply of human and financial resources. The global economic slow-down also exposed China to more international treaty obligations and global integration risks. When facing the quick rise of wages, most small- and medium-sized firms in non-State sector began to struggle to survive in the market. While wages grew about 15% or more after 2005, labor productivity grew less than 10% and inevitably started a descent. A large number of firms in the non-State sector were not able to remain profitable and quitting manufacturing sector which had been in decline even before 2008. On the other hand, there were monopolistic State-owned firms in upstream industries (telecom, energy, oil industries) making higher profits in domestic market. The tendency was reinforced by a financial system dominated by State-owned banks which stymied the development of the non-State sector by

The original version of this chapter "From Industrial Policy to Upgrading Strategy: Dilemma of Local Developmental State in China's Pearl River Delta" was published in *China Economic Policy Review*, Vol. 3, No. 1 (2014) 1450006 (32 pages), DOI: 10.1142/S179396901450006X"

W. Zhao, *Remade in South China*, IPP Studies in the Frontiers of China's Public Policy,
https://doi.org/10.1007/978-981-95-7277-9_7

prioritizing State-owned enterprises and big firms. Within such an economic structure, Chinese entrepreneurs found no way forward and had no interests to re-allocate their capital and other factors of production to the sectors where industrial productivity ranked higher. To survive, they were often driven to invest in speculative activities such as real estates and even become money lenders in black credit markets (Zhao & La Pira, 2013).

After the global financial and economic crisis, the Chinese government saw the danger of falling into the "middle-income trap," which was generally due to the incapability of developmental State to resist the pressure of particular interest groups in a fast-changing society, such as increasing cost of ordinary labor, more social welfare demands by emerging middle class, and the monopolization of financial resources by power elite class. Over time, such a situation of social conflict would stick industries in the position of producing low value-added products with high costs of inputs, and lead the whole economy to uncompetitive edge. The government searched for new model of development to address the burdens of limited resources and deal more explicitly with inter-relationships and balance between economic, social, and environmental policies. The whole policy package is termed as "industrial transformation and upgrading," which was a new challenge to developmental State and industrial policy on (Whittaker et al., 2008):

1. how to address different "stages" targets simultaneously: developing forward and backward linkage; reinforcing existing sectors and extending their value chains; entering into new sectors and creating new activities;
2. how to creating an "innovation or technology system" conducive to global engagement in global value chain, technological learning and technological upgrading;
3. how to create coalitions with domestic and international parties, often at regional or local levels; and
4. how to undertake industrial upgrading at both firm and industrial level, and what should be the generic strategies and effective policy rationales of government action.

Since long time, neo-liberal ideas were embedded in international institutions such as WTO and certain areas in EU. However, the financial crisis since 2008 demonstrated that the nation-State remained the most powerful actor in maintaining business organization; it was recognized that in most OECD countries that the State should have authority and resources to intervene in order to sustain economic activity. For industrial upgrading in emerging economies, the strategic choice of industrial upgrading also often implied an investment-driven phase of developmental.

Compared with other developing economies that have experienced incremental industrial upgrading and successfully climbed up along the global value chain, the most striking part of China's industrial upgrading was the key and dominant role played by the government, both at central and local level. China announced its National Plan of Mid- and Long--Term Science and Technology Development (2006–2020) and showed its ambition to transform the country into an innovative nation by 2020. The industrial upgrading policy of Chinese government was above all translated in massive investment in science and technology infrastructure, in order to achieve rapid technological leap forward in strategic sectors, to support the best State-owned enterprises, and to build up national champions in innovation.

The Pearl River Delta of Guangdong as Core Region of Industrial Upgrading and Transformation

At local level, China's Pearl River Delta (PRD) in Guangdong Province, the so-called World Workshop, became the core place of experimentation of industrial transformation and upgrading policy. The rapid development of the Pearl River Delta was due to economic globalization and the strategies of American, European, and Asian companies of outsourcing from low-cost labor-intensive regions in the 1990s. The PRD grasped the opportunity of industrial diffusion and quickly became the world's processing and manufacturing center. After many years of accumulation of industrial development, the Pearl River Delta region possessed large-scale facilities of production, complete supporting industries, basic infrastructure, together with a higher degree of clustering of industrial organization. Its rich resources available for manufacturing, technological competencies and other features were even comparable to some high income national and regional economies in Asia.

However, as its industrial development model was mainly based on contract manufacturing, OEM production was characterized by companies located in the lower end of the global value chain, with low technical content and low-added value. Most companies built their advantage on low-cost capacity expansion rather on core technology innovation and own brands. They could only get a small share of the value created by the long-term growth. The economy of Pearl River Delta was dominated by export-oriented manufacturing. For example, in 2007, the exports processing with imported materials and out-bound materials accounted for 69% of all exports in PRD, and the dependence ratio on foreign trade amounted to 155%.

Local firms normally started their business through processing trade in the manufacturing sector and this kind of OEM production didn't require in-house design and innovation capability. Although the whole business of PRD was integrated into global value chains, firms were in the low end of the value chain, earning limited processing work fee. The industrial added value was 26.37% just before 2008. As pointed out in the Chap. 6, their international competitiveness of enterprises depended on low-cost production and large amount of factor inputs, rather than technological advance. Facing the situation of sluggish international market sales and rising factor costs, the profit margins were squeezed to zero and the whole industrial system seemed to be in trouble.

Therefore, since 2006 industrial transformation and upgrading was attached great importance by the Central Government and the Provincial Government of Guangdong for the regional development of PRD. As a result, in 2009 the National State Development & Reform Committee particularly prepared a Planning Outline of the Reform and Development of the PRD (2008–2020) for Guangdong Government to implement as industrial and regional development strategy. This Planning Outline was the first one among all local authorities and indicated the PRD was chosen as a pilot for experimenting new policies of industrial upgrading in China. At lower local level, the nine prefecture-level cities in the Pearl River Delta Region have been triggered to adopt strategies to accelerate the industrial transformation and upgrading. Each of the prefecture-level cities in the Pearl River Delta Region made some progress in this process, but along with it, some problems emerged. The strategic implementation at Guangdong government level and the local firm behavior level resulted in an interactive transformation among governments, enterprises, trade organizations, and other social intermediary organizations.

The Concept of Industrial Upgrading (IU)

In a very broad sense, UNIDO (2011) defines industrial upgrading as modernization of industry structure through making better products, making them more efficiently, or moving into more skilled activities. Within its framework, industrial expansion and upgrading refers to existing manufacturing activities specialization and comprise capacity expansion (scaling-up), product upgrading, process upgrading, and functional upgrading (intra-industry structural change). Industrial deepening refers to creating more backward and forward linkages and complementarities within one industry, and exploiting complementarities within on industry. Industrial diversification is shifting into new industries or moving from one industry to another (Gereffi & Kaplinsky, 2001; Humphrey & Schmitz, 2000), thus referring to the nurturing of hitherto non-existent manufacturing activities and new sectors (inter-industry structural change or inter-chain upgrading).

By summarizing the successful experience of Taiwan, H. Amsden and Wan-wen Chu (2003) argues that IU occurs when latecomer firms "compete in world markets at the stage in their development when they already have basic industry but neither operate at the world technological frontier nor still profit from low, unskilled wages." Their sustained competitiveness depends on upgrading, or improving their performance in mid-tech industries (According to CEPII, mid-tech industries include railroad and transport equipment; motor vehicles and trailers; electrical and household appliances; machinery; chemical products) and moving into high-tech sectors (According to CEPII, high-technology industries include medical and optical instruments; pharmaceuticals; radio and telecommunications equipment; information technology; manufacture of aircraft and spacecraft). For upgrading, latecomer firm has to make a three-pronged investment:

1. investing in optimal-sized plants (up-scaling);
2. investing in technology and management to develop managerial and technological capabilities (stronger);
3. investing in distribution and channels to expand production scale and scope domestically and globally (longer).

At the most basic level, the global value chains literature defines upgrading as improving a firm's position within the chain, and this is generally associated with securing more of the value-added through the production process. The most feasible avenue for upgrading includes product upgrading (producing more sophisticated goods with higher unit prices) and process upgrading (improving technology and/or production systems). Besides the technological upgrading of product and process, Frederik and Gereffi (2011) identify the way to move up the same value chain from a more marginal to more secure position by increasing the range of functions performed. For example, a turn-key or full-package manufacturer is often responsible for additional functions beyond basic production, such as design or logistics management; this is called intra-chain or functional upgrading. It often means that OEM manufacturers acquire responsibility for more value-adding activities; a switch from manufacturer to service provider may occur: from CMT to OEM to ODM to OBM to lead firm.

If the above movement from low-end to higher-end products and value chain stages is termed as firm-level upgrading, linkage upgrading is often referred as industry-level transformation. Linkage upgrading is either establishing new vertical or horizontal linkages, or the quality improvement of existing linkages. Supply chain upgrading means firm's integration to establish backward manufacturing linkages with the supply chain. Distribution channel upgrading means firm's market diversification and acquisition of new skills by serving new buyers or markets often in emerging domestic or regional markets.

For example, during the 1980s, Korea developed vertically integrated national industries through a process of sequential value chain upgrading. Korean *Chaebols* (business family) emerged as diversified enterprise growth with a vertically integrated stance toward product development, manufacturing, and marketing. In Taiwan, local manufacturers begun by supplying components and sub-assemblies, rather than finished products and asked by de-verticalized Western manufacturers to move up the value chain (Miberg et al., 2014). The strategy for Taiwan-based suppliers was to remain within the expanding set of value chain niches that had been made available, and to increase their range of competencies in contract manufacturing and design services, which expanding geographically into mainland China in an effort to respond to customer demands for ongoing cost reductions.

But the key issue is not always "functionally upgrading" and moving to more advanced functions along the value chain, but often deepening the specific capabilities required to explore new opportunities offered on the side of the stage of the value chain where the firm is currently engaged.

This requires firms to establish new or better linkages with support industries, universities, and research institutes. Without these horizontal linkages, the firm-level upgrading will soon reach its limits (Ernst, 2008).

Whatever the perspective is at the level of the local, national, or regional economy, industrial upgrading ultimately occurs at the level of the individual firm in the context of a particular value chain or sector. Without "firm-level upgrading," there is little hope that a country can push forward with an "upgrading-through-innovation" strategy (Ernst, 2014). However, firms attempting to upgrade via one of these paths often have considerable difficulty in doing so. In large part, this is due to the increasing barriers to entry that exist as company moves along the value chain: as "tangibles" [production and manufacturing] have become increasingly commoditized, "intangible" aspects of production (i.e., marketing, brand development, design) become increasingly important for the profitability and power of lead firms. It is almost certainly a pervasive trend that the barriers to entry in intangibles are growing faster than those in tangible activities (Gereffi & Kaplinsky, 2001).

Company Strategies of Industrial Upgrading in the Pearl River Delta

While the PRD local State scheduled and visioned a development goal, industrial upgrading could only be achieved through behavior changes of local firms, who were the cornerstones and real carriers of transformation. However, after the economic crisis of 2008, except very few large-scale enterprises who were able to forecast industrial cycle and make risky investment in disruptive innovation while still keep stability, most ordinary firms in the RPD were rationally living in the short run and struggle to survive. Their strategies were all spontaneous reactions to external impact, such as keeping and grasping possible orders, layoffs, lowering prices, reducing production costs, temporary closure of factories, relocating their production bases to sites where they found lower total cost of production, cancellation or suspension of investment projects, and even exit (bankruptcy or trade sale).

Figure 7.1 shows the result of a random questionnaire survey of 1200 industrial firms in the PRD regarding the efforts made by firms for industrial upgrading during 2008 and 2013. According to the statistics data, the biggest efforts of upgrading made by firms were improving quality of

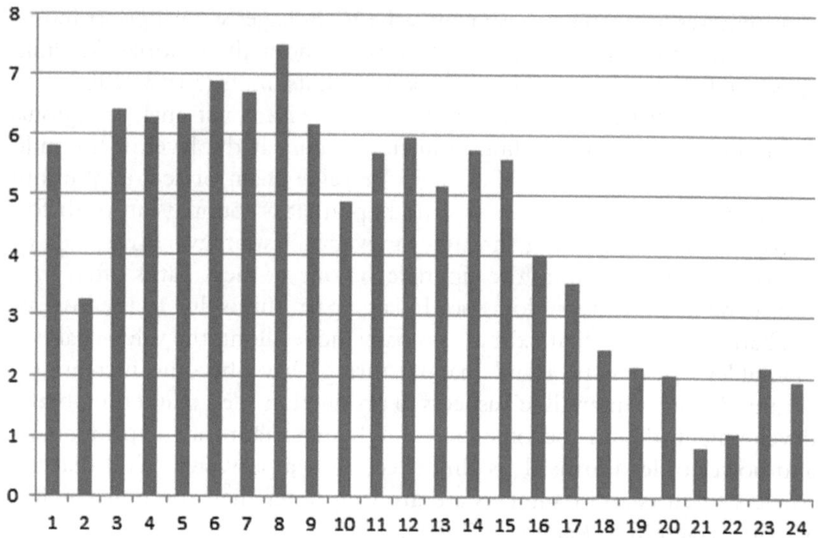

Fig. 7.1 Ranking of Strategic Behavior of Industrial Upgrading of Firms in the PRD during 2008–2013. (Note: (a) The numbers along vertical axis (0–9) represent the amount of upgrading efforts made by firms during 2008–2013, whose value varies from 0 (make no effort) to 9 (make maximum effort). (b) The numbers along horizontal axis (1–24) represent the types of upgrading effort made by firms during 2008–20,013, whose value corresponds to the following strategic behavior: (1) Investment in new production machinery and equipment/ technology. (2) Collaborative R&D with universities, research institutes and other enterprises. (3) Quality management system/system construction. (4) Optimizing inventory logistics management. (5) Optimizing the working hours management system. (6) Rules and regulation construction of safety production. (7) Employee skill training. (8) Improving quality of products. (9) Development of new products, improve the level of product differentiation. (10) Building private brands. (11) Improving enterprise's capability of independent R&D. (12) Improving after-sale services. (13) Sales and service network construction. (14) Exploring the domestic market. (15) Exploring the international market. (16) Extension to the upstream industry, such as raw material in the industry. (17) Extension to the downstream industry, such as distribution in the industry. (18) Getting into a new industry. (19) Shifting the production bases to lower cost regions. (20) Investing to build factories in other regions of the country. (21) Investing to build factories overseas. (22) Mergers and acquisitions. (23) Separation of ownership and managerial authority, the introduction of professional managers. (24) Cultivation of the entrepreneur's child to take over the Company. Source: Zhao Wei (2014). From Industrial Policy to Upgrading Strategy: Dilemma of Local Developmental State in China's Pearl River Delta, *China Economic Policy Review*, Vol. 3, No. 1 (2014) 1450006 (32 pages), DOI: 10.1142/S179396901450006X")

products (for keeping orders), internal rules and regulation construction of safety production (to reduce cost of being fined), employee skills training, quality management system construction, optimizing the working hours management system (to be aligned with new Labor Law since 2007), and optimizing inventory logistics management. Firms contributed most of their efforts on these improvement and optimization of their daily operational activities, while put the most important measures of industrial upgrading (in-house R&D, independent capability of research, collaboration for R&D, and constructing own distribution channels, etc.) at the secondary place, or even contributed little efforts (such as getting into a new industry, shifting the production bases to lower cost regions, investing to build factories in other regions of the nation, and investing to build factories overseas).

A more detailed evaluation of the practical efforts made by local firms reveals some characteristics of their strategic choices (Table 7.1). First, firms' upgrading efforts were concentrated in process upgrading and product upgrading; efforts on functional and value chain upgrading were relatively weak. Firms gave priority to the measures which could bring short-term results and immediate efficiency promotion, both in terms of price competitiveness and non-price competitiveness. Weak efforts were given to long-term strategic actions, especially in technological specialization through innovation. When firms carried out R&D, they preferred to depend on their own sources rather than cooperated with other organizations, especially universities (indigenous innovation becomes self-closed innovation).

It should be noted that the things that firms contributed most of their efforts and resources to do were not those measures that can improve firms' competitiveness most effectively. Statistical analysis of the survey data also helped identify the most significant strategic behaviors which had positive impact on overall performance of firms, including their financial, market, and environmental performances.

Table 7.2 shows the co-relationship between each major strategic behavior and the comprehensive performance of upgrading. A very simple coefficient analysis led to the conclusion that all these strategic measures had positive relationship with upgrading performance. And the most effective measures were technological innovation effort, change of operational modes from OEM to ODM or OBM, and expansion in domestic markets, whereas creating new business in new sectors and implementing common strategies such as merger and acquisition had smaller

Table 7.1 Evaluating Firms' Strategies of Industrial Upgrading in PRD

(1) Strategy of Process Upgrading

Type of IU at firm level		1. Process upgrading (improving process efficiency)	
		Activities within the chain	Linkages across the chain
General business practices		R&D; changes in logistics and quality practices; introducing new machinery	R&D; supply chain management procedures; E- business capabilities; facilitating supply chain learning
Efforts influencing short-term performance, based on:	Low-cost competitiveness	*Better rules of safety production (2); Optimizing the working hours management system (5); Investment in new production machinery and equipment/ technology (9)*	*Optimizing inventory logistics management (6)*
	Differentiation competitiveness	*Employee skill training (3); Quality management system (4); Improving enterprise's capability of independentR&D (11)*	
Efforts influencing long-term performance, based on:	Diversification through internationalization (geographic expansion)		
	Specialization through technological innovation		

(continued)

Table 7.1 (continued)

(2) Strategy of Product Upgrading			
Type of IU at firm level		2. Product upgrading (Introducing new products or improving existing products)	
		Activities within the chain	Linkages across the chain
General business practices		Expansion of design and Marketing departments; establishing or strengthening of new product development cross functional teams	Cooperating with suppliers and customers in new product development; concurrent engineering
Efforts influencing short-term performance, based on:	Low-cost competitiveness		
	Differentiation competitiveness	*Improving quality of products (1); Development of new products, improve the level of product differentiation (7); Improving enterprise's capability of independentR&D (11)*	
Efforts influencing long-term performance, based on:	Diversification through internationalization (geographic expansion)		
	Specialization through technological innovation		*CollaborativeR&D with universities, research institutes and other enterprises (17)*
(3) Strategy of Functional Upgrading			
Type of IU at firm level		3. Functional upgrading (Changing the mix of activities)	
		Activities within the chain	Linkages across the chain

(*continued*)

Table 7.1 (continued)

(3) Strategy of Functional Upgrading			
General business practices		New higher value-added chain-specific functions absorbed from other links in the chain and/or low value-added activities outsourced	Moving into new links in the chain and/or vacating existing links; establishing backward and forward linkages of supply chain; establishing new channels of distribution and new markets
Efforts influencing short-term performance, based on:	Low-cost competitiveness Differentiation competitiveness	*Improving after-sale services (8);* *Building private brands (14)*	*Sales and service network construction (13);* *Extension to the upstream industry, such as raw material in the industry (15);* *Extension to the downstream industry, such as distribution in the industry (16)*
Efforts influencing long-term performance, based on:	Diversification through internationalization (geographic expansion) Specialization through technological innovation		
(4) Strategy of Value Chain Upgrading			
Type of IU at firm level		4. Value chain upgrading (Moving to a new value chain, inter-chain upgrading)	
		Activities within the chain	Linkages across the chain

(*continued*)

Table 7.1 (continued)

(4) Strategy of Value Chain Upgrading			
General business practices		Vacating production in a chain and moving to a new chain; separating branded product division from existing production (separated branding); mixing existing production with branded products for new customers (platform branding)	Adding activities in a new value chain; creating a whole value chain through acquisition of declining brands; creating new business through innovative combination of existing chain activities
Efforts influencing short-term performance, based on:	Low-cost competitiveness	*Cultivation of the entrepreneur's child to take over the Company (22); Investing to build factories in other regions of the nation (21); Shifting the production bases to lower cost regions (19)*	
	Differentiation competitiveness	*Separation of ownership and managerial authority, the introduction of professional managers (20)*	*Exploring the domestic market (10); Getting into a new industry (18)*
Efforts influencing long-term performance, based on:	Diversification through internationalization (geographic expansion)	*Investing to build factories overseas (24)*	*Exploring the international market (12); Mergers and acquisitions (23)*
	Specialization through technological innovation		

Source: Zhao Wei (2014). From Industrial Policy to Upgrading Strategy: Dilemma of Local Developmental State in China's Pearl River Delta, *China Economic Policy Review*, Vol. 3, No. 1 (2014) 1450006 (32 pages), DOI: 10.1142/S179396901450006X"

Note: The number in parenthesis represents the ranking, i.e., the degree of practical effort of upgrading made by local firms, varying from 1(highest ranked efforts of upgrading made by firms) to 24 (lowest ranked efforts of upgrading made by firms)

Table 7.2 Co-relationship between Upgrading Behaviors and Firm Performance Improvement (sample of 1200 firms)

Upgrading Behavior of Firm	*Coefficient with Firm Performance Increase*
Technological Innovation Efforts	0.6270
Change of Operational Modes from OEM to ODM to OBM	0.5380
Expansion in Domestic Markets	0.4957
Optimization of Production Operation	0.4258
Internationalization of Business	0.4018
Enhancing Purchase and Logistics Management Capabilities	0.3546
Implementing Generic Corporate Strategies	0.1883
New Business Creation in New Sectors	0.1800

Source: Zhao Wei (2014). From Industrial Policy to Upgrading Strategy: Dilemma of Local Developmental State in China's Pearl River Delta, *China Economic Policy Review*, Vol. 3, No. 1 (2014) 1450006 (32 pages), DOI: 10.1142/S179396901450006X

effectiveness on improving firms' performance. Optimization of production operations and enhancing purchase and logistics management capabilities were not the most effective measures which could upgrade firms' performance, but were the strategic focus where firms made most of their efforts.

Strategic Policy of Industrial Upgrading

Though IU is by nature the behavior of firms, most of the practical experiences in East Asia show that industrial upgrading has never been achieved by firm alone. It is always a result of joint efforts made by private and public sectors. In fact, IU is a special task of developmental State. Wade (1990) and Amsden (1989) identified some basic elements of developmental state such as "getting prices wrong," "picking winners," "State-imposed discipline," "subsidies," "backyard competition," "import substitution," "forced exportation", P. Evans (1995) characterized it as "embedded autonomy" and "State-society synergy." Compared with regulatory state, welfare state, predatory state, and even central planner in developing countries, the distinct roles played by developmental State in industrial upgrading can be described as "broker" of private investments and "entrepreneur" of national projects. It is in this field of how to overcome the upgrading obstacles that the developmental State interferes.

The Role of Developmental State in Industrial Upgrading

Developmental State emphasizes the role of State bureaucracies in eliciting higher rates of private investment (Amsden, 1989; Evans, 1995; Johnson, 1982; Wade, 1990; World Bank, 1993). Rational, risk-averse entrepreneurs will avoid making long-term investments in plant and equipment if they face a corrupt, unpredictable bureaucracy unlikely to provide complementary public investments. Competent bureaucracies can help individual entrepreneurs overcome coordination problems that may be crucial in instigating new activities. They can also turn informational resources into public goods in ways that increase the likelihood and effectiveness of investment (Rodrik, 1995). In such case, bureaucracies act as "honest brokers" in overcoming collective action problems among entrepreneurs. Furthermore, the bureaucracy itself is organized for gathering information and providing advice and incentives that help local firms to better thread their way through the labyrinth of rapidly changing world markets. Thus, the developmental States means also the ability of governments to push entrepreneurs into investing larger shares of their profits by "disciplining" them (Amsden, 1989) and the ability of public agencies to stimulate more risky but ultimately rewarding forms of investment through selective subsidies and protect selected sectors.

In contrast to a regulatory State in market economy, a developmental state intervenes more directly and deeply in the economy through a variety of means to promote the growth of new industries and to reduce the dislocations caused by shifts investment and profits from old to new industries, far beyond the so-called market-friendly policy targeting transversal functions, such as macro stability, saving interest rates, education promotion, export orientation (World Bank, 1993). In industrial upgrading, many initiatives to enter into new manufacturing brands come primarily from the government. Developmental State's role is rather a kind of special entrepreneur that creates new sectors than a simple central planner of resource allocation. Its functions are quite similar to those of an entrepreneur of innovation: perception of a new economic opportunity, evaluation of the profitability of the new opportunity, gaining command of financial resources, plant design, technology acquisition, construction supervision, recruiting and training new personnel, coordination of relationships with suppliers and purchasers, etc.

Framing Government Strategy for Industrial Upgrading

In more conventional words, developmental State pursues proactive industrial policies and almost all the important upgrading behavior at firm level can be regarded as a consequence of government interventions. The question therefore is what kind of industrial policy can be effective for government to coordinate and direct firms toward upgrading efforts. Through the discussion of the role of developmental State, it is evident that the so-called market-friendly or market-conforming horizontal industrial policy aiming at improving general business environment or "framework conditions" such as skills, innovation, and operational efficiency is far from enough to promote industrial upgrading.

New upgrading policy measures are all selective industrial policy by nature. And based on Taiwan's experience, H. Amsden and Wan-wen Chu (2003) identified in more detail two types of government strategy for industrial upgrading: big State-firm leading strategy and State-led networking strategy. Effective industrial upgrading depends on the mixture of the two.

State-firm leading strategy puts selective policy to a more extreme end: government plays a role of planner, entrepreneur, and manager in targeting specific sectors and technologies to create and accumulate industrial capabilities through direct investment in the chosen sectors, establishment of big State-owned firms, development of endogenous technology, and reorganization of existing firms into big groups. The typical example of such kind of strategy is the "strategic industrial policy" promoted by UNIDO (2006) since years.

Strategic industrial policy is the proactive approach to selective industrial policy which is the government interventions aimed at steering intra- and inter-sectoral structural change of industries toward a country's sustainable economic growth. The purpose is to promote and create a competitive industrial sector through development of large nationally owned firms covering upstream and downstream activities along the value chain.

The policy process includes: industrial diagnosis (identifying manufactured products and sectors which would be competitive in international markets), policy design (selecting policy instruments; prioritizing resources and coordinating interventions through program and projects), projects implementation and policy evaluation. Strategic industrial policy is characterized by its sectoral targeting, arms-length technological learning, focus on process improvement in manufacturing, development of vertically integrated national industrial firms, nurturing of national champion firms, sequential implementation of import substitution and export promotion policies, and formation of cooperative government-business relationships.

Particularly, H. Amsden and Wan-wen Chu (2003) proposes the following big State-firm leading strategic measures for industrial upgrading:

1. Promote "industrial complexes" or "urban economic commons" or "growth poles" with public R&D investment in nationally-owned firms.
2. Promote firms' moves in many industrial and service sectors, often with sector-specific and even firm policy instruments, and in higher value-added parts of global value chains.
3. Promote outward FDI and internationalization of large firms which chase hot products developed by first movers, push up production of specified items quickly, and exploit scale economies before profit margins become paper-thin. Only large firms can product in large volumes and are big enough to be of interest to first-mover firms as subcontractors or potential partners.

State-led networking strategy counts on local and foreign-invested small- and medium-sized firms. Policy measures are for forming local industrial clusters and linkages through government's help providing infrastructure, capital, land, labor, technology resources and market access (Zhao et al., 2011). The policy tools include fiscal measure, investment promotion, incentive scheme, universal but functional tools (HR, land zoning, export, technological development, etc.). In this sense, the State-led networking strategy can be found near what M. Porter and J Rivkin (Porter & Rivkin, 2012) recently proposed as competitiveness policy to improve the quality of the US business environment, including improving skills (create or expand an apprentice program to train workers; create or expand a training program to upgrade the sills and productivity); upgrading supporting industries (join consortia that help small companies locally); bolstering regional strength (participate in a cluster competitiveness initiative); adopting management practices that strengthen company locations; supporting innovation and entrepreneurship (invest in or incubate promising start-ups); and setting the business-government relationship (advocate business-wide improvements rather than lobby for special interests).

Successful upgrading relies on a smart combination of the State-firm leading strategy and the State-led networking strategy. Put in another words, it relies on the cooperation among government bodies, large firms as champions, foreign firms in growth, and local small and medium firms in more traditional sectors. Always taking Taiwan as example, H. Amsden and Wan-wen Chu (2003) argues that even within late-comers' most "networked" sector, electronics, most transactions are arm's-length. "New" commercial technology is typically generated by government research centers and the lion's share of output is accounted for by large firms (with sales in the hundred-millions or billions of dollars), not small ones.

Most latecomers' high-tech sectors are characterized by the production of mature products and the inability to create brand-name recognition in foreign markets. In the fastest-growing latecomers, high-tech industries tend to be dominated by nationally owned firms, and governments continue vigorously to promote such firms as well as "new" high-tech market segments. In fact, the experience of Taiwan in both electronics and modern services strongly suggests that as latecomers upgrade, they begin to look increasingly like advanced economies insofar as their nationally owned business enterprises become larger in scale and more global in scope, and their markets become more concentrated. In the whole story of upgrading, large nationally owned firms are the backbones, but a well-coordinated network of local firms around is also a necessary supplement. Industrial upgrading needs both.

The above review of existing theories of government strategy shows that for industrial upgrading in emerging economies; the role of a developmental State is vital. However, industrial upgrading can only be achieved through concrete changes of firm behavior. So, the effective government policy for upgrading shall be well integrated with firm development. This can be done through implementing State-firm leading strategy supplemented by State-led network strategy. While in reality, as demonstrated by the province of Guangdong, developmental State often faces serious challenge in elaborating and implementing appropriate strategies for promoting industrial upgrading.

Government Policy of Industrial Upgrading in Guangdong

Guangdong Province was the scene of a great industrial and economic take-off since the launch of economic reforms in 1978. The province and its core region of Pearl River Delta, which were largely agricultural before, benefited from an arsenal of incentives to promote export and foreign direct investment. It quickly became the "laboratory" of the market economy in China (OECD, 2010). Special Economic Zones and many highly specialized industrial clusters emerged in several cities of the Pearl River Delta (e.g., Foshan, Dongguan, Zhongshan), and gradually became the world's most competitive territories in industries such as ceramics, furniture, or hard drives and integrated circuits. However, from 2008, factors such as rising land prices and wages, environmental degradation, and competition from other Chinese provinces, threatened the future of this growth model.

The industries in the Pearl River Delta had been highly integrated in global value chain. But the process was always "invisible," "on backstage," and "quiet," that is to say, Chinese companies rarely created brand in the international market, though most products were made in the Pearl River Delta. This firm development model was different from the international experiences of Japanese or even South Korean firms. Driven by the global industrial chain, the firms in PRD in the years before economic crisis had actually experienced a gradual and continuous upgrading. But it seemed this path was reaching its limits. In response, provincial authorities began to implement a series of industrial policies to steer investment strategies of local firms, trying to push them into higher value-added activities. Changes in the labor market, vocational training, relationship between firms and the local system of R&D are were at the heart of the new regional dynamics.

Local Policy Evolution from Cluster to Upgrading Investment

In terms of industrial policy, China shared more similar characteristics with Taiwan rather than with Japan or Korea since China, like Taiwan, also had an economy of dual structure that divided the public and non-public sectors (Seung-Wook Baek, 2005). Guangdong Province was the arena where businesses flourished, financed with capital from Hong-Kong and subsequently from Taiwan. From late 1990s, a multitude of "product-based" towns and villages agglomerating hundreds, sometimes thousands of firms of a single type product emerged. These industrial cities, teeming with private-public mixed firms proliferated and even became the symbols of success in China. Yet, the industrial clusters in Guangdong were not created by the policy of the State.

As discussed in the Chaps. 4 and 5, the peculiarity of the clusters in its region of Pearl River Delta was the symbiotic relationship between business, entrepreneurs and local governments, which had slowly shaped a specific model of industrialization. The unique aspect of this region was that it was neither planned nor even predictable, but what had appeared are entrepreneurial firms grouping together by product and industrial sectors (Zhao et al., 2011). The local governments in Guangdong grasped immediately the emergence of the PRD industrialization model and elaborated a series of supporting policies. Overtime, the industrial policy experienced an evolution from policy toward specialized product towns or industrial clusters to regional innovation system building, to the particular promotion of Industry-University-Research alliances, and to the new national industrial upgrading policy after 2009.

In 1998, the provincial Department of Science & Technology began to implement a policy called "Innovation Experimental Pilots of Specialized Town." The Government identified more than 60 pilot clusters in Guangdong and allocated 300 thousand Yuan (30 thousand US dollars) to establish public "Innovation Centers" for developing generic technologies for the firms included in each pilot cluster. In 2005, a United Commission of the provincial government implemented a policy called "Upgrading Demonstration Zones of Industrial Cluster." 15 zones of clusters were identified and the policy package put emphasis on infrastructure construction of the park zones with hardware investment from government; regional brand building with industrial exhibitions organized by government; and technological innovation promotion through the established public innovation centers, test facilities, and innovation projects of platforms built up by government.

After 2005, industrial cluster policy was fully elaborated at city and township level. For example, in three specialized towns of Xiqiao (textiles and garments), Humen (shoes and garments) and Dalang (woolen textiles), local governments implemented exactly the same policy measures. They built own Technological Innovation Centers in charge of consulting, distribution of knowledge and technologies, applied research, quality control, support in promoting products, and finding customers for local firms.

They organized whole-sale market exhibitions and industrial fairs for local firms to get access to foreign clients. They built up technical schools and infrastructures for trade logistics. They provided award and official recognitions to backup local firms. As before, they also subsidized local companies for some operations. And finally, they controlled the size and speed of industrial investment by local firms: elimination of unproductive internal competition, allocation of complete supply chain in one place, organization of vertical integration among firms, and diversification into other kinds of products.

These local cluster policy measures later were approved by the Chinese Central Government and were diffused in other regions of China. Moreover, with the suggestion from Ministry of Science & Technology, more measures of building a regional innovation system were added to cluster policy after 2007, including:

- Policy toward firms' technological innovation: R&D tax credit, government purchase, building R&D centers in big firms, initiating key S&T projects in firms.
- Policy of public R&D centers and platforms: building of Shenzhen national high-tech innovation center, South China Pharmaceutical Innovation Center, Guangzhou international biological island, and 100 key labs, engineering centers, and engineering laboratories as innovation platforms.
- Policy toward national universities: promoting the creation of campuses or branches of national key universities and research institutes in Guangdong. For example, the Chinese Academy of Science created 6 key branch laboratories in Guangdong.
- Policy of promoting industry-university-research (IUR) alliances: setting up "Demonstration Firm of IUR Cooperation"; more than 50 IUR Innovation Alliances of Ministry and Province as platforms of innovation. For example, in Shunde City, which later became a subsidiary district of Foshan City, there were 12 R&D Platforms set up with introduced universities; Shunde City also created an Industrial Design & Research Institute for Guangdong.

The crisis in 2008 had a huge impact on industrial policy orientation of the Pearl River Delta. Though some local authorities continued their cluster-based innovation policy system, like Dongguan City's "Science & Technology Dongguan Strategy" and Shunde City's "Urbanization-led

Industrial Upgrading Strategy," the provincial government asked immediately policy guidelines from the Central Government to deal with the changing situation. Some typical strategic changes at firm level were labor substitution by equipment, diversification of export market, focus on domestic market, and increasing functional capabilities. During 2007 and 2010 the province of Guangdong adopted an "emptying the cage to change the birds" policy, which in fact was to relocate some labor-intensive and low-cost manufacturing firms in the Pearl River Delta to other regions in Guangdong or even in other provinces.

This industrial relocation policy was soon replaced by the new industrial transformation and upgrading policy elaborated in 2008–2009 by the Central Government in the Planning Outline of the Reform and Development of the PRD (2008–2020). The new policy was a typical strategic industrial plan in suitable to the stage of investment-driven development. It promoted investment of big projects and big State-owned enterprises as carriers of key programs to change Guangdong's industrial structure. It concentrated technological resources in public research institutes and universities, and set up a series of indicators such as ratio of R&D over GDP and energy consumption per capita to evaluate the performance of industrial upgrading. Guangdong's former industrial cluster policy was progressively marginalized in the new policy framework because they dealt mainly with traditional sectors which didn't fall in targeted structure of industrial upgrading. The planned new industrial structure was characterized by heavy weights of tertiary sectors (service, information, finance, etc.) and advanced manufacturing sectors, particularly of equipment manufacturing.

The Strategic Plan of Industrial Upgrading in Guangdong

According to the new official development strategy made in 2009,[1] the primary goal of industrial upgrading was to build up a modern industrial system in the PRD. "System" here meant that the industrial structure should be complete, composed by modern production-oriented service sectors (finance, industrial design, supply chain and logistics, exhibitions, etc.), advanced manufacturing industry (modern equipment, automobile, steel & iron, petrochemical, ship building, nuclear equipment, wind power equipment, aircrafts, trail transportation equipment, mechanical

[1] The Planning Outline of the Reform and Development of the PRD (2008–2020).

equipment, etc.), as well as traditional sectors with advantage (textile and garment, food and beverage, furniture, paper making and paper products, toys, electric appliances, ceramics, plastics, medical equipment, etc.).

"Modern" meant that the whole industry should be based on upgraded indigenous capacity of innovation. All sectors shall be upgraded and transformed by application of high-tech, especially IT technologies, advanced appropriate technologies, public knowledge and patented technologies, and modern management technologies. The advanced manufacturing industry would become very intensive in terms of technological input and capital, and integrate emerging sectors with high-tech content, such as high-end new electronic information products (e.g., super-speed optic fibers), energy-saving and environment-friendly products (electric vehicles), LED, solar panels, biological pharmaceutical products, oceanic engineering, new materials.

Sectors where the PRD traditionally had advantages would be transformed and upgraded through more integration in the industrial value chain. Firms within these sectors would occupy higher value-added functions in global production chain (e.g., R&D, marketing) and their modes of production will be upgraded from OEM to ODM or OBM.

People can see immediately that many of the above policy elements would become later the key parts of the national master plan of Made in China 2025, published in 2015.

For Guangdong government, the above policy goals were concretized into development mission objectives to senior officials at both provincial and city levels in terms of 28 quantified indicators. For each chosen sector, the government set up detailed planning and time table. There were totally 22 specific plans including infrastructure construction, industrial location integration, adjustment and promotion of ten key industries, development of supply chains, and development of sector of renewable energies, etc. The government also elaborated 26 supportive policy packages, including fiscal measures, list of service sectors to be supported, measures for fusion of information technology and industrialization, measures for promoting indigenous innovation, measures of reform of R&D system, etc. With public investment and under government direct management, the government planned and implemented the investment of 73 (later extended to 84) key industrial projects, R&D programs and infrastructure projects, such as Zhanjiang Steel Project, Ship building and repairing project, nuclear equipment project, new energy car program.

Table 7.3 summarizes the major policy instruments of industrial upgrading. With these concrete measures, the local government of Guangdong expected that by 2012, total number of firms with more than 10 billion Yuan (2 billion US dollars) turnover should reach 100; among them 8 firms should exceed 100 billion Yuan (20 billion US dollars) turnover. The local government of Guangdong also had the ambition that by 2012, 3–5 Chinese MNC with turnover of 100 billion Yuan (20 billion US dollars) and global influence can appear, and by 2020, this number of Chinese MNC could be increased to 20.

A detailed analysis of the policy measures of Guangdong local governments can show that it does more than the "normal" industrial policy and its style of governance was very developmental State. The local government's IU targets focused on inter-value chain upgrading (new industry creation) and efforts were made for building up firms' long-term specialization. For doing this, policy measures focused on technological innovation, R&D, and university research, but lack of geographical diversification consideration, especially the internationalization process of business. Government mainly relied on SOE as implementing units and administrative organizations as supervising units.

Through direct intervention and heavy investment, the local governments of Guangdong had become the biggest "entrepreneur," "investor" and "organizer" of industrial upgrading movement. Key industrial projects with huge investment were selected, and were supplemented by investment in public R&D and technological development programs, and supported by complete infrastructure building and renewing projects.

At lower level of government, the strategy of promoting industrial upgrading was concretized into a series of implementation details according to local specific situations, while the rationale of overall strategy was kept. Table 7.4 lists out the New Upgrading Policies of Shunde City Government in 2013 as an example. The similar policy and measure packages could be found across all the local governments in the Pearl River Delta.

Table 7.3 Guangdong Government's Strategic Instruments for Industrial Upgrading

Policy for Value Chain Upgrading		
Type of IU perceived by the government (policy target)		Upgrading along value chains (including firms' process upgrading, product upgrading and internal functional upgrading)
General Government Policies		– Sustain the upgrading of local suppliers – Facilitate the interactions among local firms, universities, institutes and other intermediaries – Assist SMEs in meeting international standards through regulatory framework – Provide public goods in critical bottleneck areas (infrastructure, labor skills) – Facilitate access and diffusion of knowledge and protection of IPR – Etc.
Government measures influencing short-term performance of firm, based on:	**Low-cost competitiveness** **Differentiation competitiveness**	– Fiscal measures to promote modern industrial system in Guangdong – Give priority to develop modern service industries (finance, exhibition, logistics, IT service, outsourcing bases, etc.) – Assign Dongguan City as "national processing industry transformation pilot zone" – Continue some specialized product cluster policy
Government measures influencing long-term performance of firm, based on:	**Diversification through firm internationalization**	
	Specialization through technological innovation	– Regulations on indigenous innovation promotion in Guangdong – Government procurement policy for innovation & own proprietary products – "Opinion on deepening science & research system reform" – Government innovation lead funds
Policy for Industrial Structure Upgrading		

(*continued*)

Table 7.3 (continued)

Policy for Value Chain Upgrading		
Type of IU perceived by the government (policy target)		Upgrading the whole industrial structure (creating or adding higher added-value sectors): including firms' external functional upgrading, inter-value chain upgrading, linkage upgrading
General Government Policies		– Encourage overseas investment of leading local companies to expose them to leading-edge innovations and management approaches – Promote access to new markets and value chains – Promote entrepreneurship and innovation in the PRD region – Attract international lead firms into local clusters – Generate dialogues at various levels among multiple participants – Etc.
Government measures influencing short-term performance of firm, based on:	**Low-cost competitiveness**	
	Differentiation competitiveness	– All kinds of infrastructure projects – Industry-University-Research alliance and cooperation programs
Government measures influencing long-term performance of firm, based on:	**Diversification through firm internationalization**	
	Specialization through technological innovation	– Solar battery R&D project; petro--chemical projects; automobile projects; general air crafts and aerospace industrial park; medical and biological industrial park – Sino-Singapore Knowledge City; CAS institutes in Guangdong – Introducing 3-5 foreign famous universities to cooperate higher education; building 1-2 national first class universities

Source: Zhao Wei (2014). From Industrial Policy to Upgrading Strategy: Dilemma of Local Developmental State in China's Pearl River Delta, China Economic Policy Review, Vol. 3, No. 1 (2014) 1450006 (32 pages), DOI: 10.1142/S179396901450006X"

Table 7.4 Main Policy Instruments of Industrial Upgrading by Shunde Government

Policy Category	*Policy Instruments*
Policy Programs for Firm Growth & Innovation	• « Dragon Flying » Project: 300 selected big firms • « Star Lighting » Project: 1000 selected small firms • « Backbone » Enterprises: 18 specific measures (e.g., supporting R&D institute building of Midea) • Incubators for entrepreneurs: 1 at national level, 3 at provincial level
Developing New Industrial Parks	• Connecting Midea Group zone and GD Industrial Design City zone • Constructing industrial parks of advanced manufacturing (5200 Chinese hectares): 1. Exhibition Park of innovations of digital-controlled machine tools 2. Production base of intelligent manufacturing: already assigned by MIIT as "Pilot Base of Informationized Industrialization of Equipment Industry"; 10 Robot factories, etc. • Constructing new parks of sectors of service to industry (320 thousand square meters): 1. Zones for firms in internet service of logistics/supply chain 2. Zones for firms of E-commerce • Constructing new parks of S&T and service 1. Southern Intelligence Valley (7.5 square kilometers): technical college; research institute; pharmaceutical industry; incubators; new urban area, etc. 2. Sino-German Industrial Service Zone (26 square kilometers): introducing high-end service companies for industrial sectors 3. High & New Tech & Industrial Development District (39 square kilometers): new urbanization with newly introduced firms; at provincial level
Creating Public Service for Innovation in Cooperation with Other Organizations	1. Introducing more national universities: 10 universities of 985 program and 40 university alliances 2. Building up on-line resource platform: website construction for all relevant organizations within the program 3. Building key platforms of innovation: allocate major resources to 7 selected R&D platforms/alliances between firms and research institutes

(*continued*)

Table 7.4 (continued)

Policy Category	*Policy Instruments*
HR and Social Policy	1. "1+10" program: 10 measures for introducing 10 innovation teams; 100 leading R&D staff; 1000 highly qualified talents; 10000 qualified staff 2. Social security benefits (education; fiscal subsidies; S&T support; housing aids; employment aids, etc.) to new permanent residents who accumulate enough marks; 3. Training system: short-term and long-term; within and beyond Shunde; qualification system; professional clubs; 4. Participating in projects of new business creation by immigrants.
Financial Support Policy	1. Create polite VC; 2. Create guarantee funds; 3. Create with existing banks some S&T specialized banks; 4. Set up policy company of financing & investment, etc.

Source: Zhao Wei (2014). From Industrial Policy to Upgrading Strategy: Dilemma of Local Developmental State in China's Pearl River Delta, China Economic Policy Review, Vol. 3, No. 1 (2014) 1450006 (32 pages), DOI: 10.1142/S179396901450006X"

Integrating Government Policy and Business Strategy for Industrial Upgrading

In the region of Pearl River Delta, the original idea of industrial upgrading was firstly put in agenda even before the 2008 crisis by the Provincial Government because it found unavoidable for the labor-intensive export processing firms to transform or upgrade themselves:

1. to transfer and relocate the processing activities to the regions around and outside the PRD;
2. to extend the industrial chains. Ideally the export processing firms shall transform from OEM mode of production to subcontract the design work or even carry out independent design activity. Firms shall create their own brands while expanding foreign as well as domestic markets.
3. to establish abroad production bases, marketing centers, research institutions and trade and economic cooperation. Capable firms shall possess overseas assets, master the key technology of foreign

SMEs through mergers and acquisitions, and build up own research institutions and marketing channel network in foreign countries;

4. to participate in the international division of labor in the global value chain by engaging in higher value-added activities and functions, such as supply chain integration management, brand management, and product innovation.

Industrial upgrading as a policy concept was then extended to more macro level of whole industries as a policy goal of transforming the existing industrial structure to a more modern one, highlighted by service industry, advanced manufacturing, emerging high-tech industries, besides the traditional export processing sectors. Technological innovations, particularly indigenous innovations would be used as a weapon to create this high-value-added modern industrial system. Local government was then the initiator and planner of the industrial upgrading in Pearl River Delta, as well as the most important propulsion.

However, the industrial upgrading strategy of government also had some challenges. In the reality of PRD region, the long-term expectations of local firms were dramatically modified by 2008 economic crisis and the subsequent market fluctuation. Facing the sudden increase in stocks and a shortage of working capital, most firms took a withdrawal and conservative strategy, instead of making efforts in technological innovation, international expansion and new business investment, as showed by the above results of questionnaire survey. Long-term projects were abandoned by private firms, especially those innovation projects with high risk and big capital investment. Firms' continuous upgrading and improvement in the period of stable economic growth was interrupted by crisis and replaced by all kinds of short-term reactions: cutting costs, business contraction, market shifting, finding ways for economy, and even closing down. The goal of private business sector was survival and money saving, not upgrading and innovation.

On the contrary, the Guangdong Government held its long-term perspective during crisis and recession. The government realized that once the crisis is over, the PRD needed an industrial foothold built on its long-term competitiveness of innovative firms in the world market. Having less confidence on firms' vision and determination of investing and upgrading, the Guangdong Government stepped directly in many high-stake and complex project investments, especially in new sector creation.

Besides, since industrial upgrading was initiated from the beginning by government as a political-economic course, it seemed to the government to be very natural to count on itself to find paths of upgrading the industries, not counting on existing firms mostly in traditional sectors. This was the reason why for the local governments in Guangdong, the industrial upgrading target contained mainly creation of new sectors through big projects of cooperation between SOE and public research organizations coordinated and directed by the local governments in the PRD, which became totally developmental State. The dilemma for such a local developmental State in industrial upgrading was that the more they put their hands directly on upgrading, the farer it was away from the initial objective of transforming the local firms in traditional sectors, since the majority of firms reacted to short-term impact toward other directions without being well integrated in the upgrading policy framework of government.

So, the real challenge of the industrial upgrading in the Pearl River Delta was that the Government should come up with a way to substitute the short-term expectation of firms with the long-terms expectations of the Government, so that the firms could make long-term investment in the key areas which were essential for the next round of world industrial competition, such as technology development, internationalization and new industry creation.

To meet this challenge, after setting up its upgrading goals for the whole industry, the Government identified the most effective firm behaviors which could lead to achieve these goals and elaborate the according policy measures to reinforce, stimulate or spread out these "best practices." The problem of government policy on industrial upgrading in the PRD was that most of the upgrading efforts at the firm level were the extension of government action, and most of the behavior of firms themselves fell outside the policy framework and purpose. In another word, there was too much "big State-firm leading strategy" and not enough "State-led networking strategy." In the government-made upgrading projects at firm level, there was also a tendency that the local super developmental government used more and more policy tools in the former planned economy to try to restructure a market economy composed by firms inserted in global value chain.

The experience of many rapid industrializing economies like South Korea and Taiwan showed that the IU goals of government could be achieved with according efforts made by firms. Normally, under pressures from competitors, firms had intrinsic motivation to carry out continuous improvement and constant technology upgrading in order to gain more market share or scale-economy. After reaching a certain level of profitability, firms could choose a variety of strategies to become more competitive, such as organic growth, technical innovation, diversification, market expansion, mergers and acquisitions, alliances, corporate venturing, manufacturing process optimization, being listed in stock market. If government could come out with appropriate industrial and technology policies, create favorable business environment, and provide supplementary support and guidance, a large number of firms would be able be transformed and upgraded smoothly and economic growth model can be changed.

Table 7.5 indicates the government goals of industrial upgrading and the corresponding supportive strategies of firms to fulfill the policy objectives. These firm strategies of upgrading are summarized from the

Table 7.5 Coherent Government Policies and Firm Strategies for Industrial Upgrading

Government Policies of IU	Modernization of industrial structure: driven by service sector and modern industrial sector; the latter contains mainly advanced manufacturing sector, strategic emerging sector, high-tech sector, and transformed traditional sector **Upgraded and integrated activities of value chain:** engaging in high added-value sections in global value chain (R&D, design, marketing, branding, etc.); massive transformation of firms from assembles production or OEM to ODM or OBM
Firm Strategies of IU	**Upgrading capabilities of technological innovation**: Actively engaging in technology, product and process development while establishing extensive cooperation relations with various scientific and technological organizations **Upgrading capabilities of international development**: Based on own technological and market capabilities, entering in high-value-added activities in global value chain; fully internationalization in functions of human resources, organization system, production operation, marketing and branding, technology development, and supply chain management **Upgrading capabilities of creating new business sectors for growth**: Create new business models in new sectors in using own technological or commercial advantages; the forms can vary from spin-off, intrapreneurship, business renewal to vertical integration and diversification, etc.

Source: Zhao Wei (2014). From Industrial Policy to Upgrading Strategy: Dilemma of Local Developmental State in China's Pearl River Delta, China Economic Policy Review, Vol. 3, No. 1 (2014) 1450006 (32 pages), DOI: 10.1142/S179396901450006X"

successful experience of other Asian economies, especially these of the Taiwanese firms. They are also justified by the above analysis on key measures influencing positively the firm performance of the questionnaire survey in Guangdong.

Thus, what the local developmental State in Guangdong needed was a more balanced strategy framework integrating the big State-firm leading projects and the State-led networking of local firms which could benefit from the spillovers of the upgrading projects of the former. This was not simply to avoid the risk of "State crowding out private," but to integrate in the upgrading framework the main traded sectors composed by existing local firms. These traded sectors were traditionally export-oriented, globalized in backward and forward linkages, and served as primary drivers of PRD economic growth. They could play a crucial role in fostering development by underlying all incremental growth and new business activity. Without being chosen as major target for upgrading, they were left in a business environment composed by increased labor costs, more tightly controlled utilization of land, rising prices of raw materials, reduced access to financial resources, and leveled up environmental criteria.

With the progress and deployment of industrial upgrading, the integrated strategy became eventually more balanced. It was above all more sector specific. For example, policy could promote more rather than less internationalization of the traditional export-oriented firms, which had been proved to be an effective way of firm upgrading. In fact, there existed various pathways of OEM producer upgrading through more international expansion. OEM or ODM spin-offs was the separation of branded product division from contract manufacturing and creating own brands. OEM or ODM start-ups was founding of factory-less (fabless) product firms that relied on global value chain for a range of inputs including production. Mixing of contract manufacturing (OEM) mode and own branded products (platform brands) for contractors was another way. Global expansion through acquisition of foreign declining brands could help upgrading. Mixing OEM and foreign brands acquired was also a step toward higher end of the value chain, etc.

Conclusion

After the financial crisis in 2008, the Pearl River Delta region, China's "factory of the world," was losing its comparative advantage and in urgent need of industrial transformation and upgrading. The regional governments, both at provincial and lower levels, developed a new agenda of industrial development, aiming at adjustment of economic structure. The former cluster policy in Guangdong then faded away. In the new era of China's investment-driven development, the local governments in Guangdong became the biggest investors, organizers, and operators of industrial restructuring projects, i.e., a super local developmental State. It counted on investment in large industrial projects which were concentrated on technological innovation activities and infrastructure sectors.

However, in the beginning, except the "emptying the cage for changing the birds" policy during 2007–1010, less consideration had been taken about geographical diverse of firms' expansion, especially in trade and international development. Meanwhile, most of the existing firms in the Pearl River Delta had rather short-term priorities on how to reduce production costs, how to solve the problem of survival, how to shift from production-for-export to domestic-market-development, and how to deal with the worsening business environment, etc. These strategic choices of companies were somehow in contrast to what was encouraged by the governments, such as huge investment in long-term R&D projects.

It was a big challenge for the local governments in Guangdong to find a coherent development model integrating its State-firm leading strategy and the latent State-led networking strategy. The governments reacted to the situation by going back to the fundamental aspects of firm behavior to find what kind of efforts would match well with the upgrading goals set by government and it constituted the new starting point of policy design.

As for the big State-firm leading projects and emerging sectors, the local governments learnt more from experience and lessons of developed economies such as US, Germany, and Japan (Berger, 2013; Herrigel, 2010) in terms of innovation-driven strategy. Government officials got more training on innovation management. New structures such as policy-oriented venture capital funds were progressively created to execute the function of strategic integration in managing innovation projects and R&D investment in cooperation with existing leading companies in the market. Government then redirected its focus on building concrete innovation ecosystems such as new industrial park, new incubators, and new technological zone, rather than search for abstract innovation system design. Geographic planning in the PRD served in fact as a concrete tool of innovation policy-making. The Guangdong local governments later created a series of R&D and innovation platforms, mixed of public and private funds, but also with big and small sizes. Some big public R&D

platforms like the famous Industrial Research Institute in Taiwan emerged, as well as the various industry-research-university alliances or networks at lower level of cities. All these important changes in strategy are the subjects of the following chapters that we are going to elaborate more in detail.

References

Amsden, A. H. (1989). *Asia's next giant. South Korea and the late industrialization*. Oxford University Press.

Amsden, A. H., & Chu, W.-w. (2003). *Beyond late development: Taiwan's upgrading policies* (p. 224). The MIT Press.

Berger, S. (2013). *Making in America: From innovation to market (with the MIT taskforce on production in the innovation economy)* (p. 264). MIT Press.

Ernst, D. (2014). *Upgrading India's electronics manufacturing industry: Regulatory reform and industrial policy, East-West Center special study* (p. 108). Honolulu.

Ernst, D. (2008). Innovation offshoring and outsourcing: what are the implications for industrial policy? *International Journal of Technological Learning, Innovation and Development, 1*(3), 309–329.

Evans, P. B. (1995). *Embedded autonomy: States and industrial transformation*. Princeton University Press.

Frederik, S., & Gereffi, G. (2011). Upgrading and restructuring in the global apparel value chain: Why China and Asia are outperforming Mexico and Central America. *International Journal of Technological Learning, Innovation and Development, 4*(1/2/3), 67–95.

Gereffi, G., & Kaplinsky, R. (2001). The value of value chains: Spreading the gains from globalisation. *IDS Bulletin, 32*(3).

Herrigel, G. (2010). *Manufacturing possibilities: Creative action and industrial Recomposition in the United States, Germany, and Japan* (p. 336). Oxford University Press.

Johnson, C. (1982). *MITI and the Japanese miracle: The growth of industrial policy, 1925–1975*. Stanford University Press.

Miberg, W., Jiang, X., & Gereffi, G. (2014). Industrial Policy in the Era of Vertically Specialized Industrialization. In J. Salazar-Xirinachs & R. Kozul-Wright (Eds.), *Industrial Policy for Economic Development: Lessons from country Experiences*. Palgrave Macmillan.

OECD. (2010). *OECD territorial reviews: Guangdong, China 2010* (p. 310). OECD Publishing. https://doi.org/10.1787/9789264090088-en

Porter, M. E., & Rivkin, J. W. (2012). *Prosperity at risk, findings of Harvard Business School's Survey on U.S. Competitiveness* (p. 23). HBS Project Report 2/2012.

Rodrik, D. (1995). Getting Interventions Right: How South Korea and Taiwan Grew Rich. *Economic Policy, 20.*

Schmitz, H., & Humphrey, J. (2000). Governance and *upgrading: Linking industrial cluster and global value chain research.* IDS Working Paper 120, IDS.

Seung-Wook, B. (2005). Does China follow "the east Asian development model"? *Journal Of Contemporary Asia, 35*(4), 485–497.

UNIDO. (2006). *Supporting industrial development: Overcoming market failures and providing public goods, UNIDO research Programme.* UNIDO.

UNIDO. (2011). *Industrial policy for prosperity—Reasoning and approach* (p. 41). Working paper 2011/2 of development policy, Statistics and Research Branch (DPR).

Wade, R. (1990). *Governing the market: Economic theory and the role of government in Taiwan's industrialization.* Princeton University Press.

Whittaker, D. H., Zhu, T., Sturgeon, T. J., Tsai, M. H., & Okita, T. (2008). *Compressed development* (p. 44). MIT IPC Working Paper 08–005.

World Bank. (1993). *The east Asian miracle: Economic growth and public policy.* Oxford University Press.

Zhao, W., & La Pira, F. (2013). Chinese entrepreneurship: Institutions, Ecosystems and Growth Limits. *Advances in Economics and Business, 1*, 72–88. https://doi.org/10.13189/aeb.2013.010204

Zhao, W., Arvanitis, R., & La Pira, F. (2011). Innovation policy and local cluster of entrepreneurs in South China. *International Journal of Management and Enterprise Development, 11*(2/3/4), 109–126.

CHAPTER 8

Regional Innovation Ecosystems from Below

Introduction

Since the year 2015, China has entered the stage of innovation-driven development. China's significant improvement of innovation performance during this phase is characterized by the geographically clustered regional innovation systems around the major metropolitan areas such as Beijing-Tianjin-Hebei region, the Yangtse River Delta around Shanghai, the Pearl River Delta around Shenzhen and Guangzhou, as well as a group of smaller but rapidly growing cities. Prior to 2020, before the outbreak of the COVID-19 pandemic, some indigenous innovation capabilities already emerged in regions such as Beijing, the Yangtze River Delta, the Pearl River Delta, and the Chengdu-Chongqing area, with a clear and strong tendency to become the influential technological centers.

Now, Beijing has become the center of technology innovation and has a large R&D talent pool. It is home to 26 of 112 key national universities designated by the Ministry of Education and research centers of global firms headquartered in the Zhongguancun district of north-eastern Beijing. Shanghai has the largest concentration of life science companies

This chapter is rewritten from a paper "Ecosystem as Policy Strategy: The Making of a Bottom-up Regional Innovation System in South China" to be published in *L'industria. Rivista di Economia e Politica Industriale*, 2026.

W. Zhao, *Remade in South China*, IPP Studies in the Frontiers of China's Public Policy,
https://doi.org/10.1007/978-981-95-7277-9_8

and the R&D operations of 11 of the 14 largest global pharmaceutical companies, many in its Zhangjiang Science and Technology Park. There are also contract research organizations to serve both Chinese and global companies with trials and other outsourced services in Shanghai.

As for Guangdong, its regional innovation system is mainly found in the core metropolitan area of the Pearl River Delta (PRD), composed of Shenzhen together with other cities such as Guangzhou, Zhuhai, Dongguan, Foshan, Zhongshan, Huizhou, all characterized by hardware innovation. The Pearl River Delta, traditionally known as the "world workshop in China," has become in recent years the most innovative manufacturing cluster, highlighted by the fast-growing strategic emerging industries such as IT, household appliances, LED lighting, robotics, and new energy vehicles and batteries. Shenzhen had 11,200 high-tech companies at national level, with high-tech sectoral industrial added value of 735.9 billion Yuan, 32% of Shenzhen total GDP. Shenzhen's export value has been on top of cities in China for the last 30 years, with almost 50% being high-tech products. Compared to the rapidly developing new cities like Shenzhen, old cities in the Pearl River Delta like Guangzhou and Foshan have longer tradition of industrial and research activities, but are all under transformation to develop more in emerging sectors and new technologies. In the transformation from the "world's factory" to an innovation-driven economy, the Pearl River Delta has eventually created a dynamic regional innovation system characterized by a high concentration of innovation entities, resources, and networks within its geographic space.

In the above regions of China, both thinking and practice of innovation policies have made progress with the rapidly improved regional and corporate innovation performance. It is evident that the Chinese State government and its innovation-driven development strategy played an important role in triggering the building of national innovation system (Appelbaum & Parker, 2008; Guo et al., 2016; Prud'homme, 2016). Meanwhile, new policy terms, such as "innovation chain," "innovation platform," "innovation ecosystem" and "innovation cluster," not only appeared in the documents of central government, but were also widely adopted and implemented by local governments. Many local governments, especially those in Guangdong, worked out, in a bottom-up way, some specific policy solutions to create ecosystems and platforms for promoting innovative activities, greatly helping local firms become creative and take the innovation path. These policies under the banner of innovation-driven development became more comprehensive and hybrid, surpassing traditional industrial policies, R&D policies, and science policies. The Chinese local governments gradually formed a new generation of regional innovation policies in practice (Zhao, 2023; Conle et al., 2021, 2022).

This chapter and the Chap. 9 will respectively concentrate on ecosystem policy and platform policy and how they are implemented at local level. Before we go there, it is worthwhile to have a general view on the main characteristics of the new generation of regional innovation policies in China. These new practical approaches of regional innovation development with Chinese characteristics can inspire other emerging and catch-up economies for their policy-making.

China's New Regional Innovation Policy: Characteristics

Policy as Practice

Though China entered into its desired stage of innovation-driven development already in 2015, it is until very recently that people begin to realize that the Chinese central government has shifted the innovation governance model from national science programs to the local government policies, which were more responsible for building high-tech parks or zones, local infrastructure, and other physical support related to innovation.

In fact, Chinese local governments were the "hidden-but-visible hands" behind its remarkable innovative rise, "translating" the innovation-driven development strategy of central government to concrete local policies and practice. They adopted policies for encouraging the co-location of public science institutions and innovative firms in high and new technology industrial zones and incentivizing universities and public research institutes to pursue the commercialization of S&T knowledge. They also strived to attract and capture technological and knowledge resources outside their own regions by integrating these resources in regional spatial planning, land development and urbanization construction (Wu, 2007, 2018; Zhang & Wu, 2019; Zhang, 2015).

Research on the role of Chinese local government and innovation policy has focused on both inputs such as patents and R&D expenditures and outputs such as firm performance and production outcome to evaluate the policy impact on regional innovation capacity and system evolution (Li,

2009; Yang, 2015; Boeing, 2016; Guan & Yam, 2015; Li & Georghiou, 2015; Wang & Wang, 2017). Some research also begins to reveal the planning, facilitating, and functioning roles of both central and local governments in industrial upgrading and innovation (Gruss & ten Brink, 2016; Zhang & Wu, 2019). But, due to difficulty in field access in China, most research have to assume that the innovation policy would be implemented eventually as stated by written document, leaving the process and practice of innovation policy by local government remain a "black-box."

Against this backdrop, innovation policy, which is implemented by local governments in China, shall be examined through participative observation of the de facto behavior of local governments themselves, not by checking only their written policy documents. Putting in another word, since the Chinese innovation policy can be found more in the practice and conduct of local governments than in the planning documents or official statements made by State leaders, and inspired by the management approach of "strategy as practice" (Bartels, 2018; Whittington, 1996, 2006), innovation policy in China shall be taken as practice and implementation process managed by local governments.

For example, the Chap. 9 will discuss the policy relevance of the new experimentalist form of "innovation platform" in regional innovation practice. All data and material of the case were collected directly from local government of the district. It reveals that at the very local level, innovation policy as practice is a highly mixed-up and integrated process composed of steps from targeting emerging industries, to constructing platforms, and to developing new clusters, during which the most important policy concept of "innovation platform" is used in a distinctive way by local government to effectively foster regional innovation-oriented development. In general, local government intervenes heavily in or even "manages" every step of the implementation process with specific policy approach and instrument. Managing regional development as a whole process of innovation, the entrepreneurial Chinese local government indeed plays a role of meso-level organizer equivalent to the innovation project manager in business sector.

Platform and Ecosystem

In terms of substance and instrument of innovation policy, existing research is concentrated on allocation and effectiveness of China's R&D subsidies, use of procurement, and other financial incentives (Boeing,

2016; Li & Georghiou, 2015; Guan & Yam, 2015; Guo et al., 2016). While in practice, Chinese local governments have recently invented and used widely a variety of new policy concepts, such as innovation chain, innovation ecosystem, innovative cluster, innovative district, innovation platform, and intelligent manufacturing system.

Among these emerging concepts and approaches of implementing regional innovation policy, "innovation platform" is doubtfully a most popular one. For local government officials, innovation platform represents all kinds of organizations situated at the interface between science and industry, including "innovation alliances," "industry associations," "innovation service platforms," "program platforms," and "innovation centers," etc. These platforms often perform functions of technological R&D, incubating, facilitating, intermediating, and pro-actively contributing to science-industry transfer and interaction, by soliciting and combing openly the external resources from key actors, such as universities, research institutes, and industrial firms. Some rare research has highlighted the ideal types and functions in technology transfer of the Chinese innovation platforms (Zhang et al., 2018; Conle et al., 2021), but their direct implication in innovation policy has to be clarified by more empirical analysis.

Similar to the concepts of "innovation chain" (Zhao, 2022) and "innovation platform"(Zhao, 2023), the notion of "innovation ecosystem" has also evolved in the policy practices of local governments in China. Local governments at all levels have established numerous "innovation clusters," "manufacturing parks," "science and technology parks," "development zones," "economic zones," "innovation districts," "characteristic towns," "innovation corridors," and "innovation valleys" as new geographic spaces for building the so-called innovation ecosystems. These innovative "spaces" have attracted and concentrated a growing number of innovative entrepreneurs, R&D projects, platform institutions, and startups, thereby constituting a region's competitive advantage.

Holistic Innovation Policy

Innovation platform and innovation ecosystem have become not only key policy concepts proposed in central government documents, but also the guiding principle, policy approach, and even a way of thinking in policy-making. This has made the new concepts an integral part of China's emerging regional innovation policy system with distinct Chinese characteristics. For example, in practice, local governments in the Guangdong

Province have operationalized the "innovation ecosystem" in a unique policy pathway, forming a relatively comprehensive policy system that integrates both horizontal policy tools and vertical governance structures.

Horizontally, since local governments generally view the "innovation ecosystem" as an economic and social environment conducive to innovation, they have adopted constructing an "innovation ecosystem" as the overarching policy goal. They have implemented various cross-sectoral and cross-functional policy measures covering innovation platforms, innovation spaces, innovation resources, technological entities, and industrial planning, thereby forming a comprehensive or "holistic innovation policy."

Multi-Layered Governance

Vertically, since local governments at multiple administrative levels—ranging from provincial and municipal to district, township, and even grassroots industrial parks and community-level administrations—implement innovation policies within their respective jurisdictions, the "innovation ecosystem policy" in Guangdong exhibits a multi-level governance structure. Furthermore, different levels of government prioritize horizontal policy tools differently.

The multi-level and cross-sectoral policy implementation for building a local "innovation ecosystem" has resulted in an unintended but significant outcome. From the perspective of firms, the policies of Guangdong local governments weave a dense and intricate network of supporting institutions and organizations. From the broader perspective of its Pearl River Delta as an administrative and geographic region, the regional innovation system increasingly resembles an ideal "ecosystem," reducing uncertainty, creating more opportunities, and effectively fostering the development of innovation projects and activities. Our findings highlight these local characteristics and operational mechanisms of China's emerging regional innovation policy system, and can offer valuable contributions to both the theory and practice of the holistic innovation policy.

Bottom-Up Approach

In academia, the rise of "innovation platform" and "innovation ecosystem" as new policy concepts has sparked an increasing number of empirical studies on China's regional and local innovation systems (Sun et al.,

2019; Ma et al., 2019; Huang et al., 2020; Tang et al., 2014). However, most previous research on China's innovation policies has primarily adopted a "top-down" perspective, focusing on the national innovation system and traditional industrial policies while analyzing policy documents issued by the central government. As a result, there has been relatively little attention given to local innovation systems, which serve as the "building blocks" and "cells" of the broader macro innovation system (Fu et al., 2012). Consequently, in-depth studies on how central government policies are applied and implemented as regional innovation policies by local governments remain limited, and little is known about the policy implementation processes at the bottom that shape the operation of regional innovation systems.

This book, from the very beginning, proposes to adopt a "bottom-up" approach to treat the innovation subject in China. This chapter takes the region of the Pearl River Delta in Guangdong as a case to examine how local governments construct regional innovation systems around the emerging policy concept of "innovation ecosystem," or how local governments in practice use the ecosystem-centered innovation policy as new-generation instruments to manage and promote innovation, entrepreneurship, projects, and venture development within the region. We will see that the innovation ecosystem-related policies were implemented at three geographic levels: local grassroots, urban districts, and the whole region. Together, they constituted a system or web of "innovation ecosystem policy" and had effective impact on business firms. With the formation of a system of local innovation policies, a regional innovation system emerged from "below."

"Innovation Ecosystem" as New Policy Approach

As an emerging innovation policy strategy and pathway, policies based on the concept of the innovation ecosystem exhibit two key characteristics. First, they are spatially bound, meaning that the "innovation ecosystem" is inherently linked to some specific geographic areas. Second, they are systemic and holistic, as they transcend functional domains and integrate various components of the innovation system within a given policy space, forming a complex policy system at the regional level. These two characteristics are particularly relevant when analyzing the innovation strategies of the local governments in China: the first relates to its administrative jurisdictions, while the second pertains to the mix of policy instruments.

Defining Innovation Ecosystem and Policy

The term "ecosystem" is borrowed from biology as a metaphor to describe and analyze the conditions necessary for innovation. It encompasses the environment, networks, resources, relationships, and other external factors that innovators and stakeholders require. The concept of the innovation ecosystem has emerged in response to the rise of knowledge-intensive activities, increased communication and connectivity among individuals and institutions, the mobility of talent and financial capital, the globalization of production, and evolving labor and social relations.

Innovation ecosystems are often defined as evolving networks of actors, activities, artifacts, institutions, and relationships—including both complementary and substitutive interactions—that are critical to the innovation performance of participants or groups of participants (Grandstrand & Holgersson, 2020). The micro-level and context-specific perspective distinguishes the innovation ecosystem concept from the more macro-structural national innovation system framework. It is often characterized by the following features:

1. Geographic and Localized Nature: Innovation ecosystems are inherently linked to specific spatial or geographic regions, aligning closely with the location of key innovation actors such as firms, entrepreneurs, and research institutions. However, their boundaries are fluid and may shift depending on actors' subjective definitions and the dynamic nature of innovation processes.
2. Non-Linearity of Innovation: Unlike the traditional "innovation chain" metaphor, which suggests a linear progression from research to commercialization, the innovation ecosystem perspective conceptualizes innovation as a continuously evolving networked process. This approach emphasizes the ongoing acquisition of resources, knowledge, and support, which enhances the competitive advantages and scalability of innovators.
3. Coupling, Self-Organization, and Co-Evolution: Innovation ecosystems function as symbiotic networks where actors are interdependent. The system as a whole exhibits self-organizing capability, coordination among participants, and collective evolution over time.

The widespread adoption of the "ecosystem" concept has led to the emergence of several closely related and sometimes overlapping frameworks, each emphasizing different aspects of innovation (Thomas & Autio, 2020), as described in the following:

1. For example, Berger (2005) defines "industrial ecosystems" as localized systems of capabilities accessible to firms, encompassing skills, capital, pre-competitive R&D, suppliers, facilities, and industry-specific knowledge. Companies can leverage these capabilities in conjunction with their internal resources to drive innovation (Berger, 2005; Pisano & Shih, 2012). The development of such production-related capacities, which are closely linked to firms, has the potential to accelerate innovation and create employment opportunities.
2. At its core, an innovation ecosystem shares similarities with a "business ecosystem," which refers to localized social networks that coalesce around ambitious and shared business objectives—such as those in biotechnology, electronics, pharmaceuticals, and software industries. However, the innovation ecosystem concept places greater emphasis on the enabling conditions that support firms in their pursuit of innovation. These conditions are often materialized through innovation platforms, research centers, and interconnected entities, including firms, departments, and global value chains.
3. An "entrepreneurship ecosystem" represents a specific form of an innovation ecosystem that fosters business model innovation at the ecosystem level, facilitating the emergence of new firms (Stam, 2015; Spigel, 2017).
4. Meanwhile, a "platform ecosystem"—sometimes referred to as a technological ecosystem—constitutes another variation of an innovation ecosystem but focuses on the role of technological interdependencies. Platform ecosystems organize interactions among firms through a shared technological architecture and standardized interfaces ('platforms'), thereby creating a relatively stable technological infrastructure alongside a collection of complementary modules developed by ecosystem participants.
5. Lastly, a "knowledge ecosystem" describes innovation ecosystems operating at the regional level within pre-competitive environments. Knowledge ecosystems consist of universities, public research institutions, intermediary organizations, and private enterprises collaborating to generate new knowledge as a systemic output. These ecosystems emphasize the development of institutional infrastruc-

ture, including education systems, intellectual property regulations, labor policies, and mechanisms for technological R&D, transfer, diffusion, and application.

As a new policy concept, the theory of innovation ecosystems provides a fresh guiding framework for policy-making. Firstly, localized innovation ecosystems have to become targets of policy. The geographic proximity that enables frequent interactions allows innovators and other participants to establish robust local networks, with numerous connections that provide access to unique resources. The clustering of innovation ecosystems is a result of enhanced innovation capabilities, rather than the cause of such capabilities.

Secondly, the construction of innovation ecosystems has also become an objective for policy implementation. Schilling and Phelps (2007) argue that the concentration of regional innovation is not a result of "clusters," but rather a "capture" of national policy by localities. The government plays the role of a coordinator within the innovation ecosystem, helping or facilitating interactions among stakeholders to promote the co-evolution and co-creation of value, ultimately driving innovation in products and services (Iansiti & Levien, 2004). Innovation activities and public investments can create or attract essential resources for ecosystem, such as technological knowledge, financial capital, manufacturing facilities, and skilled labor. Government interventions, including investments in universities, public venture capital, the establishment of incubators, and training programs, can enhance the resources of the innovation ecosystem and foster strong networks among innovators based on a supportive cultural foundation (Adner, 2006; Adner & Kapoor, 2010; Spigel & Harrison, 2018).

The Spatial Approach of Innovation Ecosystem Policy

The regional characteristics of innovation ecosystems determine that innovation ecosystem policies must address specific geographic spaces as their policy targets (Morisson & Doussineau, 2019). The literature on innovation, particularly on innovation geography, has considered various spatial dimensions, from local or suburban areas, urban or metropolitan regions, to larger areas such as regions, nations, supranational entities, and even global scales. Scholars have proposed various concepts to describe innovation spaces with different scopes and characteristics, such as Marshallian industrial districts, Italian industrial districts, innovative places, regional innovation systems, new industrial spaces, localized learning, and regional clusters (Scaringella & Radziwon, 2018). The typical concepts include:

1. For example, the concept of "regional innovation systems" is often geographically defined by regional boundaries intended to represent an administrative division of a country (Cooke & Leydesdorff, 2006). The Silicon Valley regional innovation ecosystem consists of a venture capital-centered financial system, a highly skilled labor market, interactions between academia, government, and industry, balanced industrial organizations between large and small enterprises, an entrepreneurial culture, as well as professionals such as law firms and accounting firms (Kenney, 2000).
2. A regional innovation system can include many smaller regions, and for these smaller areas, the concept of "industrial districts" proposed by Becattini is more suitable. He defined industrial districts as a social territorial entity characterized by active communities and business populations within a natural and historical boundary. In such regions, communities and companies tend to merge differently from other environments (Becattini, 2002). In the case of the Lombardy region of Italy, where he conducted his study, connections between companies and institutions within the "sub-region" of innovation are more developed, leading to local innovation systems reflected in their specific knowledge bases. In this case, only local policies can provide highly efficient and effective support to meet the needs of companies and institutions in local communities (Muscio, 2006).
3. Similar to local innovation systems, "industrial clusters" are defined as regional agglomerations of industries and services characterized by close interactions between suppliers and users, involving various learning networks among companies and public and private actors. Porter (1998) defines industrial clusters as "geographic concentrations of interconnected companies and institutions in a particular field, including a set of interrelated industries and other entities critical to competition." Clusters are regarded as places where close communication between companies, social-cultural structures, and institutional environments can stimulate collective learning and continuous innovation embedded in society and geography (Asheim & Isaksen, 2002).

4. Also, as a new urban economic spatial ecosystem, "innovation districts" are highly concentrated geographic areas featuring advanced research institutes, R&D organizations, entrepreneurial firms, business incubators, accelerators, and financial institutions. These districts primarily exist in city centers or metropolitan areas, without clear spatial boundaries at the regional periphery. They are also physically compact, with seamless transportation, wired technology, and a mixed layout offering residential, office, commercial functions, and public services (Bruce Katz & Julie Wagner, 2015).

There are many other concepts regarding the spatial patterns of innovation, but these concepts all highlight some shared characteristics of innovation in specific geographic spaces (Scaringella & Radziwon, 2018):

1. A specific territorial industry with a unique atmosphere and varying scales;
2. A set of shared values, such as trust, mutual understanding built on a common history, culture, and conventions;
3. A diverse group of stakeholders, including companies of various sizes, research institutes, universities, and policy-makers at different stages of the value chain;
4. A strong economic foundation based on localized economies, agglomeration economies, transaction cost theory, local spillovers, and economies of scale;
5. A strong social foundation based on collaborative coexistence and competition, with a focus on social and human capital;
6. The central role of different types of knowledge (tacit and explicit), which circulate well through dissemination and are effectively absorbed through reinforced learning.

Policies targeting these specific geographic or territorial innovation spaces are often referred to as spatial innovation policies or place-based innovation policies. Different spatial scales can be seen as evolving members of a multi-level governance system, and therefore, spatial policies for innovation are crucial to the future economic development of regions (Asheim & Isaksen, 2002). In many countries, governments delineate and plan the geographic scope of innovation through spatial innovation policies, such as industrial development zones, science parks, high-tech and industrial parks, innovation clusters, special economic zones, and "supply chain cities" (Moulaert & Sekia, 2003).

In China, within the administrative boundaries of city government, innovation spaces are explicitly defined as economic and technological development zones and high-tech development zones, with different levels of these zones recognized by various levels of the national government. These development zones and industrial parks are substantive operational units managed by government development companies and quasi-governmental organizations (Zhang & Wu, 2019).

On a larger geographical scale, the Chinese government also considers entire cities or metropolitan areas as ecosystems for innovation. A frequently used policy tool in local government spatial innovation policies is land zoning. Many innovation zones require different zoning regulations from outdated land uses designed to protect health and safety, such as spatial separation for housing, offices, businesses, and manufacturing, and in some cases, a complete overhaul of existing infrastructure.

For example, Shanghai's high-tech parks expanded from six parks to 22, covering the entire metropolitan area. Su and Hung consider the Zhangjiang High-Tech Park, which represents a typical "policy-driven" approach (Su & Hung, 2009). A prominent management office is chaired by the Mayor of Shanghai. This change can be viewed as a form of branding and a policy for spreading and replicating the Zhangjiang innovation model (Zhang, 2015). The development of land zoning in Shanghai's innovation zones has promoted linkage, incorporating highly innovative companies that gain additional effectiveness through connections with knowledge centers, markets, and one another.

In the US, at the end of the twentieth century, the uprising of innovation regions such as Silicon Valley, the Research Triangle, and Boston's metropolitan "knowledge regions," as well as government investments in basic and applied sciences and public universities, meant that governments could provide institutional foundations for innovation ecosystems, laying the groundwork for the generation and commercialization of ideas, as well as the creation and expansion of companies. From a policy perspective, the "grouping approach" as a policy tool (Borrás & Tsagdis, 2008) has played a role in managing interfaces, deconstructing and organizing systems, providing learning platforms, strategic intelligence, and stimulating demand (Smits & Kuhlmann, 2004). Governments at various levels recognize that by developing their strategic capabilities, they can mobilize resources and institutions to promote local development (Cooke & Morgan, 1998).

Furthermore, as the geographic "space" or scope of innovation expands, the organization and institutional depth of policies must also increase to improve the cohesion of local economies (Isaksen & Trippl, 2017; Tödtling & Trippl, 2005).

The Systematic and Holistic Approach of Innovation Ecosystem Policy

The systemic nature of innovation ecosystems dictates that innovation ecosystem policies have characteristics of both holism and systematism, particularly in terms of policy tool combinations and policy implementation. The main objective of innovation ecosystem policies is to actively influence the environment in which innovation processes occur, making them holistic policies. These policies are sometimes referred to as "broad-based innovation policies," "systemic innovation policies," "demand-pull approaches," and "demand-driven policy tools." They are defined as integrating all public actions that influence or could potentially influence the innovation process (Edquist, 2018). Holistic innovation policies comprehensively consider all significant economic, social, political, organizational, institutional, and other input factors that affect innovation development, diffusion, and use, and coordinate all activities that influence the innovation process in a "customized" manner. These activities primarily include (Borrás & Edquist, 2019):

1. Knowledge production and R&D (Research and Development)
2. Building knowledge capabilities through education, training, and skills development
3. Formation of new product markets (demand-side innovation procurement)
4. Clarification of quality requirements (also in terms of demand)
5. Organizational changes through entrepreneurship and intrapreneurship (creation and modification of organizations)
6. Interaction and formation of innovation networks
7. Creation and modification of institutional mechanisms
8. Incubation and acceleration of entrepreneurial and small businesses
9. Innovation financing
10. Consulting services

Within a specific regional scope, innovation ecosystem policies designed according to the above holistic principles essentially constitute a complex innovation policy system. According to innovation policy theory, this system includes two aspects: "policy mix" and "policy governance," both of which are complex and diverse in nature (Magro & Wilson, 2013).

Firstly, the "policy mix" encompasses the areas of policy intervention and the combination of policy tools. In terms of policy areas or domains, innovation policies include all policies that affect the innovation process and are interconnected with various other policy fields, such as research policy, education policy, labor market policy, public procurement policy, defense equipment policy, energy policy, transportation policy, healthcare policy, environmental policy, and regional policy, as well as macroeconomic policy, among others. These policies often involve actions by many government departments and agencies. Therefore, when formulating innovation policies, integration and coordination become crucial, and the government must transition from being a service provider and regulator to being a coordinator and facilitator (Edquist & Hommen, 2008). In terms of policy tools, innovation policies typically have three types of instruments:

1. regulatory tools,
2. economic and financial policy tools, and
3. soft policy tools.

Innovation policy tools are usually combined in specific configurations, used simultaneously in a complementary manner to address innovation system challenges (Borrás & Edquist, 2013). The term "policy tool mix" is more precise than the general term "policy mix" (Flanagan et al., 2011). In the day-to-day process of policy formulation and design, the selection of policy tools is rarely driven by clearly defined goals and indicators. Typically, they may be inspired by similar interventions from other governments and chosen based on broad and inadequately analyzed intervention rationales.

Secondly, the characteristics of innovation ecosystem policies in terms of "policy governance" include the "multi-departmentality" and "multi-levelness" of the governing bodies (Guimon, 2014). Since innovation policies span multiple fields, their implementation often requires a whole-of-government approach, where various government departments participate. At the same time, within the same geographic region, the vertical division of policy power across different levels leads to overlap and accumulation of innovation policy tools from different government levels, forming a multi-level governance structure for regional innovation policies.

Sometimes, the division of powers is clear, as these levels of government have exclusive powers, while at other times, powers are shared. For instance, in Europe, support policies for incubators often come simultaneously from the EU, national, regional, and city governments. However, other policies, such as support for the public or regulatory oversight of research institutions, are concentrated at one particular level of government (Magro & Wilson, 2013). Therefore, the specificity of the national government structure is critical, and the policy tools designed and developed through its multi-level power division lead to multi-level governance of innovation policies within regions (Borrás & Edquist, 2019).

Framework of Innovation Ecosystem Policy

The concept of the innovation ecosystem itself provides a method for formulating innovation policies, starting from the perspective of innovation actors. It describes the external connections and necessary conditions at the micro level, which can serve as the targets for policy intervention. The concept of "innovation space" as the target of policy reflects both the physical and social spaces of innovation activities, as well as the geographic scope covered by the policy, and is therefore also referred to as "policy space" (Uyarra & Flanagan, 2010). Innovation ecosystem policies are holistic and systematic, encompassing a variety of combinations and specific designs of policy areas and policy tools. The organizational and implementation methods of these policies often exhibit multi-level governance characteristics. The above review of concepts and theories indicates that a systematic framework of innovation ecosystem policies within a specific region should consist of three key parts (Fig. 8.1):

1. the "space" of innovation ecosystem as the policy target,
2. the policy mix for the innovation ecosystem, and
3. the governance structure as implementation foundation.

In the following parts of the chapter, we will use this framework and employ a single case study design (Yin, 2018) to examine the innovation ecosystem policies implemented by governments at various levels within the PRD region as a whole.

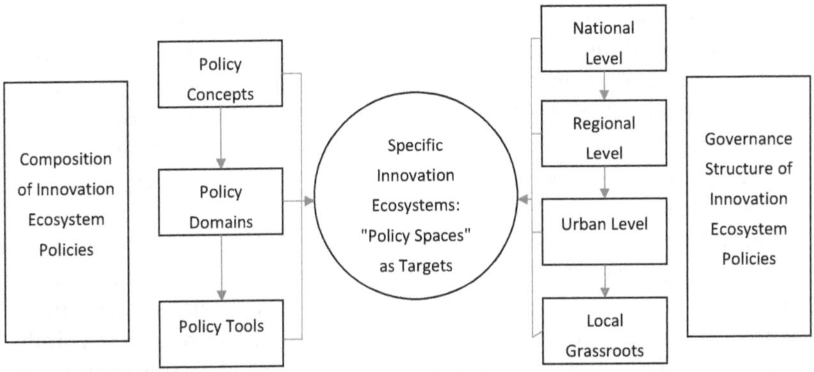

Fig. 8.1 A Framework of innovation ecosystem policy. (Source: Adapted from the framework of the innovation policy system by Magro and Wilson [2013])

The Case of the Pearl River Delta

As mentioned before, the Pearl River Delta (PRD) is located in the central-southern part of Guangdong Province. It accounts for less than one-third of Guangdong's total land area, but it is home to 53.35% of the province's population. In 2023, the combined GDP of the nine cities in the PRD reached 11.02 trillion Yuan, accounting for 81.24% of Guangdong's total GDP. According to a World Bank report, the PRD surpassed Tokyo in 2010 to become the largest urban agglomeration in the world in terms of population and area.

The PRD is now a global hub for advanced manufacturing and modern services, a key region for China's participation in economic globalization, a national base for scientific innovation and technological research and development, and an important engine for national economic development. Given that the PRD is one of the three largest urban agglomerations in China, with the highest population density, innovation capacity, and overall strength, its local innovation policies are among the most successful in China and have been widely imitated by other regions. By studying the PRD case, we gain insight into many emerging features of regional innovation policies in China.

The PRD is administratively part of Guangdong Province and is composed of nine prefecture-level cities: Guangzhou, Foshan, Zhaoqing, Shenzhen, Dongguan, Huizhou, Zhuhai, Zhongshan, and Jiangmen. These cities manage large territories, including urban districts, surrounding counties, county-level districts, and county-level cities. According to administrative divisions, different levels are designated as rural or urban, including towns, townships, villages, streets, and residential committees.[1] Amazingly, constructing an "innovation ecosystem" has been explicitly recognized by the local governments at all hierarchical levels as an overarching goal and guided various policy tools for implementation.

Our observation encompasses the entire PRD region, but we will focus more on lower-level areas (districts, towns, and cities) as specific examples for deeper analysis. Only through analyzing the public policies implemented by various government levels within the PRD region that influence or may influence the innovation process can we better capture the nature, characteristics, and effects of the PRD's local innovation policies.

The majority of the first-hand materials and data were collected through intensive field research and structured interviews with local government officials and their affiliated agencies between 2016 and 2019. During this period, our research team was involved in several strategic consulting projects for the Guangdong provincial government regarding innovation policies, which allowed us to access internal government documents and policy discussions.

We first examined publicly available information, such as research reports, annual reports, and various internal materials and statistical data provided by local governments, to develop more detailed research questions. We then visited relevant government agencies and interviewed government officials. Each in-depth interview lasted about two hours, with each visit typically lasting half a day. The local governments we interviewed included: Longgang District (Shenzhen), Shenzhen City, Huizhou City,

[1] The administrative hierarchy of local governments in China consists of five levels from top to bottom. In this article, we roughly divide them into three major levels: Regional, City/Urban, and Local.

Regional level contains:

1. Provinces, autonomous regions, and municipalities directly under the central government
2. City/urban level contains:
3. City and prefecture level cities
4. District, municipal district, county
5. Local grassroots level contains:
6. Streets, towns, townships, and industrial areas
7. Neighborhood committees, villages, and industrial parks

Guicheng Street (Foshan's Chancheng District), Shunde District (Foshan), Nanhai District (Foshan), Foshan City, Guangzhou City, Chang'an Town (Dongguan), Changping Town (Dongguan), Dongguan City, and Guangdong Province (General Office). Throughout the research process, we cross-checked between interviews and documents, holding regular discussions to verify issues or discuss new findings. In addition to formal interviews, we also used personal observations and informal discussions to corroborate data from other sources.

Local Ecosystem: Policy of Platform and Cluster

In the Pearl River Delta region, the primary policy actors at the grassroots level are government entities responsible for managing development zones, industrial parks, technology parks, and even large real estate development projects, such as management committees for these areas, as well as departments overseeing public incubation parks and incubators. Additionally, local government administrations of districts, streets, and towns and villages within urbanized areas also play significant roles, with municipal governments often involved as well. Given that grassroots governments are tasked with attracting investment and fostering local economic and industrial development, their focus is primarily on creating a favorable investment and business environment, essentially providing firms with a sound "business ecosystem."

In the context of higher-level government guidelines advocating the development of "innovation ecosystems," the policy approach at the grassroots level has shifted toward attracting more technologically advanced firms and entrepreneurial projects. In practice, grassroots governments have increasingly recognized that by introducing and establishing various "innovation platforms" and spatially clustering investment projects with platform characteristics, they can rapidly foster local industrial clusters. As a result, the main strategy of grassroots innovation policies has become the active support of platform-based innovation and entrepreneurship projects, creating "platform ecosystems" and, in turn, fostering the geographical clustering of these platform organizations (Zhao, 2023).

Ecosystem Policy of Platform

In terms of the areas covered by innovation ecosystem policies, grassroots governments focus on establishing innovation entities, particularly by creating various innovation platform organizations (called "platforms"), and developing a combination of policy tools to encourage these entities to engage in scientific and technological research and development activities. In the practices of many grassroots level governments in the Pearl River Delta, platforms serve as "hub-type" institutions that are internally multifunctional and externally well-connected. These platforms help identify the key elements of innovation within the local development process. Grassroots governments, through platform projects and organizations, essentially create new entities or potential industry participants, not limited to merely intermediary organizations for innovation activities.

Innovation platforms are, in fact, emergent and transitional organizations with various development potentials. In the future, they may evolve into technology intermediary institutions, technological infrastructures (incubators, regions, parks, etc.), investment funds or technology finance institutions, new research and development institutions, even emerging start-ups or new companies, and participants from other industries. The inherent external connections of these platforms provide them with a "genetic" tendency to form innovation ecosystems. In some cases, the purpose of establishing these platforms is to provide commercial services for other institutions and projects, serving as relatively pure innovation and entrepreneurship service institutions (such as incubators).

As the platform develops and expands, it naturally forms a small ecosystem capable of accommodating more innovation projects. Grassroots local governments thus build their industrial chains and supporting infrastructure around such institutions, gradually forming a development advantage for platforms and innovative enterprises within their jurisdictions. For example, in Changan Town of Dongguan City, the focus is on developing the mold industry, with the establishment of the National Hardware Mold Supervision and Testing Center, as well as a partnership with the Massachusetts Institute of Technology to set up the Changan Hardware Mold Research Center. Through the establishment of such innovative platforms, Changan Town has introduced new stakeholders, aiming to effectively connect the local traditional hardware mold manufacturing industry, advanced mold technology, and external knowledge experts.

Ecosystem Policy of Cluster

Another important area of grassroots innovation policy is the development of local industrial clusters. With the establishment of numerous innovation entities and platform organizations, grassroots governments have begun to build local industrial clusters based on these micro-level "units." The typical approach is when the development of a platform project requires external support in the form of a commercial ecosystem, grassroots government policies will focus on cluster development around the project. Grassroots governments gather platforms of similar industries together, forming specific small parks, such as industrial parks, science parks, and development zones, to provide the necessary foundational services. In another scenario, when the constructed project is a large-scale one that functions both as a research and development institution and an innovation service platform, the formation of external networks and the service functions of the R&D activities will simultaneously create a complex innovation ecosystem around the project. On the one hand, the platform serves as the ecosystem foundation for other projects; on the other hand, the platform itself will also have extensive external networks and connections. This type of project is particularly favored by the grassroots governments. For example, the CNC Equipment Research Institute at Guangdong University of Technology in Nanhai District, Foshan, is not only an incubator but also plays a crucial role in linking universities with enterprises for cooperation.

The emphasis on industrial clusters also signifies a shift in innovation policy from the organizational domain to the spatial domain, which characterizes local innovation ecosystems with both geographical proximity and regional scope. Industrial clusters represent the direct and immediate business environment outside of companies and serve as their fundamental innovation environment. Grassroots governments are highly experienced and skilled in land zoning, planning, and development. They establish basic administrative institutions such as offices or committees to manage these areas. The industrial cluster administrations planned and developed include industrial zones, technology parks, entrepreneurial parks, and specialized towns. Grassroots governments focus on gathering innovation platforms geographically when they are to be established and invest in the construction of the park's infrastructure (such as roads and telecommunications).

For example, in Nanhai District, Foshan, multiple emerging industrial clusters have been planned around the established technology innovation platforms: the Sanshan Qian Deng Lake area, the Nanhai Sanshui Industrial Cooperation Zone, the Foshan West Station Hub New City, Foshan National High-tech Zone, the Guangdong Financial High-tech Zone, Foshan Nanhai Electronic Information Industrial Park, and various technology innovation towns with distinct industry characteristics that can be developed by township and street-level governments. Among these, the Sanshan Qian Deng Lake area is centered around the Jihua Laboratory, with plans to create an innovative, resource-intensive, talent-concentrated, and achievement-focused eco-friendly innovation town. A series of innovation platforms, represented by the Jihua Laboratory, are planned to accelerate the industrialization of technology, bringing in high-end manufacturing projects such as the industrialization of stretching rheology technology, 3D printing, and flexible display materials. To support these technology projects, the Nanhai District government has planned a 100-acre talent apartment plot, a park greenbelt, and service areas for daily living. Additionally, specific policies have been formulated to promote the renovation of surrounding village-level industrial parks.

Industrial clusters normally consist of platform organizations and their business ecosystems. Once an industrial cluster begins to take shape, grassroots governments provide more general policies related to capital, labor, technology, and information to further enhance the cluster. For example, by establishing regional branding organizations for local marketing and promotion activities, investing in public technology development centers and testing centers, and facilitating strong collaboration among suppliers, manufacturers, and customers within the established manufacturing ecosystem.

Strong grassroots governments also formulate local industrial policies and plans, selecting priority industries and corresponding vertical measures. However, horizontal industrial policies often rely on higher-level governments. For example, in Chang'an Town of Dongguan, the policies have been tailored to attract talent and train workers in response to the newly established research and testing innovation platforms, including the international hardware mold exhibitions and joint exhibitions. Furthermore, a combination of policies is used to encourage the overseas expansion of local businesses, develop related technology services, and adjust resource allocation, thus forming resource complementarities.

City and Urban Ecosystem: Policy of District and Entrepreneurship

The spatial scope at the urban level in the Pearl River Delta is broader than that of local grassroots areas. This includes cities of a certain scale within urbanized areas, some districts within large metropolitan areas (each of which could be considered a medium-sized city on its own), or rapidly growing new development zones on the edges of urban built-up areas. Typically, the administrative levels at this spatial level are higher. The main policy actors at this level are usually municipal governments, specifically the nine prefecture-level cities in the Pearl River Delta. However, district-level governments in large cities with extensive jurisdiction (such as Longgang District and Nanshan District in Shenzhen) and governments of key development areas located further from the urban center (such as Nansha District in Guangzhou) also fall into this category. These governments have broad and comprehensive management responsibilities, but their primary functions are the construction and development of the city itself, both in terms of software (policies and systems) and hardware (infrastructure).

Key areas in urban construction include investment, land development, and infrastructure. This is especially true when the cities they manage are undergoing rapid urbanization driven by technological and business transformation. Therefore, when these cities or districts set the goal of building an "innovation ecosystem," they typically begin by emphasizing the construction and renovation of the city's hardware infrastructure to create a more attractive, modern metropolitan environment to attract innovators and entrepreneurs. At the urban level, infrastructure development focuses on urban transportation, telecommunications, and energy systems. Specific policy measures largely revolve around the establishment of various innovation and entrepreneurship incubators, incubation parks, and using these incubator spaces as integral components of urban development and renewal. The result is the creation of a unique form of urban innovation ecosystem in the Pearl River Delta, where innovation districts and entrepreneurial ecosystems co-exist and thrive within the cities.

Ecosystem Policy of District

Under the policy guidelines for building urban innovation ecosystems, the governments in various cities and districts in the Pearl River Delta have launched a range of spatial policies for developing "innovation districts," such as urban renewal, redevelopment of old neighborhoods, and the development of new districts to expand urban areas. The aim is to improve infrastructure and physical space, utilizing the diverse resources of mature urban areas to accommodate new institutions, industries, and technological projects. This has gradually spread the innovation spaces in the Pearl River Delta from "parks" on the outskirts of cities to "districts" closer to the urban core.

Before the outbreak of the COVID-19 pandemic, with the combination of entrepreneurial incubators like innovation valleys and startup bases with real estate development projects, large-scale urban projects emphasizing hardware facilities and infrastructure support for "entrepreneurial real estate" also flourished. These entrepreneurial real estate projects emphasize mixed-use land development, breaking away from traditional zoning and incremental planning. They integrate the renovation of old districts with the development of new ones, aiming to introduce more cultural and technological content into traditional urban areas with comprehensive residential, business, and service functions. This enriches the social and economic components of the district renewal. Cities have increased public planning and investment, introducing new public transport routes, designing pedestrian-friendly streets, and creating new public spaces and housing.

The planning of innovation districts emphasizes communication, cooperation, and integration, so spatial compactness and geographical proximity have become priority criteria. Each city aims to build an "urbanized science park," densely positioning research activities and business ventures in the city center to create a vibrant atmosphere. Essentially, this integrates innovation ecosystems into the city's "space" and promotes the diversification of innovation ecosystems by utilizing the high density and mixed use of city centers. To achieve this, many cities have branded their innovation districts with physical elements to enhance their visual landscape. For example, they use urban design elements such as building massing, street design, public spaces, materials, and plants; gateway signs marking entrances to the district; and digital displays, lighting, signage, and banners along key corridors, district gateways, and public spaces—each carrying the district's logo.

For instance, Longgang District in Shenzhen has embraced the innovation policy concept of "fully utilizing ample land space to transform Longgang into a huge super incubator." Taking advantage of the World University Games held in Shenzhen in 2011, the district updated important infrastructure and developed a cluster of international university campuses, ultimately attracting institutions like the Chinese University of Hong Kong. Longgang also redeveloped its old districts into entrepreneurial spaces, collaborating with real estate developers to build related communities and introducing specialized incubation service companies and incubator park management firms like Tianan Digital City and TUS Park.

Ecosystem Policy of Entrepreneurship

Similarly, the government of Chang'an Town in Dongguan has undertaken large-scale redevelopment of old factory land into incubators, accelerators, and advanced manufacturing parks. In line with the policies for innovation districts, another type of city-level policy is the establishment of various incubator platforms and venture capital institutions. These policies focus on creating various entrepreneurial parks and incubation centers to attract entrepreneurial projects, thus fostering the so-called "innovation and entrepreneurship ecosystem."

From a bottom-up perspective, the entrepreneurial ecosystem is an ongoing process of developing connections and expanding resources. The entrepreneurial ecosystem must ensure that initially lacking resources are provided to the relevant agents, such as capitalists, raw material suppliers, and skilled individuals.

The city governments in the Pearl River Delta also made great efforts to cultivate a social atmosphere conducive to innovation districts and to provide better social services for innovators. First, city governments have introduced or encouraged the establishment of professional community members not found in other types of ecosystems, such as startup accelerators, co-working spaces, entrepreneurial spaces, entrepreneurship academies, university entrepreneurship programs, crowdfunding platforms, angel investors, venture capital, and mentors. The innovation districts in city centers have successfully attracted numerous universities to settle in their districts, creating new attractions and providing a shared space for students, researchers, and entrepreneurs to innovate together.

Second, city governments have developed entrepreneurial incubation as a unique industry. As a leader of Longgang District in Shenzhen put it: "In Longgang, we provide all the necessary factors to make projects easily achieve their innovation goals." The district government has not only established multiple incubators, makerspaces, accelerators, and entrepreneurial parks but has also actively fostered venture capital companies and providers of other "innovation elements." Longgang District has specifically dedicated an entire building to gather various new R&D institutions and technology service companies, forming a tech service industry cluster. The government has also concentrated intellectual property law firms in one building, creating a "knowledge property legal cluster." Similarly, Shenzhen has established an investment service system specifically for its Futian High-tech Zone. The development zone includes 90 incubators where enterprises can enjoy policy support and professional services in areas such as land, factories, funding, human resources, and logistics.

Ecosystem Policy of City

As urban land development and infrastructure progress, geographically proximate entrepreneurial ecosystems will form larger-scale urban innovation ecosystems, such as interconnected science and technology parks and educational parks, which integrate with broader urban spaces. The new urban innovation ecosystems can then be used by local authorities as larger platforms to attract more external resources. This process is dynamic and exhibits an upward spiral trend, achieving the joint evolution of innovation districts and entrepreneurial ecosystems.

In addition to innovation districts and entrepreneurship ecosystem policies, there are other common local policy tools at the city level in the Pearl River Delta, particularly those that mobilize and connect various innovation elements. For example, Huizhou has formulated policies to encourage the establishment of enterprise-level R&D centers, with 40% of large enterprises having set up formal R&D centers. The government also encourages small and medium-sized enterprises to establish internal laboratories and nurtures high-tech startups. Huizhou actively promotes industry-university-research alliances, including collaborating to establish technology transfer centers, organizing technology trade fairs, and forming alliances between businesses, universities, and research institutes. It has set up key technology development projects or patent development projects and is advancing technological transformation projects within manufacturing enterprises.

In terms of talent attraction, almost all city governments in the Pearl River Delta have specific plans and programs for talent recruitment and introduce talent programs, with talent workstations established overseas for recruitment purposes. Regarding attracting funding, city governments have set up pilot funds, venture capital funds, and created local science and technology financial service platforms. These policies can all be considered part of the broader innovation ecosystem policies.

Regional Ecosystem: Policy of Innovation and Knowledge

The Pearl River Delta is a regional-level innovation space, but sometimes regions slightly smaller than the Pearl River Delta, such as the expanded metropolitan areas of Guangzhou and Shenzhen, can also be considered at this spatial level. This is because these large cities contain a greater number of grassroots spaces and urban spaces, which form a secondary level of innovation ecosystems. The primary policy-makers at the regional level are the Guangdong provincial government and the municipal governments of Guangzhou and Shenzhen, but there is also direct intervention from the central government, especially after the central government officially named the Pearl River Delta and the Hong Kong-Macau region as the overall "Guangdong-Hong Kong-Macau Greater Bay Area." In fact, since the central government issued the overall planning outline for the Pearl River Delta in 2009, the creation of an integrated regional innovation system for the Pearl River Delta has been the goal and concept of regional innovation policies. Therefore, broadly speaking, the policies aiming at building the Pearl River Delta's regional innovation system are considered regional-level innovation ecosystem policies.

Ecosystem Policy of Region

In terms of policy tools, regional innovation policies in the Pearl River Delta closely resemble the standard national innovation system model, which emphasizes building innovation capabilities and institutions. Since policies are primarily implemented by cities and lower-level governments, regional-level policies are typically comprehensive plans and strategies, with the central and provincial governments providing guidance and coordinating actions for local governments. In recent years, as competition between regions in China has intensified regarding innovation-driven development, the Guangdong provincial government and the governments of major metropolitan cities have become more active in securing national-level projects from the central government and leveraging research and development as well as higher education resources from other knowledge-intensive provinces. As a result, regional-level innovation ecosystem policies in the Pearl River Delta have increasingly focused on building "knowledge ecosystems."

At the regional level, the innovation policies in the Pearl River Delta cover the entire geographic area and have become highly institutionalized, comprehensively addressing various fields such as industry, trade, finance, technology, talent, and corporate research and development. Following the national innovation system model, the Guangdong Province has formulated several policies related to the construction of the Pearl River Delta regional innovation system, including the "Pearl River Delta Regional Science and Technology Innovation Integration Action Plan (2014–2020)," the "Pearl River Delta National Independent Innovation Demonstration Zone Construction Implementation Plan (2016–2020)," and the "Guangdong Province Deepening Pan-Pearl River Delta Regional Cooperation Implementation Opinion." These policies include initiatives for the sharing and opening of regional technological resources, joint tackling of major scientific and technological projects, collaboration within industrial clusters, the development of technological solutions for social and public welfare, the joint creation of talent hubs, technology-finance cooperation, and the promotion of independent intellectual property rights. Government policies also focus on enhancing the capabilities and interactions of innovation entities such as production enterprises, research institutions, higher education institutions, intermediary organizations, and local governments.

Shenzhen, with its regional influence, has a well-developed innovation policy that primarily offers public services to technology companies and their innovative activities throughout the city. These services include financial services for high-tech companies (such as a diversified capital market), legal and auditing services for high-tech enterprises, human resource services (such as talent attraction, labor markets, and talent policies), management of the technology trade market (such as high-tech exhibitions), investment services through high-tech zones, supply chain development for high-tech companies, and assisting technology companies in connecting with international markets and customers. For Shenzhen, the municipal government plays a key role in the innovation ecosystem, while the city itself acts as a space or "entity" that gathers various innovation participants to pursue shared goals. The city must present an innovation environment conducive to fostering innovation.

Guangzhou, on the other hand, has developed innovation policies around emerging pillar industries such as next-generation information technology, smart and new energy vehicles, biomedicine and healthcare, as well as emerging industries like intelligent equipment and robotics, rail transportation, new energy and energy conservation and environmental protection, new materials and fine chemicals, and digital creativity. These policies include:

1. encouraging innovation (such as technology innovation centers, industrial innovation centers, and national key laboratories),
2. developing industries (cultivating innovation-driven industrial clusters around industrial chains),
3. tackling technological challenges,
4. establishing innovation carriers (specialized technology innovation transformation agencies, technology service organizations, high-tech zones),
5. developing science and technology finance (equity investment funds, technology loans, competitions, and listing of technology companies), and
6. talent recruitment.

Regional Planning

Another important aspect of the Pearl River Delta's regional innovation ecosystem policy is the comprehensive and integrated planning that combines industrial planning with technological planning, based on large platforms and spatial carriers within the region, such as innovation zones, clusters, urban areas, and cities. Higher-level local governments can deploy and coordinate policies and actions of lower-level governments according to the planning.

For instance, in 2017, the Guangdong provincial government formulated the "Guangzhou-Shenzhen Science and Technology Innovation

Corridor Plan," which proposed the construction of an internationally first-class science and technology industrial innovation center by 2050. The plan presents a spatial layout of about 180 kilometers in length, covering a total area of 11,836 square kilometers, featuring "one corridor, ten cores, and multiple nodes." This includes the ten core innovation platforms: Guangzhou University Town—International Innovation City, Pazhou Internet Innovation Cluster, Guangzhou Sino-Singapore Knowledge City, Guangzhou Science City, Dongguan Songshan Lake, Dongguan Binhai Bay New District, Shenzhen Airport New City, Shenzhen High-Tech Zone, Shenzhen Bantian Science and Technology Park, and Shenzhen International Bio-Valley, as well as 37 other innovation nodes like Guangzhou International Bio Island Park, Tianhe Smart City, Shenzhen Qianhai Shenzhen-Hong Kong Modern Service Industry Cooperation Zone, Shenzhen Bay Super Headquarters Base, Dongguan Neutron Science City, and Dongguan Shui Xiang New City. The Science and Technology Innovation Corridor is an innovation regional urban cluster or city cluster organized with "science and technology innovation" as its development theme, with a "corridor" as its spatial organization, essentially forming a regional, complete science and technology innovation ecosystem.

Ecosystem Policy of Knowledge

The Guangzhou-Shenzhen Innovation Corridor is, in essence, a systematic policy by the Guangdong provincial government to integrate innovation entities and resource concentration points scattered across the Pearl River Delta (Zhan et al., 2023). With the central government's decision in 2019 to build the Guangdong-Hong Kong-Macao Greater Bay Area, the plan for the Innovation Corridor expanded spatially to Hong Kong and Macau, forming two science and technology innovation corridors: "Guangzhou-Shenzhen-Hong Kong" and "Guangzhou-Zhuhai-Macau." This concept allows the Guangdong-Hong Kong-Macao Greater Bay Area to emerge as a new regional innovation system or ecosystem.

Recently, the focus of the Pearl River Delta's regional innovation ecosystem policy has shifted toward attracting high-end innovation resources from outside the region, particularly research institutions, including universities and research institutes. As the innovation ecosystem in the Pearl River Delta expands spatially—from industrial parks and clusters to regions, cities, and even beyond the Pearl River Delta—governments have placed greater emphasis on high technology density and diversity. Higher-level governments are increasingly leveraging the modernized cities and cultural environments within the Pearl River Delta to attract science and technology industries, R&D headquarters, research centers, universities, and institutions from outside the region to invest.

The entry of these high-tech and knowledge-intensive institutions has created new infrastructures across the Pearl River Delta, and it could even be said that they represent a "knowledge industry." This includes universities, engineering colleges, R&D institutions, corporate R&D laboratories, small R&D companies, government laboratories, as well as various consulting firms and professional financial companies. As a result, regional innovation ecosystem policies have increasingly become oriented toward constructing a "knowledge ecosystem." Large cities like Guangzhou and Shenzhen have also established industry-guided funds to bring in scientific, technological, and industrial resources from other regions, thereby forming a "knowledge ecosystem" in the city. This shift represents an upgrade of the entire regional innovation system in the Pearl River Delta from a manufacturing-based system to a knowledge-intensive system.

PRD'S New System of Innovation Ecosystem Policy

In recent years, the concepts such as "innovation ecosystem," as well as "innovation chain" and "innovation platform" have increasingly become focal points in research on regional innovation system, holistic innovation policy, and even the EU's Smart Specialization Strategy. These concepts have led to the development of various policy instruments to support the creation and growth of innovative firms. The theory of regional innovation system suggests that by clustering innovators, local industrial clusters, and technology research institutions within a specific territory, and by fostering their interactions and linkages, the level of regional industrial innovation can be enhanced (Chaminade & Lundvall, 2020). Therefore, in addition to establishing innovation centers and institutions to provide services, the PRD region also supported innovation infrastructure, such as the construction of technology parks and research centers. Other policy instruments aimed to facilitate collaboration, coordination, and integration among various innovation actors, such as encouraging partnerships between firms and universities through collaborative projects and researcher mobility, as well as promoting interaction with financial systems.

Ecosystem Policy Mix

Under the guiding policy concept of building a local innovation ecosystem, governments at all levels in the Pearl River Delta have formulated the corresponding policy measures in various functional areas, forming a regional innovation policy system. This system is holistic and comprehensive in terms of policy mix:

1. The policy areas covered extend beyond traditional science and technology to include land use zoning, regional and urban planning, economics, industry, capital, human resources, R&D, fiscal incentives, intellectual property protection, infrastructure, education, trade, and both domestic and international cooperation—encompassing nearly all government functions.
2. The policy tools are varied, including both rigid regulatory measures such as laws and regulations, and economic and financial incentives. Additionally, there are soft approaches such as organization, coordination, mobilization, and information sharing.
3. Since innovation ecosystem-oriented policies are implemented by nearly all levels of local government, from grassroots to towns, districts, cities, and provinces, the governance structure of this policy system is multi-tiered. The "space" targeted by the policy —the innovation ecosystem— is also multi-level, ranging from projects, platforms, and industrial parks to development zones, industrial clusters, innovation districts, innovation cities, innovation corridors, and even regional innovation systems.
4. Further, the innovation ecosystem policies developed at different levels of government are often repetitive in many ways, but they do have different focuses. At the grassroots level, such as parks, towns, and streets, the priority of the innovation ecosystem is the development of innovation entities and platform organizations, as well as the development and use of physical innovation spaces. At the city or district level, for general prefecture-level cities and larger urban areas, the focus is on the construction of physical innovation spaces, as well as the establishment of various entrepreneurial incubation and acceleration facilities to fill these spaces. At the regional and major metropolitan levels (e.g., Guangzhou, Shenzhen), innovation ecosystem policies focus on comprehensive planning, institutionalizing various innovation policy measures, and introducing more

advanced innovation elements and resources from external sources. This division of labor with different focuses at each level has naturally formed, and it leads to overlapping and complementary innovation policies in the Pearl River Delta, resulting in a comprehensive and multi-tiered innovation policy system (see Table 8.1).

"Dense" Policy Network

Due to the overlapping geographic scope of the policy "spaces" and the target innovation ecosystems that each level of government aims to build, rather than being isolated, this policy system resembles a concentric circle structure formed by multiple layers of spatial regions. At the core of this structure are entrepreneurs, projects, and enterprises. From the micro perspective of firm or entrepreneur, the innovation ecosystem it inhabits is supported by a dense and robust policy network. The "density" of the network arises from the fact that the policies encompass various functional areas that cover the elements and resources required for innovation. The "thickness" of the network stems from the fact that the policies come from different administrative levels, corresponding to different geographic levels of local governments.

Within the specific innovation ecosystem of an enterprise, the existence of such a supportive policy network significantly increases the "organizational and institutional thickness" (Asheim et al., 2011; Tödtling & Trippl, 2005) of the innovation environment in which the enterprise operates, enabling innovation resources such as talent, ideas, and physical resources to cross certain thresholds. The innovation process is characterized by trial and error, uncertainty, a scientific foundation, complexity, experimentation, and accumulation, meaning the risk of failure for individual enterprises is substantial. The overlap of policies across different fields and levels may lead to an "oversupply" of innovation policies, but the dense and robust innovation policy network makes it possible to conduct a sufficient number of innovation attempts. As a result, the probability of new projects and startups in the Pearl River Delta receiving funding and resource support increases, and the risks and uncertainties associated with entrepreneurial innovation are reduced.

For example, Fenghua-Zhuoli is a company in Shishan Town, Foshan City, in the Pearl River Delta, which utilizes innovative 3D printing technology to provide equipment for the mold market. The company needed substantial funding during its startup phase. Thanks to multi-level

Table 8.1 The System of Innovation Ecosystem Policy in the Pearl River Delta

Policy tools and mix Policy governance levels	*Policies for developing innovation organizations and platform institutions*	*Policies for building innovation spaces (clusters, development zones, physical buildings, infrastructure, etc.)*	*Policies for connecting and utilizing innovation resources and factors*	*Horizontal or functional policies (education, labor, capital, services, etc.)*	*Vertical industrial policies or programs for developing target industries*	*Measures for anchoring external technology and knowledge organizations*	*Innovation ecosystems constructed as policy "spaces"*
Regional-level governing bodies (Prefecture--level cities, Provincial government)	*** **Example**: Shenzhen vigorously develops emerging research and development (R&D) institutions, becoming the source of China's new R&D institutions.	*** **Example**: Shenzhen opens high-tech zone investment services, including 90 incubators. Enterprises can enjoy support and services in areas such as land, factories, funding, human resources, and logistics within the development zone.	** **Example**: Shenzhen assists enterprises in establishing connections with international markets and customers.	**** **Example**: Shenzhen provides financial services for the development of high-tech enterprises (diversified capital markets), legal and auditing services for high-tech companies, human resources services for technology companies (attracting talent, labor market, and talent policies), and establishes a technology trade market (high-tech exhibitions).	*** **Example**: Shenzhen supports key enterprises in the supply chain of high-tech enterprises and export promotion.	***** **Example**: Shenzhen introduces research institutes established by domestic universities such as Tsinghua University. Knowledge ecosystem, regional innovation system.	Knowledge ecosystem, regional innovation system.

City/ District-level governing bodies (Governments of large towns, districts, and medium-sized cities)	**** **Example**: Longgang District develops new types of R&D institutions and research and testing institutions.	***** **Example**: Longgang District uses the infrastructure built for the World University Games to create an international university campus cluster city; the old urban area is transformed into a makerspace; professional incubation companies and incubation parks (such as Tianan Digital City, Qide Technology Park, etc.) are introduced.	*** **Example**: Longgang District establishes a dedicated technology achievement transformation promotion center and entrusts the operation and management of this government department to a professional commercial company.	*** **Example**: Longgang District's human resources policies include setting up overseas talent workstations and talent introduction plans. The financial system supports government pilot funds, VC/PE, and technology financial service platforms, etc.	*** **Example**: Longgang District vigorously develops policies to promote the science and technology service industry (law firms, accounting firms, etc.).	** **Example**: Longgang District introduces the Chinese University of Hong Kong to establish a Shenzhen campus.	Innovation district, entrepreneurial ecosystem.

(*continued*)

Table 8.1 (continued)

Policy tools and mix Policy governance levels	*Policies for developing innovation organizations and platform institutions*	*Policies for building innovation spaces (clusters, development zones, physical buildings, infrastructure, etc.)*	*Policies for connecting and utilizing innovation resources and factors*	*Horizontal or functional policies (education, labor, capital, services, etc.)*	*Vertical industrial policies or programs for developing target industries*	*Measures for anchoring external technology and knowledge organizations*	*Innovation ecosystems constructed as policy "spaces"*
Local grassroots governing bodies (Governments of industrial parks, science parks, zones, clusters, towns, and streets)	***** **Example**: Chang'an Town established the National Hardware Mold Supervision and Inspection Center and the MIT Chang'an Hardware Mold Research Center.	**** **Example**: Chang'an Town transforms old factories into incubators and accelerators for the mold industry.	*** **Example**: Chang'an Town hosts the International Hardware Mold Expo and related exhibitions.	*** **Example**: Chang'an Town's investment fund for the hardware mound industry, talent attraction, and training policies.	** **Example**: Chang'an Town encourages local enterprises to expand overseas.	*	Platform ecosystem, industrial clusters.

Legend: * represents the number of corresponding policies at this governance level, therefore, * very few, ** few, *** average, **** more, ***** many

Source: Author

government policies, in addition to financial institutions and shareholders, the company received industrial land from Shishan Town, an innovation and entrepreneurship team project from Foshan City, and project funding from the Guangdong Provincial Department of Science and Technology. In the product development phase, the company faced decision-making challenges related to market selection and exploration. With public information service platforms set up by governments at various levels, Fenghua-Zhuoli was able to access ample information from different sources, comprehensively assess opportunities and risks, and make decisions by dividing the R&D direction into two aspects: upgrading the existing sand mold printing technology and investing in emerging technologies like ceramic and metal 3D printing.

"Ecosystem" as Policy Thinking

In the Pearl River Delta region, with the substantial increase in the number of innovative entrepreneurs, projects, platforms, and firms, a large number of new innovation spaces have emerged, such as "innovation clusters," "manufacturing parks," "science and technology parks," "economic zones," "innovation districts," and "characteristic towns." Local governments' innovation-driven development policies are also moving beyond outdated industrial, R&D, and science policies, becoming more comprehensive and mixed. The case of the Pearl River Delta reveals some qualitative characteristics of innovation policies at the regional level in China: innovation ecosystem-oriented, with multi-level governance structures in spatial and regional aspects, involving multiple policy areas, and having already formed a relatively complete policy system.

Local governments generally perceive innovation policies as tools to build the comprehensive innovation environments. However, when building an innovation ecosystem becomes the goal of local innovation policies, the innovation ecosystem is not only the expected form of innovation "space" as a policy target, but also a more systematic way of thinking and methodology when local governments formulate innovation policies. The grassroots, urban, and regional-level governments in the PRD focus on innovation ecosystem policies through project platforms, industrial clusters, entrepreneurial incubation, innovation districts, knowledge ecosystems, and regional innovation systems, weaving a dense and robust policy network for regional innovation systems, creating organizational, policy, and institutional advantages for regional innovation development. The formation of this policy system is more the result of proactive policy actions taken by local governments from the bottom up, representing the shift of China's regional innovation policy system from a central-planned, vertical, selective industrial policy approach to a more market-oriented, horizontal, and functional innovation policy approach or strategy.

Conclusion

Geographically, the engine of China's innovation power now is regional innovation system. At the policy level, the experience of the PRD shows that the construction of a regional innovation system requires the support of a regional policy system. Narrower technology innovation policies should be integrated with other regional innovation policies (such as industrial chains, platforms, clusters, agglomerations) to form a regional "package of innovation policies," generating a comprehensive effect through the construction of a multi-level policy governance structure that drives regional innovation development.

At the conceptual level, the PRD case clarifies the scale and connotation of the innovation ecosystem concept in the reality of public policy. From a bottom-up perspective, the regional innovation system in the Pearl River Delta is not a single-level innovation ecosystem, but rather a composite formed by the interlocking and nesting of multi-level innovation ecosystems continuously enriched by internal multi-level innovation policies. Based on the dense and robust innovation ecosystem policy system, this composite structure, consisting of institutions, organizations, infrastructure, information, business networks, industrial parks, industrial clusters, and cities, has also become dense and robust, forming a unique regional advantage in terms of innovation systems for the Pearl River Delta in Guangdong.

References

Adner, R. (2006). Match your innovation strategy to your innovation ecosystem. *Harvard Business Review, 84*(4), 98–107.

Adner, R., & Kapoor, R. (2010). Value creation in innovation ecosystems: How the structure of technological interdependence affects firm performance in new technology generations. *Strategic Management Journal, 31*(3), 306–333. https://doi.org/10.1002/smj.821

Appelbaum, R., & Parker, R. A. (2008). China's bid to become a global nanotech leader: Advancing nanotechnology through state-led programs and international collaborations. *Science and Public Policy, 35*(5), 319–334.

Asheim, B., & Isaksen, A. (2002). Regional innovation systems: The integration of local 'sticky' and global 'ubiquitous' knowledge. *The Journal of Technology Transfer, 27*(1), 77–86.

Asheim, B. T., Boschma, R., & Cooke, P. (2011). Constructing regional advantage: Platform policies based on related variety and differentiated knowledge bases. *Regional Studies, 45*(7), 893–904.

Bartels, K. (2018). Policy as practice. In R. Hoppe & H. Colebatch (Eds.), *Handbook on policy, process and governing* (pp. 68–88). Edward Elgar Publishing Ltd.

Becattini, G. (2002). From Marshall's to the Italian "industrial districts": A brief critical reconstruction. In A. Q. Curzio & M. Fortis (Eds.), *Complexity and industrial clusters.* Physica-Verlag HD. https://doi.org/10.1007/978-3-642-50007-7_6

Berger, S. (2005). *How we compete: What companies around the world are doing to make it in the global economy.* Doubleday.

Boeing, P. (2016). The allocation and effectiveness of China's R&D subsidies - evidence from listed firms, Research Policy, published online, https://doi.org/10.1016/j.respol.2016.05.007.

Borrás, S., & Edquist, C. (2013). The choice of innovation policy instruments. *Technological Forecasting and Social Change, 80*(8), 1513–1522.

Borrás, S., & Edquist, C. (2019). *Holistic innovation policy: Theoretical foundations, policy problems, and instrument choices.* Oxford University Press.

Borrás, S., & Tsagdis, D. (2008). *Cluster policies in Europe: Firms, institutions, and governance.* Edward Elgar Publishing.

Chaminade, C., & Lundvall, B.-Å. (2020). Science, technology, and innovation policy: Old patterns and new challenges. In *Oxford Research Encyclopedia of Business and Management.* Oxford University Press. Retrieved from oxfordre.com/business.

Conle, M., ten de Brink, T., & Zhao, W. (2022). Innovation platforms as a tool for anchoring non-local knowledge: Smart specialisation strategies in Guangdong, China. Industry and Innovation. https://doi.org/10.1080/13662716.2022.2132919.

Conle, M., Zhao, W., & ten de Brink, T. (2021). Technology transfer in emerging knowledge-based development: New R&D institutes in Guangdong, China. *Science & Public Policy, 48*(1), 132–144.

Cooke, P., & Leydesdorff, L. (2006). Regional development in the knowledge-based economy: The construction of advantages. *Journal of Technology Transfer, 31*(1), 5–15.

Cooke, P., & Morgan, K. (1998). *The associational economy: Firms, regions, and innovation*. Oxford University Press.

Edquist, C. (2018). Towards a holistic innovation policy: Can the Swedish National Innovation Council (NIC) be a role model? *Research Policy, 48*(4), 869–879.

Edquist, C., & Hommen, L. (Eds.). (2008). Small country innovation systems: Globalisation, change and policy in Asia and Europe. Edward Elgar Publishing.

Flanagan, K., Uyarra, E., & Laranja, M. (2011). Reconceptualising the 'policy mix' for innovation. *Research Policy, 40*, 702–713.

Fu, W., Revilla Diez, J., & Schiller, D. (2012). Regional innovation systems within transitional context: Evolutionary comparison of electronics industry in Shenzhen and Dongguan since opening in China. *Journal of Economic Surveys, 26*(3), 534–550.

Grandstrand, O., & Holgersson, M. (2020). Innovation ecosystems: A conceptual review and a new definition. Technovation, 90–91, 102098.

Gruss, L., & ten Brink, T. (2016). The development of the Chinese photovoltaic industry: An advancing role for the central state? *Journal of Contemporary China, 25*(99), 453–466.

Guan, J., & Yam, R. (2015). Effects of government financial incentives in firms' innovation performance in China: Evidences from Beijing in the 1990s. *Research Policy, 44*(1), 273–282.

Guimon, J. (2014). Regional innovation policy and multilevel governance in developing countries: Between a rock and a hard place. *Innovation, Technology & Entrepreneurship*, World Bank Policy Note, October 2014, (6).

Guo, D., Guo, Y., & Jiang, K. (2016). Government-subsidized R&D and firm innovation: Evidence from China. *Research Policy, 45*(6), 1129–1144.

Huang, X., Ma, L., Li, R., & Liu, Z. (2020). Determinants of innovation ecosystem in underdeveloped areas: Take Nanning high-tech zone in Western China as an example. *Journal of Open Innovation: Technology, Market, and Complexity, 6*, 135. https://doi.org/10.3390/joitmc6040135

Iansiti, M., & Levien, R. (2004). *The keystone advantage: What the new dynamics of business ecosystems mean for strategy, innovation, and sustainability*. Harvard Business School Press.

Isaksen, A., & Trippl, M. (2017). Innovation in space: The mosaic of regional innovation patterns. *Oxford Review of Economic Policy, 33*(1), 122–140.

Katz, B., & Wagner, J. (2015). *The rise of innovation districts: A new geography of innovation in America*. Metropolitan Policy Program at Brookings.

Kenney, M. (2000). *Understanding Silicon Valley: The anatomy of an entrepreneurial region*. Stanford University Press.

Li, Y., & Georghiou, L. (2015). Signaling and accrediting new technology: Use of procurement for innovation in China, Science and Public Policy, published online, https://doi.org/10.1093/scipol/scv044.

Li, X. (2009). China's regional innovation capacity in transition: An empirical approach. *Research Policy, 38*(2), 338–357.

Ma, L., Liu, Z., Huang, X., & Li, T. (2019). The impact of local government policy on innovation ecosystems in knowledge resource scarce regions: Case study of Changzhou, China. *Science, Technology & Society, 24*(1), 29–52.

Magro, E., & Wilson, J. R. (2013). Complex innovation policy systems: Towards an evaluation mix. *Research Policy, 42*, 1647–1656.

Morisson, A., & Doussineau, M. (2019). Regional innovation governance and place-based policies: Design, implementation and implications. *Regional Studies, Regional Science, 6*(1), 101–116.

Moulaert, F., & Sekia, F. (2003). Territorial innovation models: A critical survey. *Regional Studies, 37*(3), 289–302.

Muscio, A. (2006). From regional innovation systems to local innovation systems: Evidence from Italian industrial districts. *European Planning Studies, 14*(6), 773–789.

Pisano, G., & Shih, W. C. (2012). *Producing prosperity: Why America needs a manufacturing renaissance.* Harvard Business Review Press.

Porter, M. E. (1998). Clusters and the new economics of competition. *Harvard Business Review, 76*(6), 77–90.

Prud'homme, D. (2016). Dynamics of China's provincial-level specialization in strategic emerging industries. *Research Policy, 45*(8), 1586–1603.

Scaringella, L., & Radziwon, A. (2018). Innovation, entrepreneurial, knowledge, and business ecosystems: Old wine in new bottles? *Technological Forecasting and Social Change, 136*, 59–87. https://doi.org/10.1016/j.techfore.2017.09.023

Schilling, M. A., & Phelps, C. C. (2007). Interfirm collaboration networks: The impact of large-scale network structure on firm innovation. *Management Science, 53*(7), 1113–1126.

Smits, R. E. H. M., & Kuhlmann, S. (2004). The rise of systemic instruments in innovation policy. *International Journal of Foresight and Innovation Policy, 1*(1/2), 4–32.

Spigel, B. (2017). The relational organization of entrepreneurial ecosystems. *Entrepreneurship Theory and Practice, 41*(1), 49–72.

Spigel, B., & Harrison, R. (2018). Towards a process theory of entrepreneurial ecosystems. *Strategic Entrepreneurship Journal, 12*(1), 151–168.

Stam, E. (2015). Entrepreneurial ecosystems and regional policy: A sympathetic critique. *European Planning Studies, 23*(9), 1759–1769.

Su, Y. S., & Hung, L. C. (2009). Spontaneous vs. policy-driven: The origin and evolution of the biotechnology cluster. *Technological Forecasting and Social Change, 76*(5), 608–619.

Sun, S. L., Zhang, Y., Cao, Y., Dong, J., & Cantwell, J. (2019). Enriching innovation ecosystems: The role of government in a university science park. *Global Transitions, 1*, 104–119.

Tang, L., Sharpira, P., & Meng, Y. (2014). Developing an innovative materials enterprise in China: A nanotechnology small business case study. *Chinese Management Studies, 8*(2), 201–217.

Thomas, L., & Autio, E. (2020). Innovation ecosystems in management: A conceptual review. In R. Aldag (Ed.), *Oxford research encyclopedia of business and management*. Oxford University Press.

Tödtling, F., & Trippl, M. (2005). One size fits all? Towards a differentiated regional innovation policy approach. *Research Policy, 34*(8), 1203–1219.

Uyarra, E., & Flanagan, K. (2010). From regional systems of innovation to regions as innovation policy spaces. *Environment and Planning C: Government and Policy, 28*, 681–695.

Wang, C., & Wang, L. (2017). Unfolding policies for innovation intermediaries in China: A discourse network analysis. *Science and Public Policy, 44*(3), 354–368.

Whittington, R. (1996). Strategy as practice. *Long Range Planning, 29*(5), 731–735. https://doi.org/10.1016/0024-6301(96)00068-4

Whittington, R. (2006). Completing the practice turn in strategy research. *Organization Studies, 27*(5), 613–634. https://doi.org/10.1177/0170840606064101

Wu, F.-L. (2018). Planning centrality, market instruments: Governing Chinese urban transformation under state entrepreneurialism. *Urban Studies, 55*(7), 1383–1399.

Wu, W.-P. (2007). State policies, enterprise dynamism, and innovation system in Shanghai. *China. Growth Change, 38*(4), 544–566.

Yang, C. (2015). Government policy change and evolution of regional innovation systems in China: Evidence from strategic emerging industries in Shenzhen. *Environment and Planning C: Government and Policy, 33*(3), 661–682.

Yin, R. K. (2018). *Case study research design and methods* (6th ed.). Sage Publications.

Zhan, W., Yuan, Q., Li, G., Yang, J., & Gu, J. (2023). From "world factory" to "innovation bay": Evolution and typology of innovation spatial units in the Pearl River Delta. *Journal of Urban Planning Studies, 2023*(4), 110–118.

Zhang, F. (2015). Building biotech in Shanghai: A perspective of regional innovation system. *European Planning Studies, 23*(10), 2062–2078.

Zhang, F., & Wu, F. (2019). Rethinking the city and innovation: A political economic view from China's biotech. *Cities, 85*, 150–155.

Zhang, Y.-L., Li, R.-Y., Liu, Y.-X., Xu, Z.-H., & Zhang, G.-Y. (2018). Research on the status of new R&D Institutions in Guangdong Province (in Chinese). *Science and Technology Management Research, 13*(2018), 124–132.

Zhao, W. (2022). Industrial upgrading from below: Can Chinese local manufacturing firms reconfigure global value chains? In G. Gereffi, P. Bamber, & K. Fernandez-Stark (Eds.), *China's new development strategies*. Palgrave Macmillan. https://doi.org/10.1007/978-981-19-3008-9_7

Zhao, W. (2023). Local government as integrative organizer: The policy practice of constructing innovation platforms in South China. *Innovation and Development Policy, 5*(1), 73–99.

CHAPTER 9

Innovation Platform as Project: Business Model and Policy Tool

Introduction

Chapter 8 argues that the regional innovation system in the PRD of Guangdong is composed from lower-level innovation ecosystems. As an academic concept, a regional innovation system is a smaller-scaled national innovation system with a geographical area larger than a city but smaller than a country. It contains economic, social, political, and institutional relationships among universities, research labs, venture capital banks, and government agencies responsible for various sectors that can generate collective learning processes within relevant technical or functional areas (Morisson & Doussineau, 2019).

Regional innovation systems actually emphasize the spatial logics of co-location of innovation actors, such as externalities, agglomeration economies, and proximity effects. The perspective of regional innovation systems has now shifted focus from institutions at the national level to more local actors, institutions, capacities and interactions in innovation processes, such as "industrial clusters," "learning regions," "innovative milieux," creative cities and local territories. Regional or local social networks and

---

The original paper "Local Government as Integrative Organizer: The Policy Practice of Constructing Innovation Platforms in South China" was published in *Innovation and Development Policy*, 5(1), 73–99.

W. Zhao, *Remade in South China*, IPP Studies in the Frontiers of China's Public Policy,
https://doi.org/10.1007/978-981-95-7277-9_9

organized platforms can enable denser information flows, mutual learning and economies of scale among companies, private and public knowledge institutions, educational institutions, etc. Some innovation management authors like to refer here to the notion of "open innovation" (Chesbrough, 2003).

Related to but different from the "innovation ecosystem," "innovation platform" is another important and popular term now employed widely by both policy makers and business executives in elaborating their innovation strategy. By definition, innovation platforms can refer broadly to new organizational forms underlying rationale of network effects and interactive learning, such as collaborative networks, associations, alliances, intermediary or boundary-spanning organizations, and incubators (Flanagan et al., 2011). Specific regions are important spaces for the emergence of new combinations of factors of production, especially knowledge, as geographical proximity can help bridge distances (Boschma, 2005; Menzel, 2015). A large body of literature on innovation platforms discusses the importance of platforms for the development of regional innovation systems.

Platform as Policy Tool

In terms of innovation platform policies, many literature acknowledges that platform policies at regional level can accompany the discovery process of innovation and entrepreneurship and support the formation and adaptation of complementary resources around cross-sectoral innovation platforms (Asheim, Boschma, & Cooke, 2011), thus addressing various problems faced in regional innovation-driven development, such as lack of industrial and innovative capacity (Capello & Kroll, 2016), lack of public-sector entrepreneurs (Estensoro & Larrea, 2016), lack of innovation mediation (Pinto et al., 2015), lack of regional governance capacity (Kroll, 2015), and significant difficulties in integrating private and public stakeholders (Estensoro & Larrea, 2016). However, even though "innovative platform thinking" (Harmaakorpi et al., 2011) has entered into regional policy debates, there is still little empirical study on platform policy models. In this regard, the leading research is the "Platform Approach to Regional Innovation Policy" proposed as a regional innovation policy model (Asheim et al., 2011). It is an innovation platform method model elaborated by Harmaakorpi (2006) and collaborators, based on experiences of Scandinavian countries, particularly Finland's Lahti region. The model can serve to unlock the region's growth potential by connecting disparate but related knowledge fields and actors.

To use platforms as a tool for facilitating entrepreneurial discovery in regional innovation requires first of all a consideration of platform governance structure. In particular, it involves identifying who are responsible for coordinating the processes and activities of the platform. Possible stakeholder actors include governments, professional innovation intermediaries, and participants from diverse backgrounds who perform selected intermediary functions (Howells, 2006). Thus, platform provides an organized context for co-defining thematic priority areas and coordinating regional capacity development (Pekkarinen & Harmaakorpi, 2006), involving the creation of innovation networks and the pursuit of upgrading activities. Nevertheless, in the Platform Approach to Regional Innovation Policy, central or local government is only one of the actors participating in the platform and does not necessarily play a leading role.

Platform as Business Model

In terms of substantive policy tools for innovation platforms, research focus has been on whether platforms should choose a top-down or bottom-up decision-making process, and about prioritization and coordination of change activities (Foray, 2018). Harmaakorpi (2006) analyzed how innovation platforms in Lahti Region of Finland identified priority areas and coordinated implementation. He found that the established platforms involved a wide range of stakeholders and experts from the private and public sectors who assess regional resources and capabilities with the aim of defining, in a bottom-up fashion, priority areas connecting industries, areas of expertise or megatrends (Harmaakorpi et al., 2011; Uotila et al., 2012). It is concluded that private or (quasi-) public "systemic intermediaries" from below actually managed platform discovery and implementation by acting as brokers and coordinators of interactions between regional innovation actors (van Lente et al., 2003; Parjanen & Hyypiä, 2018; Janssen et al., 2020).

While the existing literature has discussed the operation or initiation mode of platform policy, in general, except for the relatively complete model of "platform approach to regional innovation policy," research by far has not yet proposed an alternative model. The specific steps, methods, and paths of how to operationalize the academic concept of platform into practical policy or business model remain in a "black box." In Guangdong, for policy makers, innovation platform often means a practical approach or way of thinking to establish local linkages among innovation resources; while for business firms, innovation platform means concreate organizations which can perform specific functions of intermediating different actors for innovation activities. Interestingly, both policy-makers and business people take "platform" as something equivalent to "project" or business model to build and develop. It is from here that thousands of innovation platforms emerge when the Chinese economy enters the innovation-driven stage.

Platform Policy Model of Guangdong

We already argued in the previous chapters that the driving force behind the regional innovation dynamics in China is local governments' various down-to-earth policy practice of implementing the national innovation-driven development strategy. The concepts of innovation chain, innovation ecosystem, and innovation platform were simply mentioned in central government's policy document as policy instrument frameworks, leaving the substantial content and operational approaches to be filled and concretized by local governments. The conventional division of policy responsibilities between the subnational and national levels is that the central government controls the areas of national interest (e.g., national defense, health, security) and allocates budget to R&D, especially to basic research, while the local governments oversee technological development, diffusion of existing technologies, and allocate budget to other types of innovation support. While the central government has launched innovation platforms at the national level, to support China's drive for indigenous innovation in specific techno-industrial sectors (Li et al., 2011), platform policies more commonly relate to the regional level.

The local governments of Guangdong Province have used numerous policies to support innovation, ranging from direct government investment, tax refund, mediation, infrastructure, talent subsidy, and technology investment of leading new products, to government-sponsored research institutes for the generation and transfer of advanced technology, incubation of entrepreneurs, venture capital funds, training, and consulting services, etc. Moreover, a primary focus of innovation policy in Guangdong has been in the domain of building various "spaces" of innovation, such as development and economic zones, scientific parks, and industrial clusters. In fact, after the Chinese central government intervened in cooperation with local governments by selecting the most promising special economic zones and science parks around the country and providing them with additional funding and support, regional governments continue to offer a range of complementary policies for these "spaces," including free land allocation, infrastructure, and facility support, as well as enhanced public services.

Local governments in Guangdong often cluster "innovation platforms," including start-up firms, R&D facilities, university branches, incubators, training centers, quality control agencies, technology diffusion centers, testing laboratories, venture capital funds, and other extension services in industrial parks, science parks, and technology development zones of same location, in hoping to promote inter-firm and inter-institutional linkages, and to attract more R&D resources from other regions outside. Platforms in Guangdong are not only treated explicitly as policy targets, but also used as a conceptual instrument by local governments for implementation.

As policy targets, innovation intermediaries and incubators are the precedents of the so-called innovation platforms in China (Wang & Wang, 2017). Now the scope has extended to more organizational forms, including "innovation and research centers," "engineering centers," "innovation alliances," "industry associations," "science and technology service institutions," incubators, and other intermediary organizations. According to the strategic policy document "Construction Plan of Science & Technology Innovation Platforms System of Guangdong" (2016), official "innovation platforms" include key labs (national and provincial levels), technological innovation centers (national and provincial levels), engineering technology research centers (national and provincials levels), and various forms of science and technology service platforms, such as technology transfer platforms (technology transfer institutions; industry-university-research alliances; technology property rights exchange institutions), public service platforms (sectoral alliances of technological innovation; service centers of science and technology innovation; R&D and design service institutions; inspecting, testing, measuring and standards service institutions; sectoral productivity promotion centers), and other innovation service platforms (innovation centers; makers spaces; incubation parks and bases; business schools; innovation and incubation centers within Hi-tech zones, specialized towns, and industrial parks; science & technology thinktanks). Guangdong has become the "homeland" of different innovation platforms in the strategic emerging industries.

The Implementation Process of Platform Policy

Based on experiences of innovation policy implementation in Guangdong, especially project-level empirical materials from the Nanhai District that we are going to check in detail, the overall Chinese policy approach to promote and drive innovation-oriented development can be characterized as three staged but interwoven processes, with platform construction as its core part:

1. Targeting strategic emerging industries and breaking down the industrial development plan into concrete new projects. The planning activities in this stage go beyond the narrowly defined science, technology, and innovation policy, but mixed up with sector and cluster development strategy.
2. Constructing innovation platforms. This is the core part of the whole policy practice. Local government uses "platform" as a conceptual tool guiding the new projects to adopt the operational model as well as organizational form of platforms. Thus, "innovation platform" has become a dominant policy guideline of local officials for innovation project selection and resource allocation. New projects are initiated, transformed, and constructed into platforms as much as possible.
3. Developing projects/platforms to form spatial clusters of development. The "platformization" of projects results in large number of new ventures functioning as innovation platforms, with multiple external linkages and multiple internal functions. Local government takes use of these projects and platforms to develop new local clusters by leveraging more industrial and knowledge linkages and resources. Although the efficiency of such a pragmatist policy approach is still questionable, it does create new actors of innovation and foster the more technology-based development in the region.

In this new innovation policy model, Chinese local government does not only take care of the local environment and context for new projects, but also intervene directly in every project stage during the whole process from industrial targeting, platform building, and cluster development, playing a role of innovation manager in business sector. The policy practice in local China is a mixture of the market-based, horizontal, and functional innovation policy approach, with the old-style promotional, vertical,

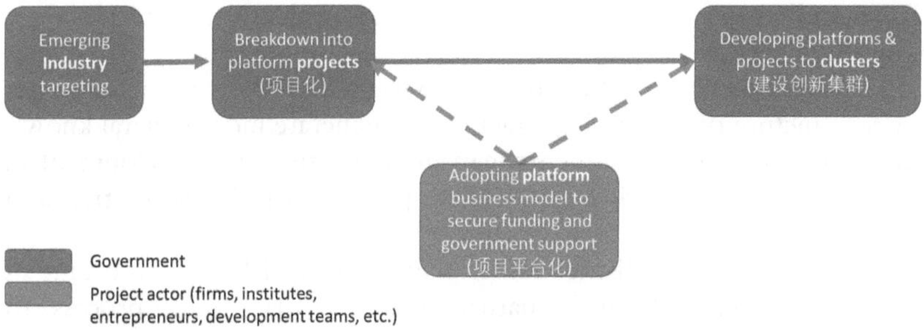

Fig. 9.1 A Process Model of Innovation Platform Policy of Guangdong. (Source: Zhao, W. (2023). Local government as integrative organizer: The Policy practice of constructing innovation platforms in South China, *Innovation and Development Policy, 5*(1), 73–99)

and selective industrial policy approach. Figure 9.1 outlines the practice pattern of innovation policy.

Compared to the previously mentioned Nordic "Platform Approach to Regional Innovation Policy" in Europe (Harmaakorpi, 2006; Harmaakorpi et al., 2011; Uotila et al., 2012), this definition of platform policy covers a broader scope, not only the platform construction itself, but also includes industrial targeting and clustering, which are traditionally regarded as areas of industrial policy and cluster policy. Additionally, this policy model from Guangdong provides more operationalized steps for local authorities to follow and more detailed policy measures in each step, as illustrated by the following case of Nanhai District.

Focusing on Nanhai District

We've known that the Pearl River Delta in Guangdong is composed by nine prefectural cities, which have their own subordinated districts or towns with government as policy-maker at each level of the administrative echelon. Covering all the nine prefectural cities in the Pearl River Delta, our field observation is carried out mainly at the level of districts and towns, but also includes municipal level of some cities. During 2015 and 2019, we undertook a series of policy research and consultation projects with local governments, including Yuexiu District of Guangzhou, Longgang District of Shenzhen, Nanhai District of Foshan, Changping

Town and Changan Town of Dongguan, Zhongshan City, and Huizhou City, etc.

Detailed observation at district or township level was conducted to get a better picture of local policy practice and generate more general knowledge on how local governments manage innovation and development in their administrative territories. Here we pick up just Nanhai District as a case to focus on.

Our choice of the district rather than municipal level as the unit of analysis stems firstly from the nature of the country's policy process. In China, *"policies are typically designed at the central, provincial and municipal levels, [whereas] counties and districts are responsible for their implementation on the ground"* (Schubert & Alpermann, 2019, p. 212). As we are interested in how innovation policy is implemented in practice, we consider the district to be the administrative level at which the policy process is deployed.

The choice of Nanhai as our focus is also because numerous research platforms, public service platforms, incubation platforms, and industry-research-university alliance platforms have been established recently in the district, and we had direct access to many project-level material and data which can be used for case-in-case analysis. In fact, our analysis strategy is a bottom-up process, i.e., we start with case analysis of four concrete platforms from their initiation to full operation, and then we construct a general picture of how relevant policies are implemented on these platforms. For this reason, we adopt an embedded case study design to explain the regional implementation of innovation platform policies (Yin, 2018). While our unit of analysis is at the district-level, we dig into specific innovation platform projects which are district policy targets. And in choosing the platform project case, we maximize their heterogeneity in terms of origin of shareholders, nature of activities, initial design, and size, in order to find their "platform commonalities."

In the fieldwork, besides the interviews with senior Nanhai district government officials of General Administration Office and Science & Technology Department, we conducted interviews with four industrial firms and three innovation service institutions, representing different innovation platform types within the emerging industries. The multiple-methods approach adopted makes triangulation possible, particularly the verification of testimony of the information gathered from interviews, which was triangulated with secondary material of local government guidelines, reports, and plans, as well as questionnaire survey findings accumulated previously by the local research team. The following content illustrates in a step-by-step way how local innovation policy is implemented around the key practice of constructing platforms in Nanhai District.

Targeting Industry and Project

Nanhai District is situated in eastern bank of the Pearl River Delta, about 25 km from the provincial capital, Guangzhou. It has about 3,032,000 inhabitants and a surface of 1074 square km. The district comprises one urbanized subdistrict and six towns. As one of the most dynamic urban areas in Foshan City, Nanhai District has an industrial output value of 174.612bn Yuan and a GDP of 317.662bn Yuan with a growth rate of 6.9% in 2019. Under the "Made in China 2025" master plan, Nanhai proposes to become the core area of a global-oriented national manufacturing innovation center, realizing a new combination of "world technology + Foshan intelligent manufacturing + global market," with objective to the total industrial output value of the entire region will reach 1 trillion yuan within 5 years. Since 2017, focusing on the goal of "upgrading industrial parks, building new cities, and developing new economies," Nanhai launched the program of "New Global Maker City" and used it as the general guideline for economic and social transformation and upgrading, to build Nanhai an exchanging and cooperation nexus between global innovation resources and the Pearl River Delta manufacturing industry.

The industries in Nanhai, specially manufacturing, are sparsely distributed across the whole district area. By the end of the 2010s, its industrial production was 77% of GDP and research and development expenditure was more than 2.6% of it. With an output value of over 243 billion Yuan, the industrial sector of Nanhai District was composed mainly by metal products, electrical machinery and equipment manufacturing, automobile manufacturing (excluding FAW-Volkswagen), non-ferrous metal smelting and rolling processing industry, equipment manufacturing industry (general equipment, computer and communication, special equipment), and the "traditional" manufacturing industries (waste resource utilization, non-metallic minerals, furniture, rubber and plastic products, products industry, textiles, etc.). Having the ambition to become a district with industrial output of trillion Yuan, Nanhai District has targeted five sectors as the main pillars of its "modern industrial system." The five interrelated sectors as shown in Fig. 9.2 include:

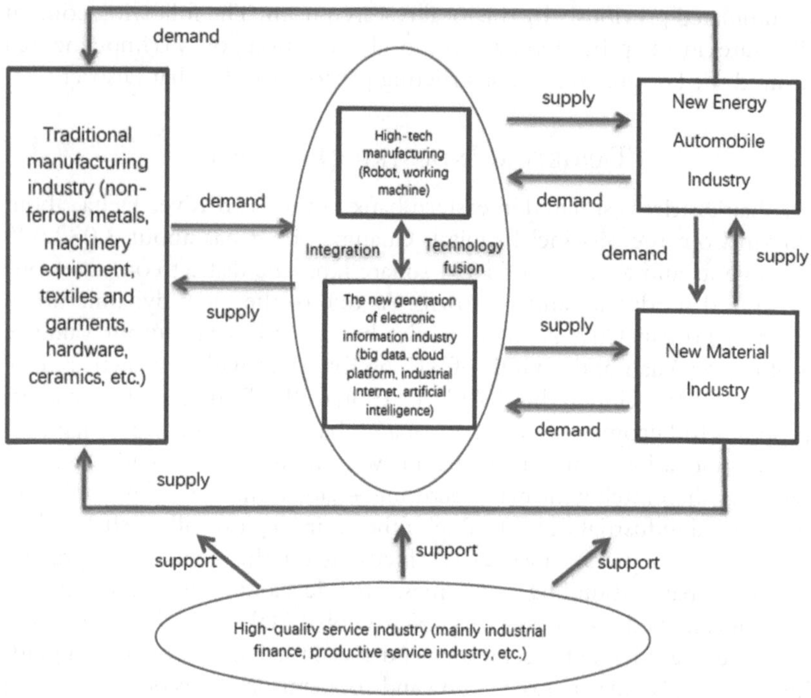

Fig. 9.2 Strategic Emerging Industry Targeting in Nanhai (2 "high" + 3 "new"). (Source: Zhao, W. (2023). Local government as integrative organizer: The Policy practice of constructing innovation platforms in South China, *Innovation and Development Policy*, *5*(1), 73–99)

1. high-tech manufacturing (machine and equipment, components, robots, materials for electronic components, software, sensors, controlling machine),
2. the new-generation electronic information industry (digital consumer electronics, IT, digital technology, telecommunication, formed and fabricated materials, as well as big data, cloud platform, industrial internet, artificial intelligence),
3. new energy automobile industry,
4. new material industry (including fuel cells, material measurement equipment, ingredients, metal molds, material manufacturing equipment, etc.), and

5. high-quality service industry (mainly industrial finance, productive service industry, etc.).

Method of Strategic Industrial Planning

For implementing the strategy of new sector development, local government usually breakdown the whole industrial planning into various projects. Thus, creation of new sectors is often operated as creating projects of new business ventures. To achieve the new goals of regional development in Nanhai, local government hoped that the emerging sectors created by new projects can also benefit its "traditional" manufacturing industries for upgrading (non-ferrous metals, machinery equipment, textiles and garments, hardware, ceramics, etc.) through establishing supplier or user linkages.

For example, the new projects in advanced equipment manufacturing industry based on robots and machine tools, combined with projects in electronic information industry, are expected to supply digital manufacturing systems to the firms in traditional sectors and promote their technological upgrading. At the same time, the new approach of industrial planning and targeting emphasized the innovation-driven aspect of sector development. Following the so-called principle of "fusion of industrial chain and innovation chain," local governments were able to integrate industrial policy and technology policy to identify and target more precisely the key industrial and technological areas of each identified emerging sector to develop.

The new approach of innovation-driven sector targeting started with detailed intra-sector value chain analysis of the planned industry in order to identify the different segments and linkages, from upstream suppliers of inputs and providers of specialized infrastructure, through manufacturers of complementary products and related industries, to downstream channels and customers. Value chain analysis often resulted in redefinition of sector borders and refined targeting of specific segments as development field. Many local governments chose the development of new energy, new materials, electronic information, and the bio-pharmaceutical industry as strategic emerging industries.

Different from the traditional way of industrial planning, the new approach contained a parallel step called "deploying innovation chain according to targeted industrial chain." Based on each targeted emerging sector or segment, local governments had to identify and target the new technology areas or "key enabling technologies" (e.g., advanced manufacturing, clean energy technology, ICT, nanotech, and biotech), the corresponding technological intensive activities (e.g., research, design, quality & test, training, information, technical support, and headquarter functions, etc.), and the actors or organizations (e.g., firms, entrepreneurs, research labs, universities, standards-setting agencies, think tanks, vocational training providers, and trade associations, etc.) as project sources and initiators.

For example, Huizhou City identified new energy vehicle industry as strategic sector and targeted specifically battery production and other key components manufacturing for new energy vehicles, such as motor management systems, on-board chargers, off-board charging equipment, drive motors, electronic control integration, and electric air conditioners, as segments to develop. The city government therefore planned industrial clusters as production and supporting base, and elaborated incentive measures to attract investments from heavyweight companies, OEM manufacturers, and technical teams of smart mobility.

Nanhai District set robot and advanced equipment as strategic emerging industry and aimed to promote the development of integration and application of robots in assembly lines of local firms. It worked out specific policy packages, launched call for projects in the field, and contacted actively universities, firms, investors, technology teams, and research institutions to solicit their investment and engagements.

Constructing Platform as Project

For Nanhai governments, since the expected projects would be situated at the interface between the industrial targeting and technological activities planning, platform was regarded as the most appropriate institutional and organizational form or business model to be adopted by projects for achieving the objective of creating new sector through applying new technologies. Platforms are various organizations having multiple functions internally and multiple linkages externally. Innovation platforms perform functions aimed at facilitating, intermediating, and pro-actively contributing to science-industry transfer and interaction. Therefore, platform as defined by Nanhai has become an important precursor to the formulation of specific projects with policy support under new industrial targeting.

Among local governments in Guangdong, the concept of platform as a policy guiding thought was so prevalent that the Nanhai government almost pushed every new project to adopt the platform business model and become a platform project, then provided funding and other support to the project actor. From the standing point of project actors, they also knew that their projects would have more opportunities to get approval and resources from government if the rolling out form is some kind of "platform." Thus, there was a variety of project actors willing to form innovation platform, such as firms, technology centers, research institutes, universities, schools, technology teams, public or private, national-level, provincial level, or city-level.

And in terms of types of innovation platforms, they are not limited to "intermediary" organization such as technology transfer center, but rather covering all kinds of new projects, including science and technology innovation service platforms (innovation alliances, industry associations, incubators, and technology intermediaries testing, intellectual property services, investment and financing, training, technology trade, technological information consulting, industry diagnostic, exhibition, etc.), research and technology development institutions (R&D laboratories, engineering research centers, university campuses, new R&D institutes), and business and manufacturing firms which industrialize and commercialize the new technologies.

Functions of Innovation Platform

The platforms created as such normally have multiple functions, including R&D, engineering, new technology transfer and diffusion, production technology demonstration, testing services, technology business incubation, establishing alliances, providing training and education, financing and investment arranging, patent licensing, etc. But for Nanhai local government lack of strong knowledge base in its region, platform is important for implementing the innovation-driven development in three aspects.

1. First, platform is an institutional vehicle to attract investment from outside the region and leverage the external resources (talent people, knowledge and information, capital, equipment, etc.) to develop relevant technologies of the targeted sectors. These specific resources are often in the hands of State-owned enterprises, State universities, technological centers, private enterprises, overseas returnees, etc., located elsewhere.

2. Secondly, the platforms themselves can become master platforms to attract further resources. As a platform could bring various linkages and interactions with different sectors and technological fields, they have the potential to become immediate innovation environment for other projects and to be transformed into transcending ecosystems which accommodate more platform projects.
3. Thirdly and most importantly, since these "innovation platforms" are embedded and integrated in the whole course of developing the strategic emerging industries, often they not only provide normal technology, information, and manpower supports to industrial firms, but also engage themselves more and more directly in the technology development and manufacturing operation like business firms. A platform can easily evolve to become a business firm as main body of emerging sector, so the development of platforms has also become the rise of industrial sectors themselves. The essence of the innovation platforms is the emergence of new projects that integrate scientific and technological resources from various stakeholders (government, industry, academia, research, capital, service provider, and user, etc.) to realize the creation of the targeted new sectors through industrialization of scientific and technological outcomes.
4. Finally, as innovation platforms is a multi-functional organization transcending different sectors, their growth can have many possible prospects and bring to the region industrial specialization and differentiation in the future.

This "platform as project" approach in Nanhai District has been widely used by other local governments in the Pearl River Delta of Guangdong. In fact, project-based platform formation is the primary policy target when innovation policy is implemented in Nanhai, as shown by the four cases below.

Business Models of Innovation Platform

Daji New Material Technology

Daji New Material Technology (Daji) was a private company that invested in Nanhai during 2018–2019. The company owned some new material technology for spraying amorphous alloys and nanocrystalline alloys, as well as some technology for producing cold spraying equipment. Thus, the business line of Daji spanned across the fields of new materials and advanced equipment manufacturing. The entrepreneurial team of founders was composed of a serial entrepreneur who had already created several private ventures in Shenzhen, a marketing specialist, a retired production engineer, and a scientist from Metallurgical Materials Institute of Hunan, which is a neighbor province to Guangdong. In fact, the public-owned Metallurgical Materials Institute of Hunan Province is the technology source of Daji.

Daji got the exclusive license from Hunan Institute of Metallurgical Materials for implementing this patented technology in production. Daji was attracted by Nanhai's huge aluminum profile industry and furniture industry which provide a potential market for the application of the new metallurgical material technology, and its overall environment of industrializing scientific and technological achievements. Initially, Daji's venture plan was just a factory producing and processing hard materials and new alloy materials for mold producers in local mechanical industry. However, local government thought that the project had bigger potential and hoped that the project could have more substance of "technical innovation," especially the possibility to establish a research and development laboratory and be able to contact and mobilize technology resources outside the region. The local government emphasized that the current government-funded and supported projects should focus on "innovation platforms"and technology-intensive industries, rather than simple manufacturing plants.

While the patented alloy material production technology was licensed from the Metallurgical Materials Institute of Hunan, Daji did have its own patent: an emerging cold spray technology. By introducing, digesting, and absorbing Russia's advanced cold spraying technology, Daji had developed a new type of cold air power spraying device, and had completed the drawing design of the new cold spraying equipment. However, to completely realize the industrialization of this new technology, Daji needed to carry out further downstream R&D activities and promotion of cold spray technology products and services to potential users. Daji needed information on requirements of technical specifications from potential customers, including graphene coating, electronic packaging coating, porous ceramic inner wall coating, and packaging material metal coating, etc.

Daji's proprietary new cold spray technology and the specific equipment Research and Development plan aroused great interest from the local government. The Nanhai District Government decided to support Daji's investment project and establish it as a local platform for industrial upgrading and technological innovation, in condition that the venture should have the form of platform organization, involving multiple actors or stakeholders, open to the whole mold industry, and attracting more resources from outside in the future. After many rounds of discussions with the local government, Daji adopted eventually these policy instruction and requirement. Thus, an initial manufacturing project with some new technology elements was transformed into an "innovation platform," according to the local policy definition. Nanhai local government approved the project and provided a financial aid of 50 million Yuan as first stage investment. The project got other policy supports, including listing the project in local industrial upgrading program and subsidizing the team members individually through a local Talent Recruitment Program.

The realized investment of Daji project included the following main structures and functions of platform:

1. A die steel original metal production plant: manufacturing parent metal to be used in mold production and casting processes. This was the initial project plan.
2. An R&D lab: planning to undertake systematic research and testing in order to produce various functional coatings with stable performance; planning to detect local firm's demand of wear-resistant and anti-corrosion coating products, provide coating samples and online testing of their wear-resistant and anti-corrosion performance, and build preliminary reputation among client firms based on actual usage.
3. An amorphous alloy process demonstration plant: using the owned-designed equipment and production line to demonstrate Daji's proprietary process technology of cold spray; attracting more clients to purchase Daji's products and technical service; developing professional and technical training sessions.
4. An alliance of mold industry: initiated by Daji in partnership with other firms in Nanhai's mold industry, with endorsement and support of local government, to promote networking and cooperation among local firms in the fields of technology and market development.
5. An investment fund in mold industry: when conditions were met, local government would support Daji with other capital investors in setting up a sectoral venture fund to invest in new technologies emerging from broader ecosystem.

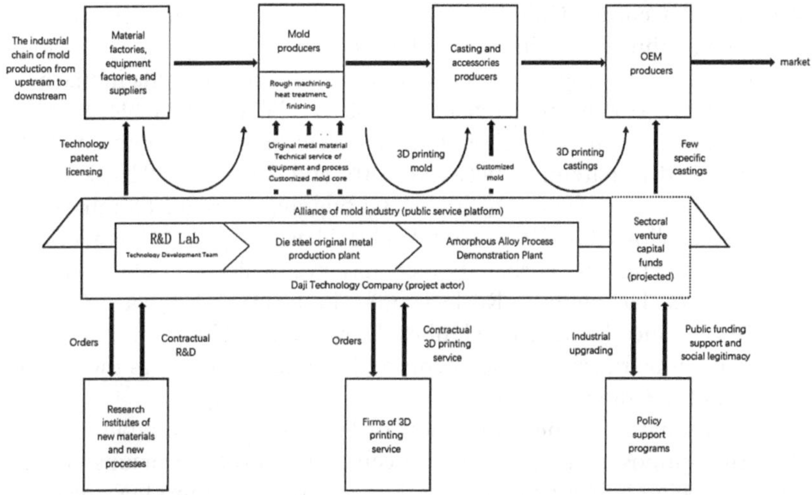

Fig. 9.3 The Platform Business Model of Daji. (Source: Zhao, W. (2023). Local government as integrative organizer: The Policy practice of constructing innovation platforms in South China, *Innovation and Development Policy*, *5*(1), 73–99)

Daji's investment project reformulated as an innovation platform was supposed to have amplified and spilled over effects of industrial upgrading over the whole production chain of mold, from upstream raw materials to downstream metal parts. Externally, Daji project would establish technological and knowledge linkages with various research centers more than the Metallurgical Materials Institute of Hunan Province, and specialized supplier relationship with 3D printing factories from a cluster in Shenzhen. Functioning as a platform, Daji project thus would become an organizational carrier of integrating local value chain of mold production and leveraging external knowledge, technical and production resources in the district of Nanhai to achieve the goal of industrial upgrading. Figure 9.3 describes the overall model of Daji project as a platform.

Huashu Robotics

The project of Huashu Robotics was initiated by Wuhan Huazhong Numerical Control Joint Stock Corporation (WHNC), a listed company owned by Central China (Huazhong) University of Science and Technology, thus belonging to the kind of State-owned firm. Huazhong Science and Technology University has been a leader in China in machine tool and CNC systems research and established WHNC in 1994. WHNC was awarded the official label of High and New Technology Firm in 2009, then engaged in patenting between 2009 and 2013. In 2013, it established its first manufacturing firm in Chongqing, Foshan (Nanhai) and Quanzhou followed in 2015. Now WHNC has altogether nine manufacturing bases and the Foshan branch has eventually become WHNC's headquarters, having four R&D centers in Foshan (Nanhai), Suzhou, Quanzhou, and Xiangyang (Hubei Province). WHNC has occupied almost all industrial robotic segments and its sales volume was the second biggest in the Chinese market.

The original investment intention of WHNC was to establish a pure platform composing a testing service center and a robot startups incubator. After being informed by the local government that another university was launching a much bigger incubation platform in exactly the same industrial segment, WHNC abandoned this initial project idea. Local governments from both Foshan municipal level and Nanhai district level suggested WHNC focusing on robot manufacturing and indigenous innovation in taking the regional advantage in manufacturing activities. Local governments promised to give full support if WHNC established a new platform based on strong R&D and manufacturing activities.

Therefore, in August of 2015, WHNC established in Foshan two robot manufacturing companies, and then shortly after co-established with Foshan government an R&D institute called Foshan Institute of Intelligent Equipment Technology. The two robot manufacturing companies were engaged in R&D integration, production, sales and service of industrial robots and core parts of robots, receiving the title of High and New Technology Firm in 2017. In terms technology and product development, their manufacturing activities relied on Huazhong University of Science and Technology, WHNC and Foshan Institute of Intelligent Equipment Technology. The R&D institute was within the factory site. The products developed by the R&D institute were industrialized in the manufacturing companies. Later it became the R&D headquarters of WHNC, with more than 100 R&D personnel.

Local government deeply got involved in turning the project of Huashu Robotics into an innovation platform. Foshan municipal government invested a lump sum of 150 million Yuan, including a 3-year founding budget for the R&D Institute which was required to be responsible for its loss after three years. In return, Foshan government got a share of 10% of the two manufacturing companies of WHNC. Nanhai district government allocated a piece of land with fiscal subsidy to the project. The R&D institute was established as a public institution belonging to government, thus having a way to access public funding for its R&D activities. The R&D institute was later granted the label of New R&D Institute which could enjoy corresponding policy support.

Huashu Robotics project was formulated from the original idea of an incubator to a powerful industrial platform composed of manufacturing facilities, R&D center, and robot utilization service and engineering activities. Through the channels of local government, the R&D institute developed technical cooperation with universities including Guangdong University of Technology concerning machine vision cloud system. The manufacturing companies also had access to the Robotics Industry Park established by Foshan government, where small firms could rent manufacturing services. Figure 9.4 highlights the cooperation between WHNC and local government on the Huashu Robotics industry innovation platform.

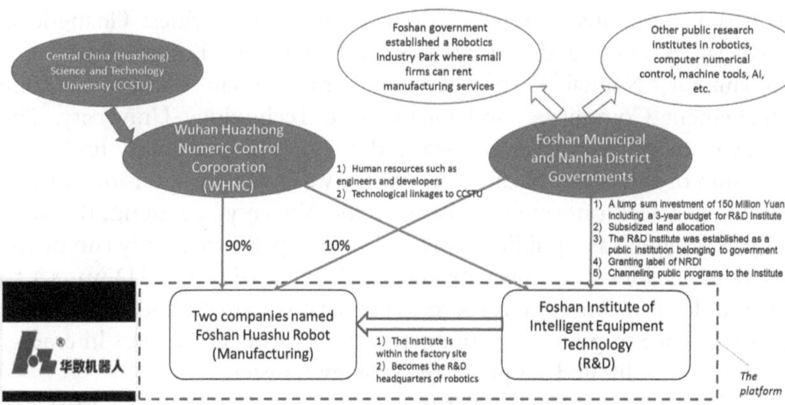

Fig. 9.4 The Platform Organizational Model of Huashu Robotics. (Source: Zhao, W. (2023). Local government as integrative organizer: The Policy practice of constructing innovation platforms in South China, *Innovation and Development Policy*, *5*(1), 73–99)

Huashu Robotics as an innovation platform created industrial, technological and knowledge linkages across the region. In the rapidly growing domestic market, it gained manufacturing clients mostly electrical appliance manufacturers, mobile phone or computer manufacturers in Shenzhen, automakers, and firms in local polishing industry in Foshan. It cooperated with many universities in R&D. For example, cooperation with Huazhong University of Science and Technology in developing core kinematics and dynamics algorithms; cooperation with Guangdong University of Technology in visual cloud system; and cooperation with Beijing Aerospace Cloud Network. Meanwhile, it also cooperated with many vocational schools, such as Huacheng, Nanhai Xinxing, and Foshan Institute of Technology, to set up laboratories equipped with Huashu robots, where students of these educational institutions could have training from Huashu R&D staff. The good performers would be enrolled in Huashu Robotics.

New R&D Institute of Guangdong University of Technology (GURD)

The official name of the new R&D institute of Guangdong Technology University (GURD) is Foshan-Nanhai-Guangdong-Technology-University CNC Equipment Cooperative Innovation Institute. It was established in 2013 as a public institution by cooperation of five parities: Guangdong Provincial Science and Technology Department, Foshan Municipal Government, Nanhai District Government, Foshan High-tech Zone Management Committee, and Guangdong Technology University. The management system of GURD was a division of responsibility under the leadership of the board of directors, which was mainly responsible for discussions and decisions on major issues. From the very beginning, the institute was designed as a public innovation service platform jointly run by the "government-industry-university alliance." The goal of GURD was set to integrate local technology resources, financial resources, and local industrial experience to guide and support manufacturing enterprises in emerging sectors, not limited simply to technology transfer.

GURD received strong government financial aid and policy assistance in all aspects. Its location was within the territory of Nanhai District Government who provided guidance for the planning and development of the park. Foshan High-tech Zone Government was responsible for the specific policies and measures implementation of the project. In the early stage of platform creation, the Nanhai District Government was responsible for the provision of the park land and factory site and invested 120 million Yuan in hardware and equipment. The government also provided strong support in connecting with talents, enterprises, and funds for the incubated firms and research teams. After the institute received the title of New R&D Institute, it received R&D project funds of 5 million Yuan.

To projects, local government even gave direct policy assistance in project establishment, investment, and bank assistance loan arrangement. At cluster level, all-layer governments recommended projects and technical teams to the platform, assisted in attracting investment, and promoted it nationwide. Nanhai government set up evaluation indicators for the institute, including the number of projects, the number of talents, the number of patents, and ventures' output value, etc., and conducted regular inspections to monitor the performance of GURD. As the most comprehensive innovation platform established in Nanhai District, GURD performed the following main functions of incubation, applied R&D, technology services, and human resources development and training.

GURD created multiple linkages in regional industrial sectors and integrated various resources. GURD established multi-level relations with governments and obtained public financial support for projects. GURD applied for more than 30 government-sponsored projects, including 5 national-level projects including the project of crowd service platform for integrated application of industrial robots, and more than 40 provincial and municipal projects including the Guangdong Semiconductor Intelligent Equipment and System Integration Innovation Center, and more than 10 projects at municipal level.

While the channel of linking to government was project financing, the way that GURD established its contacts with local firms was to set up platform organizations for specific industries, with the purpose of clustering industries in Foshan, and coupling with more semi-public institutions such as industry associations. In 2017, with the support from Guangdong Provincial Manufacturing Innovation Center, GURD took the lead of creating the Guangdong Innovation Center of Semiconductor Intelligent Equipment and System Integration. As the first integrated innovation center in Foshan City, it gathered resources from more than 10 leading industrial firms, universities, and research institutions. The center's project of developing equipment of chip manufacturing drew attention of more than 25 firms in semiconductor, including Huawei.

As the most important knowledge linkage to GURD, Guangdong University of Technology made contributions in terms of platform operation, technical support, and talent recruitment in the early stage of GURD development. Guangdong University of Technology sent teachers and professors to take charge of the management and operation of the institute, including building operational structure and personnel recruitment. GURD also established a national post-doctoral joint training program with the Graduate School of Guangdong University of Technology and signed a post-doctoral training agreement. GURD widely cooperated with schools of mechatronics, automation, and computer, and trained more than 300 doctor, master, and bachelor students.

In almost every function of platform, GURD leverage the resources of Guangdong University of Technology for cooperation: ten crowdsourcing platforms with individual professors, 3D printing technical personnel training and professionalization with the School of Continuing Education, and incubation of outstanding entrepreneurial teams with the Institute of Innovation and Entrepreneurship, etc.

Leaguer Science Park

Foshan Leaguer Science Park (Leaguer Park), or more broadly the Leaguer (Foshan) Innovation Center, was established by Leaguer Technology Group, a subsidiary specialized in technology services of the Research Institute of Tsinghua University. As a public institution, the Research Institute of Tsinghua University had to carry out business operation through its firm vehicle Leaguer Technology Group, a State-owned enterprise. Thus, Leaguer Park was in fact under the unified management of the Research Institute of Tsinghua University. Like GURD, from the very beginning Leaguer project was to build a multi-functional platform, with incubation as key business (Fig. 9.5).

The project was introduced by Foshan municipal government to Nanhai district government who provided land, initial investment, and other policy support to Leaguer Park at the initial stage of platform construction. Leaguer Technology Group was responsible for the operation of Leaguer Park as it was built up and would be eventually responsible for its profits and losses in the long run. So far, Leaguer Park still relied on government financial support and had not achieved to make profits.

Both Leaguer Technology Group and Leaguer Park invested in the incubated projects. Since Leaguer Technology Group had strong scientific

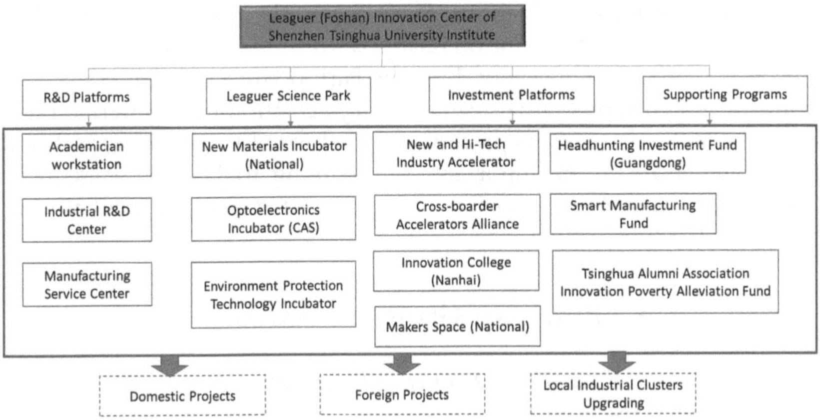

Fig. 9.5 The Platform Structure of Leaguer Park. (Source: Zhao, W. (2023). Local government as integrative organizer: The Policy practice of constructing innovation platforms in South China, *Innovation and Development Policy*, *5*(1), 73–99)

and technological background and understood better the relevant technology and prospects of the project, normally Leaguer Park would just follow Leaguer Technology Group to make the investment decision and its unified risk-control management.

Some regional industrial linkages were created through Leaguer Park. As a large-scale incubator, Leaguer Park accommodated projects in emerging fields such as intelligent manufacturing, new materials, intelligent equipment, electronic information, and biomedicine. For example, a food machine developed by one project was awarded by the Pearl River Talent Program and was used to manufacture durable and ready-to-eat food; another incubated project developed an advanced equipment that could be used for filtration; and a product team from Tsinghua University developed a new type of packaging material.

Besides the products developed by incubated projects, Leaguer Park had its own team providing technology services to serve local firms in traditional sectors. Since local firms were relatively conservative in terms of implementing innovation, the industry-research cooperation projects were only formed gradually.

Besides ties with local industrial firms, Leaguer Park also searched for various linkages with research centers, investment institutions, and other technology service organizations. Since the R&D force of Leaguer Park was still weak, it had to count on relations with universities and institutes, especially Tsinghua University. Leaguer Park offered training courses to students and entrepreneurial teams through creation of an internal business school. Some overseas professors were invited to give lecture. Local governments played an important role to bring to Leaguer Park more contacts with universities, venture investors, and even other incubators in the region.

Platform Growth Strategy

From Project to Platform

The above project cases demonstrate that in Nanhai, new projects were developed eventually to become new ventures functioning as innovation platforms (Table 9.1). For local government, quantity of projects matters, because the more there are platform projects, the more the development is regarded as being driven by innovative activities, such as R&D, venture incubation, and technological services, and the more the new projects contribute to the creation of new industrial system as planned. In fact, Nanhai attracted many projects like the cases.

From 2017 to 2019, the whole district received more than 1200 projects with investment above 100 billion Yuan each. Nanhai District has 955 national-level high-tech firms. The number of national-level in-house technology centers of firms has increased from 1 to 4, the number of provincial-level in-house technology centers has increased from 30 to 65, and the number of municipal-level in-house technology centers has increased from zero to 59. According to local statistics in 2018, there were 188 provincial engineering technology research centers, 282 municipal engineering technology research centers, and 417 district engineering technology research centers. 45% of industrial firms and all big firms with sales of 500 million Yuan in Nanhai have established in-house R&D institutions. There were 8 provincial-level new R&D institutions and 14 technology transfer centers. There were 25 technology business incubators and 12 makers' spaces. Among them, there were 6 national-level technology business incubators, 8 national-level technology business incubation units, 15 district-level technology business incubators, and 16 district-level technology business incubation units. Furthermore, there were 6

Table 9.1 Cases summary of projects becoming platforms

	Daji Material	*Huashu Robotics*	*GURD*	*Leaguer Park*
1. Initial actors of project	A team of private entrepreneurs	State-owned firm of Huazhong University of Technology	Guangdong University of Technology, provincial government, municipal government, district government, hi-tech zone government	State-owned firm of Tsinghua University
2. Initial science and technology resource	Hunan provincial institute of metallurgical materials	Huazhong university of technology	Guangdong university of technology	Tsinghua University
3. Original design of project	A manufacturing firm using patented technologies	An incubator in robot industry	An alliance of government, industry, and university	An incubator for new technologies
4. Realized venture as platform	An R&D- and manufacturing-focused innovation platform with multi-functions and multi-linkages	An R&D- and manufacturing-focused innovation platform with multi-functions and multi-linkages	An incubation- and R&D- focused innovation platform with multi-functions and multi-linkages	An incubation- and R&D- focused innovation platform with multi-functions and multi-linkages
5. Government financial aid and policy support	– initial financial support – integration in official program – integration in local industrial park – linkages to others	– capital contribution – initial financial support – land allocation – label of new R&D institute –linkages to others	– capital contribution – initial financial support – land allocation – label of new R&D institute – integration in official programs – linkages to others	– land allocation – initial financial support – integration in official programs – linkages to others

(*continued*)

Table 9.1 (continued)

	Daji Material	*Huashu Robotics*	*GURD*	*Leaguer Park*
6. Main structures and functions as established platform	– manufacturing – applied R&D – production demonstration – industrial association – venture capital fund (plan)	– applied R&D – manufacturing – technical services – technical training	– incubation – applied R&D – technical services, including technology brokerage – technical training – venture investment – industrial association – platform of platform (carrier)	– incubation – venture investment – technical services – professional training – platform of platform or innovation carrier (plan)
7. Linkages established to industrial sector	–linkages with the whole value chain of local mold industry –linkage with 3D printing clusters in Shenzhen	–industries of electrical appliance, mobile phone, and computer in Shenzhen –industries of auto parts and polishing in Foshan	– all kinds of traditional industries in Foshan and Guangdong – industries of robot, 3D printing, semi-conductor, machine vision, and intelligent equipment in Foshan	– all kinds of traditional industries in Foshan and Guangdong – industries of new materials, intelligent equipment, electronic information, and biomedicine in Foshan

	Daji Material	*Huashu Robotics*	*GURD*	*Leaguer Park*
8. Linkages established to knowledge base	– Hunan provincial Institute of Metallurgical Materials – research institutes in the field of metallurgical materials	– Huazhong University of Technology – national and local research institutes – local vocational schools	– Guangdong University of Technology – Guangdong provincial manufacturing innovation center	– Tsinghua University – via overseas offices of leaguer technology group
9. Clustering approach	Located in industrial park to be part of industrial cluster	Located in industrial park to be part of industrial cluster	Constructed as a S&T park to cluster more projects	Constructed as a S&T park to cluster more projects

Source: Zhao, W. (2023). Local government as integrative organizer: The Policy practice of constructing innovation platforms in South China, ***Innovation and Development Policy***, 5(1), 73–99

national-level makers' spaces, 9 provincial-level makers' spaces, and 160 city-level and district-level innovation and entrepreneurship teams.

From Platform to Cluster

When these projects and platforms are carried out, there is always a geographic and spatial dimension to be considered by local governments. Foshan and Nanhai governments will collect the projects and deploy them at specific locations to form industrial clusters and realize regional development. Traditionally, there have been many industrial clusters in Nanhai, in the sectors of ceramics, textiles and clothing, and aluminum. These clusters comprise almost all the upstream and downstream firms in the industrial value chains, and 90% of parts and components can be sourced locally. Nanhai district has 2 national demonstration zones of industrial cluster (textile, hardware), 4 national demonstration zones of well-known branded cluster (aluminum, underwear, electric light source, ceramics), and 5 provincial demonstration zones of industrial cluster (textile, aluminum, hardware, home appliances, underwear). In addition, there are 685 village-level industrial parks in Nanhai. Emerging clusters are in formation covering sectors such as optoelectronics, creative industry, E-commerce, and biopharma.

At the project level, local government adopted three ways to develop projects and platforms to form larger scaled industrial clusters.

1. One is clustering projects of same or related sectors in the same zones or parks, then fostering the interaction of various teams, projects, and institutions within the same zones or parks to form local clusters. For example, Daji New Material Technology Project was located in New Material Industrial Base of Nanhai, and Huashu Robotics Project was located in Songxia Industrial Zone of Nanhai Science, Technology & Industrial Park. Both clusters were endorsed by local government. The projects then could profit from the development of zone infrastructure and linkages with other institutions.
2. The second approach is that when the project itself is an innovation platform in nature, government supports the execution of project in terms of infrastructure construction and becoming a spatial and organizational "carrier" of all kinds of innovation projects. With the help of zone authorities or district governments, various kinds of innovation platforms such as makers space, incubators, forums, alli-

ances, technology transfer center, and even science parks can become themselves the infrastructure or foundation of industrial clusters. Leaguar Science Park is such an example.

3. The third approach of developing projects and platforms to become industrial clusters is that when the project itself is both "actor" and "carrier" of innovation, government supports the implementation of project more on establishing various external linkages and customized policy measures to promote the project as cornerstone of future cluster. For example, as a government-industry-university alliance, GURD was a heavyweight project combing different functions of incubator, R&D institute, investment company, and technical service firm, etc. Local governments gave supports to its site construction, financial operation, personnel recruitment, and external linkages to access resources, in hoping GURD can bring out a cluster or several clusters in the fields of robots, 3D printing, semiconductor, and intelligent equipment. The last two approaches make the platform potentially an industrial cluster.

From Cluster to Region

Platform provides the fundament for formulating sectoral transcending linkages and interactions across a range of technologies, actors, and industries. The large number of projects, platforms, and then clusters connected to each other in Nanhai eventually created multiple mass effects on regional innovation development.

1. The first effect is industrial upgrading of traditional sectors. The traditional manufacturing in Nanhai has long been based on private ownership and a lot of hidden champions in industrial segments across the country and the world. Most of them are small- and medium-sized firms, situated at the low end of the industrial value chain, with insufficient investment in technological transformation to intelligent manufacturing and low-level production technology. Path dependence makes many firms encounter difficulties in technological upgrading. Platforms link these traditional industries to the emerging advanced manufacturing sectors by interactions and continuous flows of technology, markets, information, talents, capital, and equipment, etc., stimulating the renewal of traditional firms.

2. The second effect is that new platforms in Nanhai, as both actors and carriers of innovation, do not only help existing sectors transform, but also creating a series of new sectors. The platforms as innovation carriers, such as incubators, accelerators, and science parks generate new clusters in advanced manufacturing and ensure the momentum of the industrial cluster is continuously established on new ventures.
3. The platforms as innovation actors that are in or related to a specific industrial field, including innovative ventures, R&D institutions, university scientific research institutes, technology centers, and various science and technology intermediary service agencies, etc., together with the innovation carriers, are engendering region-specific "innovative clusters" in Nanhai. They are networks integrating technology, knowledge, talents, and business projects at the levels of township or district, with local governments as critical nods and paths of linkages of the whole web, together constructing the regional advantage.

How to Manage Platform Policy

What can other developing countries or catch-up economies learn from the platform-centered innovation policy in China? As a local government, the practical experience of Nanhai district is highly attached to the particular government and policy system in China which is simultaneously centralized and regionalized. So other countries searching for innovation-driven development will have difficulty to emulate exactly what China has done. There is no panacea to achieve similar economic or technological output with the input of the same policies. But, at operational level, the policy approaches practiced by Chinese local government may provide some heuristics, especially when they are highlighted by more general thinking.

Targeting Regional Innovation Clusters

Innovation takes place primarily in local milieus with a concentration of knowledge, talents, and entrepreneurs. The recent policy experience by Chinese entrepreneurial local governments reveals the importance of creating regional clusters for a country's innovativeness. Emerging and catch-up economies shall pay more attention to regional innovation system and policy. Regional innovation system approach acknowledges the role and impact of the public sector and policy support, preferably in public-private partnerships, in developing capacity for knowledge creation and exploitation in the context of regions. Subnational governments are conceived to have responsibility to influence a variety of actors, state and non-state, individual, networked and corporate, that may be involved in policy processes.

Certainly, the conduct and creativity of local governments are profoundly shaped by local conditions and each local government should have its own innovation policy approach addressing the specific challenges, problems and opportunities found in each type of region. Chinese local government has found out its own way to leverage and valorize specific knowledge-assets in the country and achieved the so-called constructed regional advantage (Asheim & Coenen, 2006). But there exist many other policy strategies and tools which can also be useful for regional innovation, such as regional path transformation, place-based strategies, smart specialization, policy learning strategy, regional autonomy, knowledge bases, and regional governance (Asheim et al., 2016). Local authorities can take measures to build techno-poles and science hubs, to re-vitalize areas by making investments in new technology-based firms, and to foster "agglomeration effects' and "interactive learning" by developing industrial districts and clusters (Soete, 2007).

Focusing on Practice and Process of Policy Implementation

In general, innovation policy emphasizes policy instrument or tool which is the active means by which policy is implemented—the programs, organizations, rules, and regulations which affect policy outcomes. They can change over time and across space whether in terms of rationales, goals, or implementation methods (Flanagan et al., 2011). Traditional innovation policy instruments include various financial and tax measures for sponsoring basic and applied research, stimulating complementary business R&D, encouraging investment in new technology-based firms, and reinforcing intellectual property protection, etc. More recent innovation policy tools emphasize on diffusion policy including building technological service infrastructure, building science and technology parks, investing venture capital and other forms of entrepreneurship stimulation, and developing the interaction between university and industry. Other innovation policy instruments include public procurement, promoting learning organizations, and promoting consumer learning, etc. (Schot & Steinmueller, 2018).

As for instruments of regional innovation policy, the instruments cover science and technology parks building, formation of formal and informal innovation networks such as clusters, alliances, competitiveness poles and competence centers, innovation advisory services for existing firms and start-ups; innovation vouchers, schemes for talent attraction and retention, and funding for research infrastructure. Specifically, the policies that aim to improve the coordination and alignment among different actors in innovation systems often involve funding conditionality, e.g., research funding on the condition of participation with other organizations in a network. Such conditional funding can be applied to university, corporate, and public research laboratory funding (Edler & Fagerberg, 2017).

Chinese local governments take use of all these policy tools without debating on which one is optimum in the plan. Instead, they implement policy tools in a pragmatist way and integrate them in a complete implementation process that they believe adapted to local circumstances. During the process, local governments' organizational capabilities, implementation procedures, administrative structures, and officials' knowledge on how to manage innovation projects in practice are discovered and built up.

To a large degree, it is rather the implementation process as a management practice by local government officials than the central government's planned innovation policy that constitutes the regional innovation dynamics in China. Meanwhile, because of the experimental and practical nature of regional innovation policy in China, there is little consideration of the efficiency in policy choice. The effectiveness and quantity of results are more important than quality and efficiency. Local governments pursue agglomerate effects at regional level, and they achieved to have critical mass of platforms and clusters.

Using Innovation "Platforms" in a Distinctive Way

At organizational level, innovation platforms are defined as hybrid institutions which operate at the intersection of the university, industry and government institutional spheres and synthesize elements of each sphere in their institutional design. They include technology transfer offices in universities and government research laboratories, industrial liaison offices, business support institutions (science parks, business and technology incubators, start-up accelerators), and financial support institutions (public and private venture capital firms, angel networks, seed capital funds, and so on). Boundaries of these hybrid organizations become looser and innovation processes require greater sharing of tasks and knowledge (Ranga & Etzkowitz 2013; Etzkowitz & Leydesdorff, 2000). The Chinese policy definition of innovation platform is not far away from this academic conceptualization, even it is enlarged to more activities and organization. It is at the policy level that the concept of "innovation platform" gains its Chinese characteristics.

First, Chinese local governments use platform as a guideline, or "policy compass" in Chinese word, to direct their focus on project development. The platform concept is traditionally used either to describe generic technologies such as software and biotechnology, that have potential applications across a wide range of industries, or modular developments in automotive, where a limited number of platforms can be used to build a large variety of car models. A platform approach generates a context better equipped to exploit multipurpose and generic technologies (Asheim et al., 2011; Content & Frenken, 2016). If the European approach of innovation platforms is more about the combination and alignment of knowledge (Tödtling & Trippl, 2005), the Chinese local governments use the idea of "platform" as a policy guiding thought or framework to promote new path of regional development. Pushing all kinds of projects to adopt as much as possible platform business models and functions is the key part of current innovation policy in China. New projects are encouraged or even required by local governments to become eventually innovation platforms.

Secondly, since platforms are often trans-sectoral, Chinese local governments use them as future industrial generators for nurturing sectoral specialization or differentiation in the region. This approach is very similar to the Regional Development Platform Method (Harmaakorpi, 2006; Harmaakorpi et al., 2011), where innovation platforms for regional development must fulfil certain conditions: (i) important regional enterprises must be among the exploiters of building platforms, (ii) the new platforms must be able to create new business activity, (iii) there must be strong enough actors for each sector, (iv) it must be possible to name responsible organizations and people for each sector of the new platform, (v) the actors of the new platform should be able to agree on common goals and a course of action, (vi) the actors of the new platform should be able to name a credible "owner" for the platform.

Thirdly, once established, innovation platform is often used by Chinese local governments as a carrier or platform, a "handler" in Chinese word, to implement a broad mix of policy measures and instruments over specific industry, knowledge base or mode of innovation. The core idea of policies regarding innovation platforms is upgrading and renewing regional economies by stimulating connections between industries and knowledge bases (Cooke et al., 2007; Asheim et al., 2011, 2016). Platform policies create more scope and flexibility on the one hand, and the need for connectivity and the creation of systems on the other. In the Chinese context, since policy "handler" means the combination of both target (actor) and concrete context (carrier) to whom various relevant instruments can be applied, innovation platforms thus become ideal platforms for experimenting new policies. The Chinese practice corresponds exactly to the academic notion of policy platforms which highlights the articulation of an array of instruments including and integrating key components from several policy domains, and various actors, agencies and structures engaged as "carriers" (Asheim et al., 2011).

Adopting the Approach of Holistic Innovation Policy

A major challenge for policy-makers is to streamline the interaction of different levels of government in order to improve the efficiency of innovation policy. Regions and localities are also increasingly creating their autonomous innovation agencies to implement regional innovation strategies which require the development of new institutions and national-regional coordination tools (Guimon, 2014). As the responsibility for the different components of the innovation system is distributed across different areas of government, a "holistic" perspective on policy is necessary for effective coordination between different parts of government, such as the ministries responsible for knowledge creation, skills-production, finance, and so on. This fundamentally horizontal and interdepartmental nature of innovation policy calls for a "whole-of-government" approach. It depends on the establishment of efficient government machinery able to ensure the needed coordination, as well as a powerful coordinating body at the center of government allowing innovation policy to have a pervasive influence (Braun, 2008; Fagerberg & Srholec, 2009; Edquist & Leif (Ed.), 2008).

From this perspective, the Chinese approach of regional innovation policy is very integrative or holistic. Local governments at different levels, from zone, to town, to district, to city, to region, and to province, etc., are all mobilized and coordinated to participate in the whole process of regional innovation-oriented development, working from the micro level of project operation to the mesa and macro level of cluster, urban, and industrial development. This Chinese "whole-of-government" approach is due to its highly consolidated hierarchical system of administration.

Moreover, innovation policy is by nature inter-sectoral and multidimensional. It is important to integrate and co-ordinate policy areas like R&D policies, educational policies, regional policies, and even macroeconomic policies when formulating innovation policies (Edquist, 2018). Regional innovation policy requires addressing a "regional innovation system" instead of single determinant or actors, so it is often under the form of "policy package" or "policy mix" integrating actions in various functional areas—education, trade, investment, finance, and science (Vonortas & Aridi, 2012; World Bank, 2010). This "policy mix" approach suggests the intentional combination and interaction of relevant programs and instruments within a particular region. It promotes the integration of the fundamental practices, processes and mechanisms determining effective regional innovation outcomes, going beyond the more piecemeal approaches within "traditional" regional innovation policy (Flanagan et al., 2011; Borrás & Edquist, 2019).

Chinese local governments practice the "policy mix" actively in innovation. They usually use simultaneously all kinds of functional policies in various fields, such as science, education, research and development, technology, industry, labor, finance, fiscal, even infrastructure and urbanization development in a supplementary and multidimensional way. The policies and instruments may be overlapped in targeting the same projects or platforms, but since no one knows what the optimum situation shall be, effectiveness is prioritized to efficiency concern.

Becoming a Super Manager of Regional Innovation Development

Clustering and networking are important factors in constructing regional innovation advantage (Moulaert & Sekia, 2003). However, the proximity of various firms does not itself yield innovative results. Platforms are actively created regional multi-actor network nods or even innovation networks themselves. They can become the concrete actions in running the regional innovation systems, as well as lead the way to new regional paths. By constructing numerous innovation platforms with various project actors, Chinese local governments in fact create innovation networks with enough critical mass allowing the emergence of regional industry or groups of industries. They do not stay at the planning level of macro environment or institution building but are engaged in transforming projects to platforms and further developing platforms to local clusters and networks. Thus, the resulted regional innovation network is very much like the Taiwanese State-led network in the developmental State theory (Amsden & Chu, 2003).

For the non-Asian economies, what may be learnt is not the whole government-based network, but the powerful role of local government as a super "manager" during policy implementation process, who actively searches, mobilizes, and integrates financial, technological, market, and organizational resources often beyond simple project boundaries to achieve the regional innovation development.

Conclusion

The Pearl River Delta in Guangdong presents a typical example of how local government practices innovation policy and what the processes are inside the implementation "black box." Based on an in-depth study of Nanhai District in Foshan City, Guangdong and the four new investment projects, this chapter argues that Chinese local governments in Guangdong and their policy implementation practice do play a key role in constructing and developing innovation platforms, which are regarded as a cornerstone in regional innovation system (Asheim et al., 2011, 2016). In fact, Chinese local governments behave as an "integrative organizer" in managing and coordinating regional level innovation processes.

This chapter also proposes a three-step policy model of using platform as central mechanism to facilitate and promote regional innovation-driven development. The proposed model, especially the underlined policy instruments, can have wide policy implications to State or local governments. For example, the ideas of fusing industrial and innovation chains to target emerging industries, obliging new projects to adopt platform business models, transforming platforms to real industrial players, and sourcing projects from different types of organizations (firm, university, association, and entrepreneur, etc.). Local government can use cluster policy to grow the invested platform projects to a larger scale to have regional effects. Business companies can adopt the platform model as innovation strategy when creating new business with internal or external technologies.

But there is no such innovation policy, and each region shall find its own "tailor-made" approach addressing the specific challenges, problems, and opportunities (Tödtling & Trippl, 2005). By far, the innovation policy practice of Chinese local governments can only supply some heuristic approaches, far from the "best practice." Many questions relevant to the fundamental problematics in innovation theory, about innovation system, innovation platform, and regional policy, etc. have not yet full answers. For example, what the conditions of platform policy in other regions and localities in Guangdong and in China should be, and why the same "constructing-platform" approach is less effective in remoted regions, etc. These questions are related to broader policy background, such as spatial deployment of platforms, thickening situation of innovation ecosystems, and integration of clusters with various level urbanization and infrastructure development. The readers shall refer to other chapters in the book to put the platform policy in the overall structure of new generation of regional innovation policies to have a better understanding.

References

Amsden, A. H., & Chu, W.-W. (2003). *Beyond late development: Taiwan's upgrading policies* (p. 224). MIT Press.

Asheim, B.-T., & Coenen, L. (2006). Contextualising regional innovation Systems in a Globalising Learning Economy: On knowledge bases and institutional frameworks. *The Journal of Technology Transfer, 31*(1), 163–173.

Asheim, B.-T., Boschma, R., & Cooke, P. (2011). Constructing regional advantage: Platform policies based on related variety and differentiated knowledge bases. *Regional Studies, 45*(7), 893–904.

Asheim, B.-T., Grillitsch, M., & Trippl, M. (2016). Regional innovation systems: Past—Present—Future, chapters. In: R. Shearmu, C. Carrincazeaux & D. Doloreux (eds.), Handbook on the geographies of innovation (chapter 2, pp. 45–62). Edward Elgar Publishing.

Borrás, S., & Edquist, C. (2019). Holistic innovation policy: Theoretical foundations, policy problems, and instrument choices (320 p.). Oxford University Press.

Boschma, R. A. (2005). Proximity and innovation: A critical assessment. *Regional Studies, 39*(1), 61–74.

Braun, D. (2008). Organising the political coordination of knowledge and innovation policies. *Science and Public Policy, 35*(4), 227–239.

Capello, R., & Kroll, H. (2016). From theory to practice in smart specialization strategy: Emerging limits and possible future trajectories. *European Planning Studies, 24*(8), 1393–1406.

Chesbrough, H. W. (2003). *Open innovation.* Harvard Business School Press.

Content, J., & Frenken, K. (2016). Related variety and economic development: A literature review. *European Planning Studies, 24*(12), 2097–2112. https://doi.org/10.1080/09654313.2016.1246517

Cooke, P., Laurentis, C.-D., & Tödtling, F. (2007). *Regional knowledge economies: Markets, clusters and innovation*. Edward Elgar.

Edler, J., & Fagerberg, J. (2017). Innovation policy: What, why, and how? *Oxford Review of Economic Policy, 33*(1), 2–23. https://doi.org/10.1093/oxrep/grx001

Edquist, C. (2018). Towards a holistic innovation policy: Can the Swedish National Innovation Council (NIC) be a role model? *Research Policy, 48*(4), The Mayan 2019, 869–879.

Edquist, C., & Leif, H. (Ed.). (2008). Small country innovation systems: Globalisation, Change and Policy in Asia and Europe (544 p.). Edward Elgar Publishing

Estensoro, M., & Larrea, M. (2016). Overcoming policy making problems in smart specialization strategies: Engaging subregional governments. *European Planning Studies, 24*(7), 1319–1335.

Etzkowitz, H., & Leydesdorff, L. (2000). The dynamics of innovation: From National Systems and "mode 2" to a triple helix of university–industry–government relations. *Research Policy, 29*(2), 109–123.

Fagerberg, J., & Srholec, M. (2009). Innovation systems, technology and development: Unpacking the relationships. In B.-Å. Lundvall, K. J. Joseph, C. Chaminade, & J. Vang (Eds.), *Handbook of innovation systems and developing countries: Building domestic capabilities in a global setting* (pp. 83–115). Edward Elgar.

Flanagan, K., Uyarra, E., & Laranja, M. (2011). The 'policy mix' for innovation: Rethinking innovation policy in a multi-level, multi-actor context. *Research Policy, 40*, 702–713.

Foray, D. (2018). Smart specialization strategies as a case of mission-oriented policy—A case study on the emergence of new policy practices. *Industrial and Corporate Change, 27*(5), 817–832.

Guimon, J. (2014, October). Regional innovation policy and multilevel governance in developing countries: Between a rock and a hard place. Innovation, Technology & Entrepreneurship, World Bank Policy Note, Number 6.

Harmaakorpi, V. (2006). Regional development platform method (RDPM) as a tool for regional innovation policy. *European Planning Studies, 14*(8), 1085–1104. https://doi.org/10.1080/09654310600852399

Harmaakorpi, V., Tura, T., & Melkas, H. (2011). Regional innovation platforms. In P. Cooke, B. Asheim, R. Boschma, R. Martin, D. Schwartz, & F. Tödtling (Eds.), *The handbook of regional innovation and growth* (pp. 556–572). Edward Elgar.

Howells, J. (2006). Intermediation and the role of intermediaries in innovation. *Research Policy, 35*(5), 715–728. https://doi.org/10.1016/j.respol.2006.03.005

Janssen, M. J., Bogers, M., & Wanzenböck, I. (2020). Do systemic innovation intermediaries broaden horizons? A proximity perspective on R&D partnership formation. *Industry and Innovation, 27*(6), 605–629.

Kroll, H. (2015). Efforts to Implement Smart Specialization in Practice—Leading Unlike Horses to the Water, *European Planning Studies,* 23(10), 2079-2098.

Li, J., Deng, Q., & Sorensen, O. J. (2011). Building national innovation platform in China: Theoretical exploration and empirical study. *Journal of Science and Technology Policy in China, 2*(1), 58–78.

Menzel, M.-P. (2015). Interrelating dynamic proximities by bridging, reducing and producing distances. *Regional Studies, 49*(11), 1892–1907.

Morisson, A., & Doussineau, M. (2019). Regional innovation governance and place-based policies: Design, implementation, and implications. *Regional Studies, Regional Science, 6*(1), 101–116.

Moulaert, F., & Sekia, F. (2003). Territorial innovation models: A critical survey. *Regional Studies, 37*(3), 289–302.

Parjanen, S., & Hyypiä, M. (2018). Innovation platforms as a solution to the proximity paradox. *European Planning Studies, 26*(7), 1312–1329.

Pekkarinen, S., & Harmaakorpi, V. (2006). Building regional innovation networks: The definition of an age business Core process in regional innovation system. *Regional Studies, 40*(4), 401–413.

Pinto, H., Fernandez-Esquinas, M., & Uyarra, E. (2015). Universities and knowledge-intensive business services (KIBS) as sources of knowledge for innovative firms in peripheral regions. *Regional Studies, 49*(11), 1873–1891.

Ranga, M., & Etzkowitz, H. (2013, August). Triple Helix systems: an analytical framework for innovation policy and practice in the Knowledge Society. *Industry & Higher Education, 27*(3), 237–262.

Schot, J., & Steinmueller, W.-E. (2018). Three frames for innovation policy: R&D, systems of innovation and transformative change, Research Policy 47 (2018) 1554–1567.

Schubert, G., & Alpermann, B. (2019). Studying the Chinese policy process in the era of 'top- level design': The contribution of 'political steering' theory. *Journal of Chinese Political Science, 24*(2), 199–224.

Soete, L. (2007). From industrial to innovation policy. *journal of industry. Competition and Trade, 7,* 273–284.

Tödtling, F., & Trippl, M. (2005). One size fits all? Towards a differentiated regional innovation policy approach. *Research Policy, 34*(8), 1203–1219.

Uotila, T., Harmaakorpi, V., & Hermans, R. (2012). Finnish mosaic of regional innovation system—Assessment of thematic regional innovation platforms based on related variety. *European Planning Studies, 20*(10), 1583–1602.

van Lente, H., Hekkert, M., Smits, R., & van Waveren, B. (2003). Roles of systemic intermediaries in transition processes. *International Journal of Innovation Management, 7*(3), 1–33.

Vonortas, N.-S. and Aridi, A. (2012). *Innovation policy handbook* (202 pages). Center for International Science and Technology Policy, The George Washington University.

Wang, C., & Wang, L. (2017). Unfolding policies for innovation intermediaries in China: A discourse network analysis. *Science And Public Policy*, 44(3), 2017, 354–368.

World Bank. (2010). Innovation policy: Guide for developing countries (408 p.). The World Bank.

Yin, R. K. (2018). *Case study research and applications* (6th ed.). Sage.

CHAPTER 10

The Coming New Policy for Innovation-Driven Development

Introduction

The preceding chapters in Part II of this book are to describe how Guangdong has progressed from factor-driven to investment-driven and then to innovation-driven development in terms of industrial economy, reflecting the overall advancement of China's economy.

At the business level, the innovation model has evolved from the earliest closed OEM production and basic capability acquisition through technological learning, to the stages involving R&D investment, enhanced absorptive capacity, and the formation of strategic integration capabilities, culminating in the recent phase of open innovation. In sum, the innovation model of local companies has shifted from a linear innovation chain dependent on manufacturing processes to the current strategies of innovation platforms and innovation ecosystems.

At the government level, innovation policies have evolved from initial industrial clusters and specialized town policies, through R&D promotion, industry-university-research alliances, and innovation chain policies, to the latest integration of business strategies into an innovation ecosystem and platform policies.

The characteristics of these local innovation policies are bottom-up in style, that is, starting from the concrete situation of local companies, there is a close interaction and combination between business strategy and

W. Zhao, *Remade in South China*, IPP Studies in the Frontiers of China's Public Policy,
https://doi.org/10.1007/978-981-95-7277-9_10

government policy, and the joint force formed effectively promotes regional innovation and development.

In the final chapter of this book, we will first review the evolution of innovation models for local small and medium-sized companies at the micro-level through a case study of a LED company,[1] which exemplifies well the transformation from closed OEM models to open innovation platform models. The local environment in which it operates has also evolved from traditional industrial clusters to more complex innovation ecosystems.

Then, we will outline a roadmap guide for the new generation of regional innovation policies brought about by the emerging innovation trajectory in Guangdong. I hope that the summarized experience from Guangdong can inspire any economic community, government, and business company that hopes to achieve innovative development through catching up.

Business Model from Production Chain to Open Innovation System[2]

In the context of industrial upgrading, Chinese Small and Medium-sized Enterprises (SMEs) see new opportunities and challenges in this shifting from low-value to relatively high-value activities in global production networks, and knowledge-based activities through entrepreneurship, innovation, and enhanced market mechanisms. SMEs aggressively redesign their business model and their ecosystem environment to leverage their capabilities and improve their position within the ecosystem to prosper and survive.

Hongxing Innovation Valley, a pioneer LED maker in the specialized cluster in Guangdong, has undergone different stages transforming itself from a traditional OEM producer to a LED business incubator. Its new business model with new ecosystem strategy can be described as "open innovation," emphasizing openness in companies by considering external ideas, technologies, and knowledge in their business (Chesbrough, 2003).

[1] Light Emitting Diode.

[2] Most of the materials in this part is drawn from my contribution to the paper (Sonia Chikh M'hamed and Wei Zhao, 2022). From Workbench to Incubation: the Case of an Open Innovation Approach in LED Production Upgrading in Southeast China, *Revue Gestion2000*, Volume 39, number 2, 2022, pp. 141–162.

The business model refers here to the description of the system of interdependent activities that are performed by the firm and by its partners, and the mechanisms that link these activities to each other (Zott & Amit, 2010). The adoption of open innovation strategy can strengthen a company's capability to engage in a business model of incubation to transform the ecosystem.

To be precise, Hongxing Innovation Valley adopted a form of industrial upgrading by creating an open incubator in parallel to its traditional LED manufacturing activities. The nature of industrial upgrading is to capture higher added-value activities. According to the founder of the Hongxing Innovation Valley *"open innovation derives from external sources such as suppliers, customers (…) innovation cannot "stay close", in our industry we must rely on open innovation to transform, upgrade our business, to capture higher value."*

The Sector of Light Emitting Diode (LED) in China

LED is an electronic device that lights up when electricity is passed through it. They are good for displaying images because they can be relatively small, and they do not burn out. The LED industrial value chain can be divided in upstream, midstream, and downstream. Upstream includes raw materials production, substrate materials production, chip epitaxial wafers (epitaxial wafers) production, and chip making. Midstream activities include LED chip packaging and testing, related equipment production, as well as power drive, cooling base, lampshade, and other components production. Downstream activities include integrating chips to various products of application fields such as lighting products, displays, signal indications, and backlights. Each of activity can further be subdivided into multiple processes in terms of process technology. For example, chip manufacturing includes production of electric boards, chip cutting, chip testing, and chip packaging includes die bonding, wire bonding, injection molding, packaging, and testing, etc.

The structure of global LED industry has been formed progressively over time. Chinese LED brands do not play a significant role in global market. In terms of value acquisition, firms undertaking high-tech chip design and software development activities, normally positioned at the upstream end of the supply chain, capture higher value. Some new Chinese LED producers begin to play more and more important role in this filed. For example, San'an, Nationstar and HuaLei have gained significant market share and broke up the old oligopolistic structure of the global lighting industry. After 2015, the yield of downstream companies constituted nearly 80 percent of the total output of the Chinese LED industry, while that of midstream companies represented 16 percent and that of upstream companies merely 4 percent (Butollo & Ten Brink, 2018).

After years of rapid transformation, since the final LED products are now commoditized as personal computer type products, price competition in LED market is severe. Suppliers of components and product assemblers cannot get a big chunk of the whole added value. However, there exists possibility that higher value can be created by downstream producers who sell whole lighting modules and other applications. Downstream activity is very low value added due to LED as volume consumption products, but producers can enter into higher value-added fields when they begin selling LED as a lighting system to be integrated into new building construction, and providing relevant adapting and maintenance service packages, etc.

Three circumstances put the Chinese LED industry in a favorable position. First, China was already a strong production base for lighting products before the advent of LED technology. Many traditional lighting enterprises thus converged toward LED.

Second, the domestic market for lighting products is growing particularly fast. In China, people are adopting LED lighting at a rapid pace because of the gradual reduction of LED lighting price. The penetration of LED lighting is growing at a rapid pace due to supportive government policies that help out LED manufacturer and distributor to a great extent. The growing demand for LED lighting in China stimulates LED light market. Chinese LED manufacturer mainly focused on Research and Development of LED light, cost reduction, energy efficiency, environmentally friendly, and long life. In China, the demand for lower-end LED product is high, but there is also stiff competition in this segment.

Third, since the end of the 2000s the Chinese authorities have been giving particular support to the LED industry at central and especially local levels. Many Chinese LED light manufacturers are increasing their production capacity because they are getting an optimal subsidy from both central and local government. The favorable government policies of China are helping the LED manufacturer and distributor to run their business smoothly, and it will further boost the LED lighting market in the forecast period. Besides, the Chinese government has also implemented LED lighting standard that will help to produce the supreme quality of the LED product.

The LED Cluster in Zhongshan of Guangdong Province

With the rise of the LED industry in China, Zhongshan City in Guangdong Province, which is one of the nine prefecture-level cities of the PRD and has been a strong cluster in traditional lighting industry, has gradually turned to the development track of the LED industry. According to the statistics of Zhongshan Semiconductor Lighting Industry Association, in 2018, the sales of Zhongshan's LED industry were about 70.3 billion yuan, becoming an emerging industry in Zhongshan City. Lighting industry clusters of "traditional lighting + LED lighting" have been formed quickly in Zhongshan, and the output value of the two sectors has exceeded 100 billion yuan. As of June 2019, there are 8160 manufacturing enterprises involved in LED lighting products in Zhongshan City.

The Guzhen Town in Zhongshan City, where the Hongxing Innovation Valley is located, is the core cluster of lighting products manufacturing in Zhongshan. Guzhen has a relatively complete industrial system, with its lighting industry system covering from the upstream to the downstream segments of the whole value chain. The lighting industry of Guzhen started in the 1980s. Since its development, the structure of the traditional lighting industry has gradually transformed to the current structure of "traditional lighting + LED lighting."

It has formed a geographic area centered around Guzhen town, covering 3 cities and 11 towns in the surrounding area, with an annual output value of nearly 100 billion yuan. Lighting industry cluster of Guzhen has a lighting sales facility of nearly 3 million square meters and has held 26 consecutive lighting fairs, attracting more than 100 businessmen from different countries and regions. The State-level market procurement trade system has been settled here, and Guzhen builds a cross-border e--commerce cluster area recently. Guzhen Lighting Industry occupies 70% of the national lighting market. Guzhen currently has 16,000 lighting and accessories industrial and commercial enterprises, of which about 300,000 people are engaged in this industry. One out of every five people in Guzhen is engaged in the lighting industry. Products are exported to more than 130 countries and regions such as Hong Kong, Macao, Taiwan, Southeast Asia, Japan, the United States, and Europe, and it has become one of the world's largest professional lighting markets.

Guzhen has built a backbone road network system, connecting the three major highways to the Guangdong-Hong Kong-Macau Greater Bay Area, speeding up the construction of new infrastructure represented by 5G, artificial intelligence, and industrial internet. The lighting industry in Guzhen reached 6801 patents and 10,000 patents in the future. In addition, the town of Guzhen has also established a lighting college. It sets up a rapid rights protection center to protect the intellectual property rights of lighting designs. It establishes the "China Light Capital Smart Light Pole Alliance," vigorously builds, and strives to achieve the goal of making Guzhen the "China Light Capital" as well as "Smart Light Pole Industry Base" in China.

Before 2008, as a local industrial cluster, Guzhen enjoyed various advantages. It had mature supply chains of all kinds of components and spare parts for lighting products. The large quantity of production and large scope of products led to low cost and attracted international clients such as Target, Walmart, HomeDepot, Metro, and Ikea. Most firms were small organizations, flexible in production, and diversified in terms of products. But they lacked capabilities in R&D, new product design and creation, and innovation. After 2008 crisis, big clients pressed local firms to lower prices and threatened to move their supply chains elsewhere. Their commercial margins deteriorated with rising labor cost and short of qualified labor supply. Thus, Guzhen faced serious challenges of industrial upgrading since several years.

The Closed Production Chain of Hongxing

Hongxing Innovation Valley, an innovative LED business incubator, was established by Mr. Deng Qiuping, owner of two typical manufacturing factories of lighting products in Guzhen. As other small and medium--sized firms in the local cluster, the two factories of Mr. Deng were OEM (Original Equipment Manufacturing) producers, taking orders from big, branded distributors, wholesalers, and retailers and making products according to their specifications. The two factories mainly undertook general production activities such as purchasing, manufacturing, distribution logistics, and deliverance to clients, with some engineering, but absent in higher value activities such as R&D, new product design, brand marketing, and customer service. They hired more than 100 workers with sales turnover over 8 million US dollars per year.

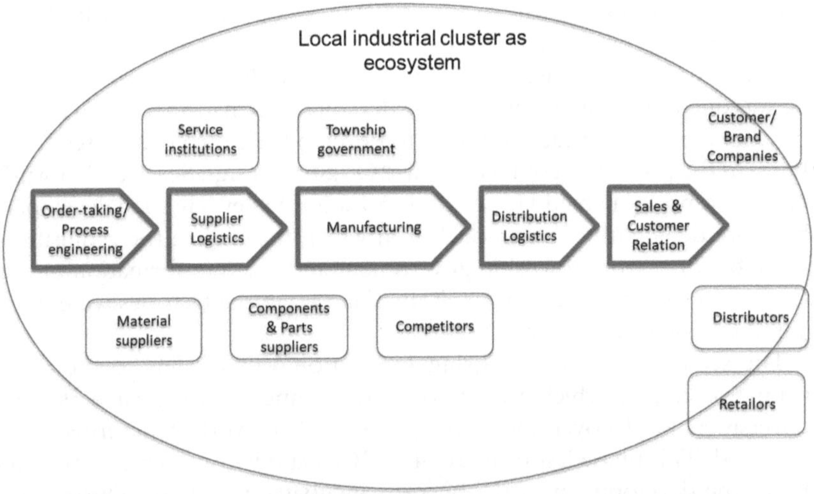

Fig. 10.1 Closed Production Chain of OEM Factories. (Source: Sonia Chikh M'hamed and Wei Zhao. (2022). From Workbench to Incubation: The Case of an Open Innovation Approach in LED Production Upgrading in Southeast China. *Revue Gestion2000, 39*(2), 141–162)

Local industrial cluster constituted a relatively closed ecosystem of the OEM factories, composed of local suppliers of materials and spare parts, with professional wholesale market often organized by township government, as shown in Fig. 10.1.

The Business Incubation Model of Hongxing

As a specialized LED business incubator, Hongxing Innovation Valley has undergoing three entrepreneurial development stages to achieve Mr. Deng's transformation and upgrading from LED manufacturing to business incubation model.

During the 2008 crisis, Mr. Deng's OEM factories were almost bankrupted due to the decline of foreign orders. From 2008 to 2014, he talked to many people that he knew to search for the solution to survive the manufacturing sectoral crisis. This first stage of "the Pre-incubation" was the creation of project idea including key transformations of the traditional manufacturer to an incubator.

In 2014, during his trip to Europe, Mr. Deng's asked himself: "how will I survive? How will my factory survive? The only way is to have more designs and more designers." He realized that his difficulty in manufacturing was due to lack of resource to hire designers. He had an idea: "why not to create a place to attract designers to develop their own businesses?" He thus had the project of establishing an "Original Design Service Platform" under a company named Hongxing Innovation Valley. He then developed the more detailed business model from which the idea of the acquisition of the building from township government and the transformation of the whole area surrounding was involved. The two initial factories were integrated to a new ecosystem.

The second stage of Hongxing Innovation Valley refers to the main incubation during which a range of activities and services, partners (i.e., universities, local government, designers) and network structuring were identified. This phase last from 2014 to 2018 and is considered to be central to the development of the business incubator programs. During this phase, the team of designers (as tenant entrepreneurs) reached over 200 designers from different countries (Italy, Belgium, Germany, etc.) and 13 universities became its key partners.

In parallel with the old manufacturing value chain, Mr. Deng in fact created a new value chain composed of an incubation platform and its open ecosystem. The platform offered design services to attract external designers to come with their own ideas to create their own business, while Mr. Deng's factories could take the industrialization part. The incubator also played role of innovation broker by organizing IP competitions and auctions for designers' new designs. The approach is implemented at an interorganizational level in which a range of various actors (i.e., designers, suppliers, distributors, universities, governments, etc.) are embedded in the new innovation ecosystem providing several entrepreneurial opportunities.

Through Hongxing Innovation Valley, many traditional manufacturers in the cluster or other lighting firms could find new product and designs originated from universities, design workshops, and research institutes. Internally, since Mr. Deng's factories could also produce newly designed products, the linkage to the designers and high-quality human resources eventually reinforced the factories' R&D and design capabilities, even became partially the in-house design and R&D activities to some degree. From 2014 to 2019, the two factories together reached an annual sales growth rate of 30% and survived in the market.

Externally, Hongxing Innovation Valley also set up various linkages with other key stakeholders under the form of alliance. Centered on its incubation platform model, it organized Design Alliance, Manufacturing Alliance, Marketing Alliance, and Data Center of LED Industry, in order to cultivate a favorable business environment for the new ventures incubated. Over time, a new ecosystem for open innovation was formed around Hongxing Innovation Valley.

The open innovation ecosystem included later 300 domestic designers from more than 30 universities, research institutes, and professional workshops; 200 foreign designers from Italy, Netherland, and Germany; numerous manufacturing firms across China, mainly located in Zhejiang Province; local suppliers of components, materials, and services; distributors, E-commerce shops, traders, and retailers; IT and internet companies; new design and new venture investors; insurance companies for IP protection; local government; etc. The incubation value chain and its new ecosystem is shown in Fig. 10.2.

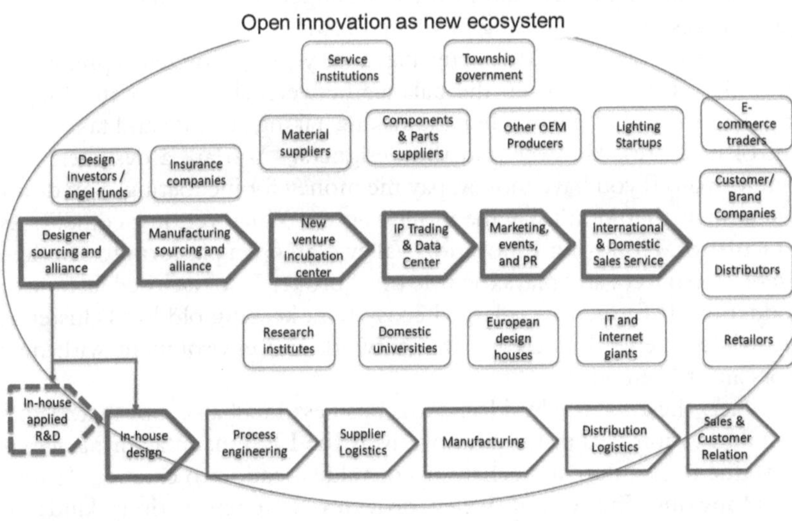

Fig. 10.2 Open Innovation Platform of Hongxing Innovation Valley. (Source: Sonia Chikh M'hamed and Wei Zhao. (2022). From Workbench to Incubation: The Case of an Open Innovation Approach in LED Production Upgrading in Southeast China. *Revue Gestion2000, 39*(2), 141–162)

The Open Innovation System of Hongxing

The third and final step of "the post-incubation" of Hongxing Innovation Valley was from 2018 to 2021. At this stage, the business incubator model has already achieved all the transitioning steps of its transformation and has started to fully perform the functions of an innovative LED incubator, i.e., incubating designers' new ventures, transacting new designs and new Ips, and upgrading in-house R&D.

The value proposition alongside with the management of the intellectual property (IP) has been identified and tested. The value creation and capture have become central to consolidate the developed ecosystem and to prepare this final step. In terms of value capturing, Hongxing Innovation Valley has tried and is trying different ways to co-create value with designers and many other stakeholders in the ecosystem. At bottom line, it charges new ventures rentals, service fees, and management fees. It organizes specific promotion fairs for new designs and charges 10% of the patent deal as commission. It signs with designers' new ventures for getting a 1–2% share of their sales once these firms begin to sell in the market. It plans to set up investment fund with some angel investors in order to have equity shares of the promising incubated firms.

As a businessperson, Mr. Deng has a very pragmatist entrepreneurial spirit, always trying to keep the balance between short term and longer term, realism and idealism. He has a risking-taking attitude and takes risk-control measures. He ever told the designers: "You are a designer; I'm open for you. If you have money, pay me money for incubating. You don't have money, then don't pay me money now… Whatever, just come!". As an incubator, Hongxing Innovation Valley is an open platform to leverage different resources and plays the role of a "broker," not a closed factory of production. It formed an enlarged ecosystem, keeping old local cluster as base while extended to create new network and environment with new actors and stakeholders.

In fact, the reason why Hongxing business incubator can materialize open innovation to transform innovatively the LED manufacturing activities is due to its internal mechanisms of value creation to external designers. Hongxing Innovation Valley provides designers various kinds of valuable services: assistance to company registration and establishment, intellectual property protection of designers, social networking and linking of designers, investing in production and manufacturing, and finding clients to customize designs. Recently, Hongxing Innovation Valley extended its showroom surface to 6000 m^2 over three floors and intended to develop international franchises. With more designers joining in, incubation proves to be an effective approach to realize open innovation in Hongxing case.

As a newly established incubator by a tradition manufacturer in the LED sector, Hongxing Innovation Valley has not reached its breakeven, though its affiliated OEM factories survived very well. During this difficult stage, the Zhongshan LED incubator has also experienced the impact of the COVID-19 pandemic which has revealed challenges to pursue the initial objectives as well as new opportunities for the LED incubator in the field of artificial intelligence (AI) and blockchain technology for LED design in the future.

The Convergence of Business and Government in Managing Innovation

In a purely technical sense, the essence of "innovation" is a transforming process, encompassing activities across multiple stages such as scientific discovery, technological invention, technological transformation, and technological industrialization, collectively forming a complete "innovation chain." The development of all industries represents a sequential accumulation of this chain. The process of transforming scientific discoveries into technological inventions gives rise to new industries; the transition from technological invention to technological transformation fosters services and organizations related to the commercialization of scientific and technological achievements, such as university and research institutions, technology transfer offices, technology intermediaries, and technology markets.

Meanwhile, the expansion from technological transformation to industrialization requires specialized enterprises and institutions engaged in various industrialization and marketization efforts, including incubators, accelerators, and shared production facilities. As an economic and social process, innovation requires diverse information and knowledge, which are nearly impossible for any individual to fully grasp in modern society but instead reside in the minds of different actors. While instances of Schumpeterian entrepreneurs completing the entire innovation process alone occasionally occur, modern practice typically involves specialized organizations based on social division of labor. Modern professionals and teams have diminished or even replaced the role traditionally attributed to entrepreneurship. These professionals and teams generally include scientists, experimental scientists, innovation engineers, feasibility engineers, product engineers, market engineers, technology operations teams, management teams, and investment teams. Their roles and importance vary across different stages of the innovation chain.

Therefore, in comparison with other types of economic activities, innovation is a process that requires more active management and governance. Innovation management involves, on the one hand, how to generate new ideas and organize their implementation, and on the other hand, how to coordinate and handle the external environment and various elements and resources necessary for the innovation process. Certainly, innovation needs entrepreneurial spirit and risk-taking behavior of firm owners, as shown by the case of Hongxing Innovation Valley and Mr. Deng, who adopted open innovation approach to redesign the business model, improve the capabilities, and restructure the ecosystem in the era of innovation-driven development.

Meanwhile, since the progress of innovation largely depends on external, extra-organizational conditions, referred to as the "ecosystem" (Ortt & van der Duin, 2008), innovation management cannot be confined solely to the firm level. It is equally crucial to have in-depth government intervention at the meso-level of industries and regions. As Chesbrough (2003) pointed out, in innovation, the boundaries between companies and their surrounding environments are constantly shifting, and innovation activities are managed by multiple participants, not just by corporate managers. Regional innovation policy, in essence, is a form of "open management" jointly undertaken by business companies and local governments regarding the innovation processes that occur outside the firm side.

Joint management of innovation process and co-value creation are the very essence of the bottom-up innovation model of Guangdong. Prior to the COVID-19 pandemic, local governments in Guangdong took various practical tools in a bottom-up manner that helped stimulate innovation vitality. This local experience may represent the embryo of a new generation of regional innovation policies that China and other economies should vigorously promote in the future.

A Guideline of New Regional Innovation Policy

Policy Objectives

The new generation of regional innovation policies should clearly aim to build a local "regional innovation ecosystem" as the primary policy goal. While this concept is similar to the traditional goal of constructing a "regional innovation system," the concept of an innovation ecosystem introduces new meanings to the policy objective.

1. First, it shifts the focus from a macro-level system to a more micro-level focus, emphasizing specific and localized innovation environments. Local governments need to provide conditions that are tailored to enterprises. From a policy perspective, an innovation ecosystem should be defined as a continuous and dynamic process system that involves increasing resources and support brought about by policy implementation, including human and financial capital, entrepreneurial knowledge, market insights, and cultural attitudes.
2. Second, it not only involves the environment and conditions but also emphasizes the cultivation and evolution of innovation actors within the ecosystem. The symbiotic relationships in the ecosystem imply that, as actors grow, they become parts of the environment that other actors can depend on. Therefore, cultivating innovation actors and fostering the innovation environment are essentially the same from an ecological perspective. This requires the government to shift from focusing on creating a "large system" to nurturing a "small ecosystem." The policy focus must shift from establishing macro-level, generalized institutions and rules to offering more personalized services that address specific issues faced by local innovation regions, projects, enterprises, and entrepreneurs.
3. Third, the innovation ecosystem emphasizes the spatial agglomeration and self-organization of innovation actors, elements, and resources. This requires the government to develop better spatial agglomeration planning while leveraging market mechanisms.
4. Fourth, the government itself is part of the innovation ecosystem, and at the outset, it is often the most critical part. The government must evolve and continually adapt to the development of the ecosystem it fosters. For example, the government can recognize the diversity of innovation paths, especially the platform-based, modular,

and networked nature of modern technological innovations, rather than being constrained by a linear view of the innovation process.

Regional innovation policies aimed at creating a "regional innovation ecosystem" should be a comprehensive system, not fragmented individual measures or an accumulation of uncoordinated policies. A complete policy system includes guiding principles, objectives, targets, governance structures, and policy tools. The design of the policy should adopt a systematic approach. Given that the innovation ecosystem is multifaceted, the innovation policy system should cover various aspects of the region, including different sectors, spatial areas, and levels of governance.

Policy Domains

Innovation is a process system composed of a series of key activities or functions, such as research, technology development, organizational mediation and platforms, industrial upgrading, labor training, capital finance, market competition, and education. The new generation of regional innovation policies must cover almost all of these areas, including entrepreneurial atmosphere, innovation culture, education, human resources, labor markets, finance, scientific and technological infrastructure, equipment, professional services, standards, regional branding, government procurement, quality control, intellectual property protection, and the internet. This is a typical "multi-functional" policy. These numerous domains also represent different facets or components of the innovation ecosystem that the policy aims to foster.

According to innovation system theory (Borras & Edquist, 2019), these system functions can be divided into four major areas:

1. Providing knowledge inputs for the innovation process (e.g., research and education),
2. Demand-side activities (e.g., public procurement or new product quality and safety requirements),
3. Creating and changing institutions and organizations (e.g., entrepreneurship), and
4. Providing support services for innovative enterprises (e.g., innovation financing, incubation).

Innovation policies should target these four areas by developing specific intervention measures, forming a policy mix that covers the entire innovation process. However, this does not mean merging urban planning, industrial planning, science policies, and education policies into one. In this sense, the new generation of regional innovation policies represents China's version of a comprehensive innovation policy.

Comprehensive and holistic innovation policies require the mobilization of various government departments, primarily the Ministry of Science and Technology, Ministry of Economy, Ministry of Industry and Information Technology, National Development and Reform Commission, Ministry of Commerce, and also include departments such as land construction, finance, human resources and social security, environmental protection, intellectual property offices, quality supervision departments, market regulatory agencies, and public transportation departments. Due to the involvement of multiple departments, local governments' implementation of the new generation of regional innovation policies is somewhat similar to a company's total quality management approach. There is no single policy called "innovation policy"; instead, it is a collaborative effort by various departments to advance the implementation of a policy mix.

Policy Targets

The overall policy target of the new generation of regional innovation policies should be the "innovation space" where innovation entities, elements, and networks are geographically concentrated. This is also referred to as the "policy space" or "space objects of innovation policy." Such innovation spaces as policy objects have two main policy associations:

1. First, they have specific geographic boundaries based on the major government policy levels;
2. Second, the urbanized physical space is the part that policy should pay particular attention to.

In terms of geography, the innovation space as a policy object can vary greatly in size and scope, ranging from the smallest projects, platform organizations, and industrial clusters, to incubators, industrial parks, science parks, small towns, and further to larger geographical areas such as communities, districts, cities, metropolitan areas, or even entire regions.

In practice, each level of local government faces spaces where resources can be mobilized through policy, priorities can be set, institutions can be established, policies can be coordinated, and policy learning and capacity building can occur (Uyarra & Flanagan, 2010). The goal of innovation policies is to shape these spaces into real innovation spaces with ecosystem characteristics.

One of the main differences between policies aimed at building "innovation ecosystems" and past policies is the shift from broad macro-level strategies to more detailed, micro-level management. For example, the "Guangzhou Value Innovation Park Construction Three-Year Action Plan (2018–2020)" planned multiple park projects around ten emerging industries. Each park was supported by policies designed with the idea of building an innovation ecosystem, including industrial policies, land policies, resource policies, and R&D policies.

Starting from grassroots projects, platforms, and parks, and with various levels of government working to create innovation ecosystems corresponding to their local administrative areas, these efforts lead to a growing, layered innovation space. In fact, a large region should be seen as a composition of overlapping spaces, with different levels of local government creating and implementing policies in these spaces. The specific innovation ecosystems created by local governments at various levels in these spaces constitute the core content of a region's innovation system.

The urbanized physical space is an essential element of the innovation space as a policy object. In addition to dense economic assets (such as innovative enterprises, R&D institutions, incubators, professional services, and living facilities) and social assets (such as community governance, activities, social organizations, and interpersonal relationships), the innovation space created by innovation ecosystem policies should also have modern physical space assets (such as parks, plazas, corporate R&D buildings, office buildings, and transportation networks). This is because talent, as the core element of innovation, is often attracted to urbanized space clusters that meet high expectations for working, living, and commuting spaces.

The new generation of regional innovation policies should be closely integrated with regional spatial planning, urban development and renewal (involving land zoning, development, urban planning, landscaping, and architectural design), and infrastructure construction to create the physical infrastructure and environment needed for modern innovation spaces.

Governance Structure of Implementation

Regional innovation policies that are guided by innovation ecosystems are suited to a multi-level policy governance structure. China's current local administrative system can roughly be divided into three levels: grassroots, city, and provincial/regional levels. If each level formulates and implements innovation ecosystem policies for the spatial scope under its jurisdiction, it will generally contribute to forming a "thicker" policy system in terms of innovation organizations and institutions within a region.

However, in practice, due to differences in power and financial resources, the innovation ecosystem policies adopted by local governments at different levels each focus on different aspects.

1. Grassroots governments tend to focus on specific project cultivation, particularly platform-type projects that can leverage more resources. Therefore, their policy path focuses on building platforms and developing local industrial clusters.
2. City governments, responsible for managing the entire city space and developing urban economies, focus their policies on urban construction and using the physical space of cities to attract talent for innovation and entrepreneurship.
3. Regional governments, with broader perspectives, focus on securing and allocating significant national resources for the region and emphasize overall regional development planning and layout.

Often, higher-level governments use the innovation spaces that are more developed within their jurisdiction as platforms and assets for external cooperation, in order to obtain more resources and generate broader regional development effects. For example, the Guangdong-Hong Kong-Macao Greater Bay Area should fully leverage the unique advantages of the innovation spaces already developed in major cities like Hong Kong, Shenzhen, and Guangzhou, to attract higher-quality human capital and better capital channels globally, thus creating a more advanced, larger, and internationally influential integrated innovation system. And this needs that there is one united government entity which can govern the Great Bay Area. Now such an entity is absent.

While the multi-level governance of regional innovation policies tends to form a natural division of labor, it is also crucial to ensure proper internal coordination and cooperation, avoiding excessive policy duplication and resource waste. In this regard, a well-designed overall policy system is key. The design of the regional innovation policy system is usually coordinated by the highest-level regional government or even the central government. In the design process, it is important to consider how innovation policies at different levels should be divided, how the various levels of government can collaborate, how policies can generate synergy, which policy measures can be duplicated, which should be avoided, and how policies can be optimized to achieve the best cost-benefit ratio, among other factors. Regional innovation policies should not be merely policies at the regional level; rather, they should be a highly coordinated system encompassing policies at all levels within the region.

Policy Mix and Toolbox

The mix of innovation policies refers to the specific combination of related policy tools. Policies such as science and technology finance, innovation talent, innovation platforms, and innovation chains are emerging policy measures at the local level in recent years. The new generation of regional innovation policies should combine and integrate these policy tools as a package for constructing local innovation ecosystems.

Local governments in coastal and developed regions of China have accumulated rich experience in innovation platform policies (Zhao, 2023). Before the pandemic, the construction of various innovation platforms had become a trend in local science and technology innovation policies. Innovation platforms, as carriers of new technological capabilities, are multi-functional, have various prospects, and establish multiple external connections as technology organizations, rather than merely serving as technology intermediaries. Local governments have made efforts to inject innovation platforms as a business model into the new technology investment projects, which are crucial to the development of key emerging strategic industries.

The policies enacted by local governments have helped platform projects gradually form their own innovation ecosystems or facilitated the establishment of new cooperation platforms among different participants in the value chain, including intermediary organizations and open innovation accelerators. Local governments have also promoted the geographical clustering of platform projects by planning and constructing various types of innovation spaces, such as industrial parks, incubation parks, and technology parks, forming industrial clusters and simultaneously expanding and enhancing innovation ecosystems at the industrial cluster level.

In this way, corresponding to different levels of innovation spaces, local governments have achieved a cycle of transformation from innovation projects to innovation platforms to innovation ecosystems, expanding to larger platforms and ecosystems, making the region a space full of innovative activities. The policy path at the regional level for innovation platforms is the process of spatial evolution and diffusion of platform organizations, integrating them into local strategic emerging industry clusters.

The concept of the innovation chain is often associated with concepts like the industrial chain, talent chain, and capital chain, as these "chains" emphasize integration in policy thinking. In terms of innovation policy in China, the innovation chain refers to the entire process from scientific research and development (R&D) to application transformation, mass production, user experience feedback, and technological iteration. It involves a variety of organizations, such as universities, research institutions, and enterprises, with different natures of involvement.

The industrial chain, or industry value chain, refers to the production technology system formed by the upstream and downstream enterprises of an industry, including various stages such as raw materials, components, product modules, integration, distribution, logistics, and services, with enterprises being the main participants. The capital chain and talent chain are metaphorical terms referring to the conditions of innovative factors that support the innovation and industrial chains.

In local government policy practices, there have been experiences in integrating the innovation chain and industrial chain, primarily in the early planning stages of emerging and future industries. For strategic emerging industries, the innovation chain should be deployed according to the industrial chain. First, an industry plan should be made to clarify the various links in the industrial chain. Then, the key technologies that need to be developed in each industrial chain link should be identified, and corresponding innovation and R&D activities should be planned based on the needs of technology development.

This integration of the industrial and innovation chains is the process of incorporating science and technology into industry development. For future industries, the innovation chain will be prioritized, which includes basic research, technological development, and application transformation, followed by forward-looking plans for several industry development scenarios. In future industries, the integration of the industrial chain and innovation chain will be more about the connection and alignment between technological innovation and industrial innovation. In the planning and implementation of the integration of multiple "chains," innovation platforms will be often used as important policy tools in combination.

Conclusion

This book aims to illustrate how Guangdong has successfully shaped a bottom-up innovation development model. The characteristics of this model are that during the development process, local government policies and corporate strategies can interact, adapt, and complement to each other, thereby generating a dynamic mechanism that drives regional economic innovation. However, government policies are not always passively adapting to corporate conditions. On the contrary, during the investment-driven development stage, it is actually the local government's industrial upgrading policies that play a positive role in fostering the strategic integration capabilities of company required for innovation. By the time of the innovation-driven development stage, Guangdong's local innovation policies and business strategies have achieved a level of integration. The new generation of regional innovation policies discussed in this chapter reflects this trend of integration.

For developing countries, the construction of regional ecosystems often entails local governments urbanizing their territories to foster an innovative environment for new business companies. Additionally, implementing holistic innovation policies at the regional level signifies a multi-level governance approach to innovation. The simultaneous implementation of policies of urbanization, clustering, industrial upgrading, and innovation development by multiple levels of government can also generate the "thickening" effect of regional ecosystems for businesses and entrepreneurs. In fact, innovation policy is not a singular policy but a series of innovative strategies and practices by local governments.

However, it should be noted that China's multi-level and replicated innovation ecosystem policy also has its limitations. Due to overlapping and repetitive levels of government, resource allocation is not satisfactory. The unique governance structure of the Chinese government makes it difficult to fully replicate its experience in other economies. One reason is that China has a large scale and multiple levels of government, and the multi-level nature of this regional innovation system is difficult for many other economies to imitate. Secondly, when the government's fiscal funds are sufficient, it is possible to build a multi-level and nested innovation ecosystem, but resource duplication and waste also often occur, resulting in low resource utilization efficiency. In the case of reduced government resources, it is difficult to continue implementing this kind of policy strategy.

At present, the local governments in China are facing severe challenges of financial situation. The stalling of the investment engine of local governments and the heavy burden of Treasury Bonds mark the end of a growth model. So far, this growth model has been described as going through a process of factor-driven development, investment-driven development, and reaching innovation-driven stage. If Guangdong and even the whole of China still hope to promote innovation-driven development through effective policies and methods, they should rediscover the original bottom-up innovation model in South China and reconstruct the regional innovation advantage all cross the country.

References

Borrás, S. and Edquist, C. (2019). *Holistic Innovation Policy: Theoretical Foundations, Policy Problems, and Instrument Choices*, UK, Oxford University Press.

Butollo, F., & Ten Brink, T. (2018). A great leap? Domestic market growth and local state support in the upgrading of China's LED lighting industry, *Global Networks,* 18(2), 285–306. ISSN 1470–2266

Chesbrough, H. W. (2003). The era of open innovation. *MIT Sloan Management Review, 44*(3), 35–41.

Ortt, J. R. and P. A. van der Duin (2008). The evolution of innovation management towards contextual innovation, *European Journal of Innovation Management,* Vol. 11 No. 4, 2008, pp. 522-538.

Uyarra, E. and K. Flanagan (2010). From Regional Systems of Innovation to Regions as Innovation Policy Spaces, *Environment and Planning C*, vol. 28, issue 4, 681-695.

Zhao. W. (2023). Local Governments as an Integrative Organizer: The Policy Practice of Constructing Innovation Platforms in South China, *Innovation and Development Policy*, 5 (2023), 73-99.

Zott, C., & Amit, R. (2010). Designing your future business model: An activity system perspective. *Long Range Planning, 43*, 216–226.

Index[1]

[1] Note: Page numbers followed by 'n' refer to notes.

W. Zhao, *Remade in South China*, IPP Studies in the Frontiers of China's Public Policy,
https://doi.org/10.1007/978-981-95-7277-9